10.20.81

D0931501

HB
2096.4
.A3
K39

POVERTY AND REVOLUTION
IN IRAN

The Migrant Poor, Urban Marginality and Politics

FARHAD KAZEMI

NEW YORK UNIVERSITY PRESS • New York *and* London

Tennessee Tech. Library
Cookeville, Tenn.

312408

Copyright © 1980 by New York University

Library of Congress Cataloging in Publication Data

Kazemi, Farhad, 1943-
    Poverty and revolution in Iran.

    Bibliography: p.
    Includes index.
    1. Rural-urban migration—Iran. 2. Iran—Social
conditions. I. Title.
HB2096.4.A3K39   307'.2   80-23374
ISBN 0-8147-4576-8

Manufactured in the United States of America

TO JANE

CONTENTS

Table

LIST OF ILLUSTRATIONS

Figure

ACKNOWLEDGMENTS

This book could not have been written without the financial support of the Joint Committee on the Near and Middle East of the Social Science Research Council and the American Council of Learned Societies and the Human Sciences Center of the Iranian Council for the Advancement of Scientific Research. I am grateful to both institutions for their generous support of my research in Iran and the United States. While in Iran, I was fortunate to receive the support and cooperation of several institutions. I am especially thankful to the various agencies of the Plan and Budget Organization and the officials of the Tehran College of Social Work for facilitating my work.

I am also grateful to many colleagues and friends who encouraged and willingly gave hours of their valuable time to help the completion of this project. I am particularly indebted to Professors Ali Banuazizi and Ahmad Ashraf for their unfailing support at every stage of my study. I only hope that I have not disappointed them. My colleagues at New York University--Professors R. Bayly Winder, Christopher Mitchell, and Richard S. Randall--freely offered their help and encouragement. I am also most thankful to Mr. Nicholas M. Nikazmerad for his assistance, patience, and good humor in moments of crisis. Finally I would like to express my appreciation to Mrs. Nancy Fernandez for her competent and efficient typing of the final manuscript. I am solely responsible for all errors of facts or interpretation.

F.K.
June, 1980

PREFACE

When I began writing this study, Iran was in the throes
of a major revolution. From afar I observed the unfolding
of events with deep concern. Millions of Iranians from
different groups and classes had banded together to put a
stop to the old regime's political, economic, and social
abuses. My personal sympathies were clearly on the side of
the masses of unarmed Iranians who risked their lives in
violent confrontations with the Shah's military and security
forces. Eventually the revolution's central aim of overthrowing the Pahlavi dynasty succeeded. However, the
postrevolutionary excesses and the inability of the government
to establish and enforce its authority leave many problems
unresolved. The increasing authoritarianiam of the new regime
and the constraints placed upon various groups other than the
religious establishment who fought in the revolution raise
many basic questions about the future of Iran. I can only
hope that the new emerging social order will not renege on
the promise of justice and egalitarianism for which the
revolution was fought.

The present study is not directly concerned with the
revolution in Iran. It is a study of the poor migrants who
left the rural areas of Iran, primarily because of the
dislocation in the agricultural sector, and settled in
squatter settlements, slums, and low-income communities of
Tehran. My analysis of the poor migrants' situation relates
to the recent events in Iran in at least two ways. First, it
analyzes the consequences of an important structural
dislocation, developed under the old regime, and its impact
on large numbers of poor peasants and their subsequent
marginal life in the urban centers of Iran. Second, it
attempts to shed some light on the process of mobilization
of segments of the politically passive poor migrants during
the course of the revolution.

The origins of the present study and my interest in the
plight of the migrant poor go back many years. It was not,
however, possible to undertake a systematic study of the poor
migrants in Tehran until the fall of 1974 when I was granted
a year's leave of absence from my teaching duties at New York
University. I subsequently spent several months in Iran and
initiated my field research.

The actual fieldwork in Tehran consisted of two separate
but complementary stages and time periods: 1974-75 and the
summer of 1977. Initially I faced innumerable problems and
difficulties in getting the project off the ground. After
two months of planning and arrangements, I was able to visit
some of the migrant poor communities of Tehran and begin the
interviewing process. Aside from visits to a few squatter
settlements in South Tehran and one known as Kashanak in the
northern part of the city, I made regular trips to five major

migrant poor areas of South Tehran. These areas are known as Javadiyih, Kuyi Nuhum-i Aban, Mihrabad-i Junubi, Park-i Vali'ahd, and Sulaymaniyih. Migrant factory workers were interviewed at the Arj Factory and at the fabric-making establishment of Park-i Vali'ahd. Moreover, second-generation migrant high school students were interviewed at the Javadiyih high school. During the 1974-75 fieldwork, about 400 migrants were interviewed. This figure includes occasional interviews with groups of five to six persons in the squatter areas.

The interview schedule was based on several prearranged and prepared questions dealing with eight broad categories: (1) family background information; (2) literacy and education; (3) living conditions in the village before migration; (4) migration; (5) living conditions in Tehran; (6) ties and relations in Tehran; (7) employment and work situation in Tehran; and (7) sociopolitical awareness. Each category in turn comprised several specific questions. After a brief pretesting, a few of the specific questions were deleted and replaced by different ones. The questionnaire was used basically to structure and give direction to the interviewing format. On several occasions, I found it beneficial to do away with the formal interview schedule and record my impressions at a later hour. There was also always ample opportunity for in-depth nonstructured conversations.

These interviews provided an important part of my analysis of the migrant poor and are reported in various forms throughout the study. What gave meaning to the first phase of the study was my participant observation and personal interactions with the poor migrants. In many ways, these were the most rewarding aspects of the research and broadened my awareness of the problems and issues confronting the migrants. These aspects also made me extremely conscious of the extensive class and status differences that exist in the highly differentiated Iranian society. My daily travels in a private vehicle from the opulent North Tehran to the poor migrant and squatter areas of South Tehran was a consciousness-raising experience of the first magnitude. Few individuals could remain unaffected after observing such fundamental and drastic differences in life styles of two groups in the same city.

The second phase of the fieldwork was undertaken during the summer of 1977. Owing to the availability of additional research funds and certain fortuitous developments, I was able to hire a group of research assistants and could thus embark on a brief but systematic survey of a sample of nonsquatting poor migrants of Tehran. The population was selected from a 1976 stratified random sample of 2,500 poor migrants from the rural areas of Iran to the capital, which was conducted by Iran's Plan and Budget Organization. This study divided Greater Tehran into 48 sections and selected a sample of approximately 50 poor rural migrant households from each section. Individual male heads of households were then subjected to extensive interviews by the Plan and Budget Organization team. Since the goals of this research and most of the questions asked were not of direct relevance to my research purposes, it was decided to choose a smaller sample from the Plan and Budget Organization's 2,500 migrants. After eliminating all migrants who had lived in Tehran for more than eight years, a systematic sample of 316 households (15%) were then selected. However, because of the recent changes in the numbering of Tehran's dwelling units and changes of residence by some migrants, it was not possible to reach every person on the list. Consequently, when the interviewing period was over, 224 completed questionnaires were available for analysis.

The questionnaire was prepared on the basis of the eight broad categories of the 1974-75 research and its later modifications. Pretesting was conducted on 5 percent of the sample, and the questionnaire was further revised. Some of the political and social class items were dropped at this stage because of the difficulties encountered in administering them. The final structured questionnaire consisted of 71 items covering a wide range of descriptive and attitudinal factors. There were also some limited opportunities for open-ended answers to a few of the questions. The average interview lasted approximately 60 minutes.

A team of five experienced interviewers and a supervisor, all of whom had previously conducted interviews for the Iranian Statistical Center and the Ministry of Labor, were hired. The interviewing staff was trained and given uniform and specific instructions regarding the goals and conduct of the interviews. They were also provided with the names and addresses of the migrant heads of households in the sample. The head of the interviewing staff supervised the actual operation of some of the interviews to ensure accuracy and uniformity. I was available throughout this period at a central location to provide consultation and advice on any potential problem areas. The supervisor and I checked the administered questionnaires at the end of each working day.

The completed questionnaires were then brought back to the United States and were coded and keypunched with the help of a research assistant who knew Persian well. Since there were very few open-ended questions, coding did not present any major problems. The cards were then used for statistical and computer analysis using the program of the Statistical Package for the Social Sciences (SPSS).

The statistical analysis also involved constructing two summarive indexes of socioeconomic status and political awareness. For each index, a set of relevant variables from the questionnaire were selected. The socioeconomic status index consisted of four relevant items dealing with income, education, homeownership, and occupational skill level. The political awareness index was constructed by summation of five elementary items gauging political knowledge. The items included knowledge about the role of the parliament, names of the prime minister and mayor of Tehran, and specific questions about the country. Each index was assigned a score of 1 or 2 based on the response to the individual items. The responses in the index were dichotomized according to the interval measure in each category indicating the respondent's extent of political awareness or socioeconomic status. Correct answers to 3 or more questions out of 5 in the political awareness index and affirmative responses to 2 out of 4 in the socioeconomic status index were the boundaries of the dichotomy. "Don't know" responses were given the lowest score of 1. Missing cases were excluded from the index and subsequent computations. Based on the respondent's score on the 1 to 2 scale, gradient indexes of political awareness and socioeconomic status consisting of low, medium, and high levels for the group as a whole were constructed. The two indexes were then used for correlational analysis with other relevant variables.

The research and writing of the present work also benefited from a number of available reports on the squatters, poor migrants, and low-income communities of Tehran. Aside from the studies by the Institute for Social Research (Tehran University) and the Plan and Budget Organization, many publications of the College of Social Work were found most useful. The difficulty of collecting reliable information on the migrant poor was partly resolved by the various research outputs of these institutions.

CHAPTER I

INTRODUCTION: MARGINALITY AND THE MIGRANT POOR

Fear of mob violence in urban centers has preoccupied city residents in many parts of the world throughout the centuries. For the city dweller of Iran, this fear has a special significance. Repeated incidents of urban riots can be readily recalled, and indeed the entire history of modern Iran is replete with examples of crowds engaged in extensive political action in city streets and alleys.

From the period of the Constitutional Revolution at the turn of the century to the present time, Iranian urban crowds have continuously served as major instruments for political change or restoration.[1] When their voices grew louder and their actions more intense toward the end of World War II, crowds gained a new preeminence in the politics of Iran. Between 1943 and 1946 the Tudeh (Communist) party sponsored major demonstrations in Tehran, Isfahan, Abadan, and some twenty other cities.[2] In 1949 the National Front spearheaded popular demands for oil nationalization through organized political activity and mass demonstrations in the principal cities. During the following four years extensive urban unrest spread throughout the country. Major urban violence surfaced again in the early 1960s resulting in many casualties and deaths.[3] The massive antigovernment riots of 1978-79 in more than fifty cities are additional proof that urban violence is not an isolated phenomenon in the history of modern Iran.

An important aspect of these riots is the fact that they were restricted primarily to the urban centers. The countryside remained generally calm, and the peasants did not participate in the periodic demonstrations, riots, and violence that were besetting their nation.[4] But unlike the peasants who, for the most part, have been passive and uninvolved in politics, several different urban groups have played major roles in the past in violence and the politics of the city. These include religious groups, the bazaar, industrial workers, and the professional mob leaders known as chaqu-kishan (knife wielders). The chaqu-kishan, with their headquarters in athletic clubs, have traditionally offered their services to politicians for pay. By hiring them, the politicians can count on large demonstrations to suit their purposes whenever they are desired. In a pattern resembling the patron-client relationship, the chaqu-kishan round up their followers through the combined influences of financial reward, loyalty, and pressure.

Mob violence led by the chaqu-kishan was a common feature of Iranian politics in the 1950s. Both the right-wing royalist politicians and the antiregime factions utilized these same mobs. In 1952 reliable observers

1

claimed "to have seen workers demonstrating for the communists, for the royalists, and for the Mossadeqist National Front on successive days."[5] In the 1960s and 1970s, the chaqu-kishan have not been able to exert a comparable influence on city politics, in large part because the regime executed a few of their prominent leaders after the 1963 riots for having sided with the opposition and having led crowds against the government. However, early in the summer of 1979 violent attacks of groups of rock-throwing and knife-wielding toughs--who identified themselves as hizbullahis (partisans of God)--on peaceful rallies of those demanding greater political freedom and women's rights were a vivid demonstration that unruly mob violence in Iran did not end with the revolution. The tactics and actions of the hizbullahis and the chaqu-kishan are far too similar to warrant the conclusion that this dramatic feature of urban politics in Iran is now terminated.

Although it is true that in most urban riots a good portion of the participants are there for reasons other than genuine sympathy with the activists, this fact does not imply that all urban mobs are bought. It would be a basic mistake, as Richard Cottam has said, to "adopt the cynical view that all Iranian mobs have been purchased."[6] The participants in urban demonstrations and riots come from various groups; indeed, many are present to support specific political causes and actions. Their motivations for participating in riots and violence are often based on what they consider to be sincere political, economic, religious, and other ideological beliefs. This also holds true for many of the demonstrations and clashes of the early 1950s.

To what extent have the migrant poor from rural areas participated in these urban riots? This question will be examined in detail in the following chapters. For now, it suffices to point out that the migrant poor are generally not active participants in the politics of the city--whether through parliamentary means or by violent political action. Although it may be true that certain elements of the migrant poor have been involved in some urban riots, this partici-pation has probably been at best sporadic. Even in the 1950s the chaqu-kishan recruited primarily in the bazaar and among the workers, not from the migrant poor. In the 1978-79 antigovernment demonstrations and riots, however, important segments of the migrant poor were mobilized and participated in the activities that eventually toppled the Shah's regime.

The Migrant Poor: Who Are They and Where Do They Come From?

Among the recent migrants to Tehran, the capital, three important groups can be differentiated. The first group consists of those migrants who are, on the whole, well-off economically and can establish themselves in Tehran without undue difficulty. They have come from Iran's other regional cities and are attracted to the capital because, as the nation's seat of government, it is the center of economic and political power. For many of them the move to Tehran is perceived to be a step to increase or consolidate their economic and political position. The pull of Tehran is in the potential opportunities it can offer them and their children for advancement in position, power, and status. These migrants have left one urban center for another, and since they have both the economic means and probably appropriate political connections, adjustment to Tehran does not present them with unsurmountable difficulties.

The second group is made up of migrants who, although not of high socioeconomic status, possess skills that allow them to at least maintain a low-middle-class life in the capital. For the most part, these migrants come from the smaller cities and towns of Iran. Some of them may have also migrated from the rural areas. However, they either have the skills or sufficient capital to be able to establish a reasonably comfortable life for themselves and their families. For these migrants, as for the first group, it is probably Tehran's pull and its envisaged opportunities that prompt their move in the first place.

The last group presents a very different picture. These are migrants of low socioeconomic background--former sharecroppers and farm laborers--who have left the countryside for the city primarily because of occupational uncertainties in the village and other, similar "push" factors. These are the poor and landless peasants who, as a result of the land reform program and deterioration of Iran's agriculture, found themselves either still without land or unable to earn enough for subsistence on the land deeded to them by the government. Thus, the majority left the countryside for the city because they could no longer maintain even a subsistence life in the village. They migrated to Tehran and to other major cities in increasingly large numbers. These are the poor migrants, the principal subject of inquiry in this book.

The poor migrants can be subdivided into two groups on the basis of their residence and occupation: (1) those who live in the squatter settlements and rarely have regular wage-earning jobs; and (2) the nonsquatting poor migrants who usually reside in rented dwellings, mostly in the slum areas of Tehran. Many of the nonsquatting migrants are employed in regular wage-earning occupations.

The poor migrants reside in large clusters in South, Southeast, and Southwest Tehran, with occasional small communities in parts of the affluent North Tehran. The total number of the migrant poor living in slums or squatter settlements of Tehran is not known. It is readily apparent that in spite of the government's efforts to curtail their numbers, squatter and slum dwelling by the migrant poor has been increasing rapidly. Estimates range anywhere from 500,000 to well over 1 million poor migrants. They suffer disproportionately the worst of urban ills, such as inadequate housing and service facilities, unemployment and underemployment, poor medical care, and the like.

These poor migrants lead a marginal life on the fringes of urban society. They are products of an economic system that has created and perpetuated their marginality, whether in the countryside as the sharecropper or in the city as the migrant poor. The migrants' marginality is attested by their socioeconomic position as underclass, by their political position as nonparticipant, and by their status position as nonprivileged. This vicious circle of marginality engulfs their lives in every step, from the village farm laborer and sharecropper to the city low-income peddler and unskilled factory worker. Their earned income may increase in every phase of this development, but only a selected few break the circle and escape marginality.

The Theory of Marginality

The concept of marginality dates back to the writings of Robert Park and Everett Stonequist, who attempted to explain the rise of a personality type, the marginal man, in situations of culture contact and conflict. The marginal man, as conceived by Park, "is one whom fate has condemned to live in two societies and in two, not merely different but antagonistic, cultures."[7] Following Park, Stonequist emphasizes the psychological marginality resulting from "culture conflict and differential assimilation."[8] For Stonequist, the marginal man is "the individual who through migration, education, marriage, or some other influence leaves one social group or culture without making a satisfactory adjustment to another [and] finds himself on the margin of each but a member of neither."[9] This individual becomes a marginal man when he experiences "the group conflict as a personal problem."[10]

Although both Park and Stonequist are interested in human migration as one of the preconditions for the rise of the marginal man, they are not concerned with the migrant poor in the cities. Stonequist makes some references to the migrant from the country who finds himself "déraciné--a man without roots, who is in danger of being blown about by every gust of circumstance."[11] However, neither Stonequist nor Park dwell much on this subject. Their primary preoccupation is with various ethnic, racial, and cultural hybrids who, because of their marginality and the experience of conflict, find personal adjustment difficult. Park and Stonequist view the marginal man positively and as a possible harbinger of advancement and progress. Park believes that by analyzing the mind of the marginal man, "we can best study the processes of civilization and of progress."[12] Likewise, Stonequist points out that it is in the mind of the marginal man "that the cultures come together, conflict, and eventually work out some kind of mutual adjustment and interpretation. He is the crucible of cultural fusion."[13]

4

Park's and Stonequist's writings on the marginal man have been the subject of much analysis and criticism.[14] Some have found the concept, or at least aspects of it, useful and have applied it to several concrete situations. Others have rejected its usefulness and value. One critic, in particularly harsh language, finds the concept of marginal man "a sociological fiction based upon a stereotype, which, like most stereotypes, is a caricature of a truth or an exaggeration and distortion of a fact."[15] Perhaps the best analysis of marginal man is to be found in H. F. Dickie-Clark's The Marginal Situation.[16] In a thorough and scholarly review of the marginal man literature, Dickie-Clark analyzes some of the concept's major problems and shortcomings. The most important among these, at least for our purposes, is the failure of Park and Stonequist to deal effectively with the marginal situation and "its relations to marginal personality traits."[17] By emphasizing psychological marginality and essentially neglecting the marginal situation, Stonequist and Park have rendered the concept of marginal man less useful for sociological analysis. The marginal situation, as Dickie-Clark points out, is "important, in its own right, as a social situation without psychological components."[18] To be in a marginal situation does not necessarily result in psychological marginality.[19]

The underlying theme of the marginal situation is concerned with those conditions under which social groups with varying degrees of income, power, and status are arranged in a relatively enduring and large-scale hierarchical order.[20] Thus, the concept of marginality as used in this book refers to a situation of inequality where the superordinate groups systematically exclude the subordinate groups from enjoying the society's chief privileges and benefits. The barriers established to separate the dominant from the subordinate groups perpetuate inequality and subject the underclass to an insecure life of economic, social, and political marginality.

In Dickie-Clark's usage, the marginal situation is a hierarchical order in which there is "inconsistency in the ranking of the individual or collectivity in any matter regulated by the hierarchical structure."[21] This emphasis on rank inconsistency for identification of marginal situations is in the tradition of Park and Stonequist who viewed marginality as a special case of experiencing conflict. Since status inconsistency creates conflict for the individual or collectivity, it becomes "the essence of the marginal situation" when experienced in a hierarchical order. Dickie-Clark further delineates three specific features of hierarchies: composition, scope, and barrier. Composition refers to the number of strata in the hierarchy and scope to to the area of behavior controlled by the hierarchy.[22] The third feature, barrier, is "the resistance offered by a superior stratum to the enjoyment by an inferior one, of their powers, privileges and opportunities."[23]

The analysis of the migrant poor in this book will not deal with Dickie-Clark's condition of status inconsistency.

5

Rather, my discussion of marginality will concentrate on the exclusion of the migrant poor in Iran by those at the top of the hierarchy--from the spheres of power, wealth, and status--and hence the impossibility of the migrant poor's enjoying those benefits and rewards that are concomitant with possession of power, wealth, and status. In this context, the poor migrants are marginals in several interrelated areas: (1) they lead an economic life that allows them to earn only a bare subsistence income; (2) they live on the fringes of the city in marginal dwelling units with insecure rights of tenancy, often without water, electricity, or the other amenities of life; (3) they do not generally belong to associations or political organizations and are nonparticipants in the political arena; and (4) they have low status and do not enjoy any special social privileges.

The Latin American Debate on Marginality

The theory of marginality as applied to the migrant poor and squatter settlements in Latin American cities has been the subject of debate for some time. Whereas some believe that the term is an apt description for the squatters and their settlements, others have seriously questioned its validity and applicability to the migrant poor and their residential units. Gino Germani explains the emergence of the theory of marginality in Latin America in the following manner:

> In Latin America the term "marginality" began to be used principally with reference to urban ecological characteristics, that is to say, to the sector of the population segregated into areas of improvised dwellings on illegally occupied land. From this point it was extended to the conditions of work and the level of life of this sector of the population. Then its marginality was perceived both in relationship to the socio-economic system of consumption of goods and services. Simultaneously it was noticed that this state of marginality included other essential aspects like political and union participation, formal and informal participation and in general its absence or exclusion from decision making whether at the level of the local community, the situation in work, or in the order of broader state and national structures and institutions.[24]

One of the first groups that attempted to develop a theory of marginality in Latin America is the Center for Latin American Economic and Social Development (DESAL) and its director, Roger Vekemans.[25] Vekemans and his associates separate Latin American populations into integrated and marginal sectors. The marginals are the underprivileged and the economically powerless groups who are also politically nonparticipant, "even in those decisions which affect them most directly."[26] For DESAL the way to alter the poor

6

sector's marginality and disintegration is to develop specific community projects and national policies "aimed at overcoming that marginality in order to allow for an integrated and democratic society."[27]

Aside from the DESAL group, Janice Perlman identifies several other definitions of marginality dealing with the urban poor in Latin America. These definitions identify marginals as (1) those living in squatter settlements, (2) the economic underclass, (3) migrants, (4) racial and ethnic minorities, and (5) nonconformists and deviants.[28] Although some of these definitions overlap, the term "marginality" is nevertheless used to describe a wide array of people and patterns of behavior in Latin America. There is, conse-quently, much dispute about the validity of the concept of marginality for discussing and analyzing the structural conditions and behavior of the migrant poor in Latin American cities.

In addition to Perlman's refutation of the marginality of the migrant poor in Rio de Janeiro, several Latin American scholars, including Wayne Cornelius, William Mangin, Lisa Peattie, and Alejandro Portes, have seriously questioned the identification of the migrant squatters in Latin America as marginals.[29] The empirical research reported by these specialists indicates that the poor migrants contribute to, and are integrated in, the national economy; participate in voluntary associations and relevant political activity; and are not living in crime-ridden communities or areas of social disorganization. Hence cultural, social, economic, and political marginality is not generally applicable to them. Perlman goes so far as to say that the migrant poor in the squatter settlements of Latin America "have the aspirations of the bourgeoisie, the perseverance of pioneers, and the values of patriots."[30] Whether this is a romanticization of the migrant poor or a description of reality is a moot point. However, Perlman admits that there is such a thing as "marginality of exclusion and exploitation" suffered by the squatters.[31] Yet one of her objections to the term "marginality" is that it has sometimes been used to blame the poor migrant for poverty and to accuse him of "low motivation and parochialism."[32]

Although it is probably true that marginality is not an accurate description of the squatters and slum dwellers of Latin America, the same cannot be said of the Iranian migrant poor. The economic, social, and political criteria used to refute the marginality of the Latin American migrant poor is not applicable to the Iranian case. The poor migrants in Tehran and other large cities are marginals in the sense that they are excluded from partaking of the benefits and privileges of the top levels of the hierarchy and are forced to lead a life of economic, social, and political marginality. It is, therefore, the structure of the Iranian socioeconomic system that has "marginalized" the migrant poor.[33]

Dependency and Marginality

It is possible to argue that marginalization of increasing numbers of poor migrants is caused by the expansion of dependent capitalism in Iran. The theory of dependency as developed originally by Latin American scholars and later modified and applied to other regions maintains that poverty of the Third World nations is the result of rapid and worldwide expansion of the industrial West. The need to extract the required raw materials for the growth of Western industry has created a dependent capitalist system outside Western metropolitan centers. Thus, backwardness and underdevelopment are not so much the result of endogenous factors in the Third World as they are the consequences of economic subordination to the West and its multinational enterprises.

It is not my purpose here to describe the multiple features of the theory of dependency or its various incarnations in any greater detail.[34] Dependency theory, however, may be relevant to the discussion of the migrant poor in Iran in at least two related aspects. These concern the center-periphery distinctions and the role of what James Petras calls the imperial state in the periphery.[35] The primary thrust of dependency theory stresses the structural inequality among nations as exemplified in the tremendous concentration of economic, and hence political power, in the advanced industrial countries or the center nations. Concomitantly, the underdeveloped, or periphery nations, are subjugated and used to perpetuate the dominance of the center through the creation of peripheral and consumer capitalism in the Third World. The center-periphery distinction also posits that the same pattern of elite dominance over exploited masses exists within both the advanced industrial nations and the peripheral countries. Thus, there is a center of the center and a periphery of the center and, similarly, a center of the periphery and a periphery of the periphery.[36]

Within the peripheral nations, development of dependent capitalism strengthens control of the urban elite over the backward rural inhabitants in the hinterlands. The pattern of predominance, with full support of the center elite of the imperial power, contributes to the growing decline of the rural areas and to the gradual destruction of agriculture. The masses of the marginalized agricultural proletariat are forced off the land and move to the urban center where capital is concentrated. The "reserve army of labor" with no technical skills finds its way into shanty towns and squatter settlements of the Third World cities where unemployment, underemployment, or marginal occupation are the common fate.[37] This labor force, relegated to lowest-income and occupational roles, ensures that wages remain low while the capitalists' profits continue to rise. Economically unable to partake either in the expanding consumerism or in the housing and land markets of the urban center, this population is doomed to a perpetuating system of marginality.[38]

The second aspect of dominance of the center over the periphery is to be seen in the process of state-building by the imperial power in the dependent capitalist nation. In the words of Petras, this process involves attempts "to prevent political decay or disintegration through the creation of a durable political order, one in which social control over the labor force permits the continuous flow of capital and the reproduction of exploitative social relations."[39] More specifically, the imperial power through various agencies (such as the military or the civilian bureaucracy) forms or strengthens those state institutions that work to preserve or increase economic control of the center in the periphery.

Applied to the Iranian case, the theory of dependency has some attraction. It can be argued that the relationship between the United States and Iran essentially resembled a center-periphery interaction. The American involvement in the Shah's state-building attempts (whether the military and security forces or the civilian institutions) and the type of wide-ranging economic activities of multinational corporations may be cited as supportive evidence for this claim. Moreover, it is possible to view the dominance of the urban areas, especially the capital, over the countryside in Iran as another proof of how the dynamics of dependent relations operate within the national boundary.

Although I do not dismiss the relevance of dependency as a factor in marginalization of the migrant poor, I am not convinced of its complete and total applicability in this particular case. One overriding problem with dependency analysis is its simplification of a highly complex problem and its frequent resort to generalizations. Peculiarities and differences of individual countries are often not given sufficient attention and are sacrificed to the requirements of overview analysis. Although the rapid development of dependent and consumer capitalism in Iran under the Shah contributed to marginalization of some poor migrants, it was not the only cause of the phenomenon. Marginality as a condition of life has been a basic feature of the Iranian poor peasantry and the low-income urban migrants for many decades. Furthermore, the pattern of urban dominance over the rural society has also been evident for a long time. In contrast to the view of some dependency theorists who claim that large capital is not invested in agriculture, in Iran extensive capital infused the countryside especially as part of the agribusiness operations. The problem was more the management and inappropriateness of these types of rural operations for Iran than the absence of capital.

Finally, the claim that wage scales remain artificially low in the urban areas is not accurate. In the urban centers of Iran, and particularly in Tehran, wage scales increased sharply for low and unskilled laborers. Hence, the "reserve army of labor" did not keep wages low for the benefit of bourgeois capitalists. The advantage of the rising wages for the poor migrants was, however, highly questionable. The increase in the cost of living and intermittent unemployment or underemployment reduced whatever benefits larger wages may

9

have brought to some of them. It therefore appears that dependency theory is relevant to the analysis of the Iranian migrant poor in the latter stages of the Shah's regime. But the development of dependent and peripheral capitalism is only a contributing and partial explanation of a complex process leading to marginalization of the migrant poor.

CHAPTER II

URBANIZATION AND MIGRATION

The Islamic City

The urban setting has always been an integral part of
Islamic life. Indeed, it has frequently been mentioned that
Muslims have viewed the city as the preferred place for
observance of their religion. Yet although this statement
is not inaccurate, the city has not always been considered as
"an exclusive center for the living of a Muslim life."[1] The
Islamic law, as Gustav von Grunebaum has indicated, "does not
concede a special status to the town."[2] A true Islamic life
is possible wherever a Muslim community exists[3]--although
preference has been given to the Muslim community in an urban
setting with its organized religious bodies, great mosques,
and marketplaces.

The medieval Islamic city--often viewed as a classic
model--was organized around what Albert Hourani calls the
"agro-city," that is, "the urban conglomeration together with
the rural hinterland from which it drew its food and to which
it sold part at least of its manufactures."[4] There was an
intricate relationship and harmony between the city and its
hinterlands. This relationship and mutual dependency has
long been documented for Islamic cities, and its inception
predates Islam.[5] With the rise of Islam, certain distinctive
features, particularly the application of the Islamic law,
were added to the agro-city. The typical preindustrial
Islamic city, as depicted by Hourani, included specific
physical arrangements.[6] It had a citadel used for defense
and security as well as a separate royal compound and a
central urban complex. The royal compound housed the state
apparatus--the royalty and its administrative offices. The
central urban complex consisted of the great mosques and
religious schools, the major markets, and the residences of
the merchants and religious bourgeoisie. The city also had
a core of residential quarters that included sections for the
major religious and ethnic groups. These sections were
separated and divided from one another. Carl Brown notes
that the Islamic city's quarters were designed "not to
generalize and ease mobility and exchange but to control and
compartmentalize it."[7] Finally, outside the quarters were
located the outer limits of the city. In these areas, recent
immigrants and the caravan quarters could be found.

The medieval Islamic city, therefore, did not conform
completely to Max Weber's definition of the city. In Weber's
classic formulation, five features are deemed necessary for
a city to exist. These are: fortifications, markets, courts
administering partly autonomous laws, distinct urban forms of

association, and at least partial autonomy.[8] Of these five
distinguishing features, two are not applicable to the
medieval Islamic city. The Islamic city did not possess
either partial autonomy or courts administering partly
autonomous laws.[9] The shari'ah (Islamic law) recognized
"no privileges for one group of believers above others,"[10]
and the city had no autonomous or "distinct territorial
status."[11] In this sense, then, the Islamic city was
different from the medieval cities of Europe as discussed
by Weber.

The Islamic cities of Iran were in many respects similar
to other Muslim cities. Ahmad Ashraf discusses four major
elements that encompassed the Islamic cities in Iran. First,
the cities had governmental organizations for political,
administrative, and military operations. Different and
related groups were entrusted with the task of supervising
social, economic, judicial, and police functions. Second,
the religious organization oversaw the operation of the
mosques, religious schools, and pious foundations (waqf) and
supervised the application of Islamic law. Third, various
occupational guilds protected and promoted their members'
mutual economic and social interests. And finally, important
sections of the city separated residential quarters of
different religious, ethnic, nationality, and occupational
groups.[12] Similar to other Middle Eastern cities, the Iranian
urban centers were agro-cities. The city and its surrounding
villages were involved in extensive relationships necessary
for their mutual survival.[13]

In the nineteenth and twentieth centuries, the
preindustrial Iranian cities entered the modern age.
Increased commercialization of agriculture; greater trade
with Europe; development of factories, banks, and an export-
oriented economy--all these factors helped to transform the
traditional Iranian city. Some urban centers such as Tehran,
Isfahan, Shiraz, Tabriz, and Yazd gained in population.[14]
Port cities such as Khurramshahr grew in size and importance.[15]
A new city, Abadan, was established at the head of the Persian
Gulf in the early twentieth century to accommodate the needs
of the Anglo-Persian Oil Company.[16] In the post-World War II
period these changes and developments were accentuated. With
the increased importance of oil and foreign trade, the
accelerated pace of industrialization, and the attempts at
greater centralization of political and administrative power,
Iran's urban centers experienced an important, and in some
cases drastic break with the past. The traditional Islamic
city with its multiple and distinct features was now past
history.

Urbanization in Iran

In the first four decades of the twentieth century, the
percentage of Iran's population living in urban areas remained
relatively steady. Toward the end of World War II and during

the following years, however, a noti
proportion of urban population occur
the time of the third nationwide cen
46 percent of the population lived i
by the Census Organization as locali
population. In the 1966-76 period,
increased approximately by 6 percent
four factors explain the sharp percen
urban population during the decade be
censuses of 1966 and 1976. There was
national population increase amountin
period.[18] Second, boundaries of some
include the surrounding villages and
portion of the rural population (380,
without actually having migrated. Th
villages increased to the point of su
These rural areas (117 localities wit
891,000) were then recognized as urba
urban population increased due to the
of villagers to major metropolitan ce
1967 about 2,111,000 migrants left th
cities. In other words, cityward mig
35 percent of the increase in total u
during this period (Table 2.2).

Although this expansion in the u
continue in the future, it should be
only a handful of the largest cities
life in Iran. This has been especiall
and a few large cities. In 1900, for
only three cities with a population of
number increased to 8 by 1948, to 10 b
and to 23 by 1976. The number of pers
100,000 or more increased from 500,000
in 1948, to 3,150,454 in 1956, to 5,67
9,900,460 in 1976. Likewise the perce
population living in cities of 100,000
from 24 percent in 1900 to nearly 58 p
63 percent in 1976 (Table 2.3). The s
largest cities was substantial in this
1948, the five largest cities--Tehran,
Mashhad, and Hamadan--contained 36.8 p
population. In 1956 and 1966, the five
Tehran, Isfahan, Mashhad, Tabriz, and
42.4 and 43.1 percent of the urban popu
If the two cities of Shiraz and Ahvaz,
of over 200,000, are added to the five
then close to 50 percent of the urban p
for by these seven cities. In the 1976
of the largest ten cities amounted to 5
residents (Table 2.4).

The case of Tehran is even more no
population, size, rate of growth, and c
economic and political power far outpac
the country. Tehran has grown from a s
sixteenth century into a bustling city

Year
1900
1910
1920
1930
1940
1950
1960
1970
1976

SOURC
Developmen
Press, 197
Iranian S
Sharshumar

Natural
Increa

Populati
City B

Populati
Urban

Rural to
Migrat

TO

SOUF
Iranian S
bih Manat

Table 2.1

Urban and Rural Population of Iran:
1900-1976 (in millions)

Total	Urban	% Urban	Rural
9.86	2.07	20.9	7.79
10.58	2.22	20.9	8.36
11.37	2.39	21.0	8.98
12.59	2.64	20.9	9.95
14.55	3.20	21.9	11.35
17.58	4.89	27.8	12.69
22.83	7.76	33.9	15.07
30.35	13.10	43.1	17.25
33.59	15.71	46.7	17.87

ES: Adapted from Julian Bharier, Economic
t in Iran: 1900-1970 (London: Oxford University
), p. 17; Iran, Plan and Budget Organization,
atistical Center, Guzarish-i Natayij-i Mugadamati-yi
i-yi Umumi-yi Nufus va Maskan, 1976.

Table 2.2

Increase in Urban Population: 1966-1976

	Total Population (000)	% of Total Increase	Average Annual Increase (000)
opulation e	2,621	43.7	262
n in Expanded undaries	380	6.3	38
n in New enters	891	14.8	89
Urban on	2,111	35.2	211
AL	6,003	100.0	

CE: Adapted from Iran, Plan and Budget Organization,
tatistical Center, "Barrisi-yi Ijmali-yi Muhajirat
iq-i Shahri." (Mimeographed.)

Table 2.3

Population Distribution in Cities of 100,000 or More: 1900-1976

Year	Urban Population	Population in Cities 100,000 or More	
		Number	% of Urban Population
1900	2,070,000	500,000	24.1
1948	4,490,000	1,986,672	44.2
1956	5,953,563	3,150,454	52.9
1966	9,794,246	5,667,012	57.8
1976	15,715,338	9,900,460	62.9

SOURCES: Iran, Ministry of Interior, Kitab-i Asami-yi Dihat-i Kishvar, Vol. 1, 1950; Iran, Ministry of Interior, General Statistics Office, Guzarish-i Khulasah-yi Sarshumari-yi Umumi-yi Kishvar, Vol. 1, 1956; Iran, Plan Organization, Iranian Statistical Center, National Census of Population and Housing, No. 168, March, 1968; Iran, Plan and Budget Organization, Iranian Statistical Center, Guzarish-i Natayij-i Mugadamati-yi Sarshumari-yi Umumi-yi Nufus va Maskan, 1976; Julian Bharier, "The Growth of Towns and Villages in Iran, 1900-66," Middle Eastern Studies, 8 (January, 1972), pp. 53-54; Mehdi Amani, "Masa'il-i Dimugrafik (Jam'iyyati-yi) Shahr'i Tehran," Sukhanrani'ha va Guzarish-ha dar Nakhustin Siminar-i Barrisi-yi Masa'il-i Ijtima'i-yi Shahri-i Tehran (Tehran: University of Tehran Press, 1343/1964), pp. 47-62.

1976. In 1966 nearly 11 percent of Iran's total population and 28 percent of its urban population lived in the city of Tehran. In 1976 these same percentages increased to 13 and 28.6, respectively (Table 2.5).

The problem of overconcentration of urban population in one or a few large cities has been discussed extensively in the sociological literature. In a seminal article in 1939, Mark Jefferson pointed to the rapid growth of one city (the "primate" city) and elaborated on the effects of this development on the social and economic life of the country.[19] Since Jefferson, scholars have been divided over the benefits and costs of overurbanization in developing countries. Philip Hauser, for example, makes a distinction between urbanization in the West and in the developing countries. He contends that:

> Urban problems and the problems of rapid urbanization are quite different in the economically advanced and the economically underdeveloped areas of the world respectively. In the economically advanced nations, urbanization is both an antecedent and a consequence of high levels of living. It both makes possible and is a manifestation of great increases in division of labor and specialization, in technology, in skill, and in productivity. In the economically underdeveloped areas, it does not usually have these properties.[20]

Hauser further makes the assertion that large population concentrations in Asia and the non-Western world "are more the result of 'push' factors due to the low level of rural living or conditions of physical insecurity, than as in the Western experience of 'pull' factors represented by job opportunities and higher levels of living."[21] Hauser and others also point to a number of economic problems that overurbanization tends to create. These include centralization and concentration of industry in one city to the detriment of other urban locations; undue emphasis on labor-intensive techniques in order to find jobs for unemployed migrants to the city; inadequate balance between agricultural and industrial development; and finally, allocation of scarce resources to power plants and factories at the expense of "social investments" such as water, sewage, and housing development.[22] Likewise, Janet Agu-Lughod in a study of Egypt emphasizes similar economic problems associated with the over-concentration of population in the two primate cities of Cairo and Alexandria. She notes that this over-concentration is "likely to emerge as the key bottleneck in any program of industrialization" in Egypt.[23]

Another group of scholars take issue with Hauser and others on the economic and social consequences of overurbanization. David Kamerschen in his comparative study of several countries finds that there is no positive correlation between rural pressure and overurbanization, and that the hypothesis that rapid urbanization adversely affects economic development cannot be sustained statistically. These two findings contrast with Hauser's major

16

Table 2.4

Population Distribution in Ten Largest Cities:
1956-1976

City	1956	1966	1976
Tehran	1,512,082	2,719,730	4,496,159
Isfahan	254,708	424,045	671,825
Mashhad	241,989	409,616	670,180
Tabriz	289,996	403,413	598,576
Shiraz	170,659	269,865	416,408
Ahvaz	120,098	206,375	329,006
Abadan	226,083	272,962	296,081
Kirmanshah	125,439	187,930	290,861
Qum	96,499	134,292	246,831
Rasht	109,491	143,557	187,203

SOURCES: Iran, Census reports, 1956, 1966, 1976.

Table 2.5

Percentages of Urban and Total Population
Living in Tehran: 1900-1976

Year	% of Urban Population Living in Tehran	% of Total Population Living in Tehran
1900	9.6	2.0
1946	20.8	5.6
1956	25.3	7.9
1966	27.7	10.8
1976	28.6	13.3

argument.[24]   Moreover, Surrinder Mehta and N. V. Sovani in
two separate studies suggest that primacy and overurbanization
may be, to some extent, beneficial to economic development.
Mehta maintains that the primate city, because of its
favorable location, tradition of market economy, and rational
economic considerations can foster economic growth. This is
due generally to the fact that the primate city is often

> the only efficient locale for non-agricultural
> production, both manufacturing and specialized
> services. This is because it has the advantages of
> a large and concentrated labor and consumer market;
> it is the focus of transportation routes; it has
> the economies of scale and juxtaposition of
> industries and specialists; it is a fertile ground
> for social and cultural change necessary for
> economic development; it is a center from which
> these innovations or new adaptations, artifacts and
> technologies introduced from the outside or of
> local origin spread and diffuse into the countryside
> and to other towns; and it is an area that receives
> migrants from the countryside thus relieving the
> farming areas of the burden of excess population.[25]

It is not my purpose here to analyze economic advantages
or disadvantages of primate cities and overurbanization in
greater depth. The most logical position to take in this
controversy is to point out that some primate cities may
hinder economic growth whereas others may foster it. There
are other factors involved in addition to primacy. Bert
Hoselitz's distinction between "generative" and "parasitic"
cities is well to the point. A city (whether primate or not)
is "generative" when it provides an impetus for economic
growth and cultural change. It is "parasitic" when it impedes
these developments.[26]   Thus, the major concern should be to
discover if a particular city is generative or parasitic.

Tehran as the Primate City

Tehran is by any definition a primate city. It is
probably also parasitic in the sense discussed by Hoselitz.
Tehran's primacy, however, has been developing slowly over
the years. The history of Tehran goes back several centuries
to when it was an insignificant small village. The Iranian
historian, A. Javahir-Kalam, points out that in the third
Islamic century two villages with the name of Tehran were
known, one near Isfahan and the other near Ray.[27]   The Tehran
of Ray was the lesser of the two villages and apparently had
no known historical significance. However, the surrounding
area, particularly Mount Damavand, was always rich with
Persian mythology and legends. The epic poet, Firdowsi,
recites many mythological stories taking place in the Mount
Damavand region.
The history of Tehran's growth is connected to the rise
and fall of the famous nearby city of Ray.[28]   As long as Ray
flourished as a great Islamic city, Tehran remained an obscure

18

village. With the sack of Ray and its terrible destruction
by the Mongols in 1220, Tehran slowly emerged as a town of
note. It was not, however, until the reign of the Safavid
king Shah Tahmasp I (1524-76) that Tehran acquired greater
importance. Shah Tahmasp ordered the construction of walls,
114 towers (for the 114 surahs of the Qur'an), and four gates
for the defense of the city. He buried a surah of the Qur'an
under every one of Tehran's towers.[29] Another Safavid king,
Shah Sultan Husayn, was sufficiently impressed with Tehran to
hold his court there during the winter months of 1720-21.[30]
The next important episode in the history of Tehran was its
six-year occupation by the Afghans. The inhabitants of Tehran
had initially managed to defeat an advance force of Afghans
but eventually succumbed to them.[31] In 1729 Tehran was freed
by Nadir Afshar, who inflicted massive defeats on the Afghans.
The Afghans, in L. Lockhart's words, "massacred many of the
notables of the city before they fled southwards."[32]

Under the Afshar and Zand rulers, Tehran continued to
grow in importance. Karim Khan Zand (1750-79) gave orders
for construction of government offices and a royal building.
For a time he even considered the possibility of making Tehran
his capital in place of Shiraz. The modern history of Tehran
begins with the founder of the Qajar dynasty, Agha Muhammad
Khan, who made Tehran his capital in 1786. From this date on
Tehran, as the seat of government, acquired great stature and
was recognized as one of the principal cities of Iran.

For some time, however, Tehran lagged behind Tabriz in
both population and commercial importance. A British foreign
office report in 1841, for example, emphasizes that "Tehraun,
although the present residence of the Court of Persia, is
only the Second or Third City of the Empire in respect to
commerce."[33] In another British report in 1868, Tehran's
population is estimated as 85,000, to 110,000 for Tabriz.[34]

The first census of Tehran in 1884 reported a total
population of 155,736, which included 8,480 categorized as
military personnel.[35] This population was dispersed in
Tehran's five major quarters of Ark, 'Udlajan, Chalehmaydan,
Sanglaj, and Bazaar (Table 2.6). There was also an
additional area outside the city walls and limits that housed
11 percent of the inhabitants. Tehran's population was
predominantly Muslim. Non-Muslims (Christians, Jews,
Zoroastrians) constituted a mere 2 percent of the population.

The population of Tehran continued to increase steadily.
By the turn of the century, Tehran had approximately 200,000
inhabitants--equal to Tabriz's population.[36] The events of
the Constitutional Revolution (1905-12), efforts toward
Westernization and industrialization, and in-migration from
provincial areas increased Tehran's importance and helped to
transform it into the country's dominant city.[37] It can
therefore be said that, owing to a variety of interrelated
factors, in the first quarter of the twentieth century Tehran
emerged as the principal and most important Iranian city.

Table 2.6

Population Distribution and
Districts of Tehran, 1884

District	Population	% of Total Population
Ark	3,014	2
'Udlajan	36,495	25
Chalehmaydan	34,547	24
Sanglaj	29,673	20
Bazaar	26,674	18
Outside City Districts	16,853	11
TOTAL	147,256[a]	

SOURCE: First Population Census of Iran, 1884. Adapted from Mehdi Amani, "Avvalin Sarshumari-yi Jam'iyyat'i Tehran," 'Ulum'i Ijtima'i, 1 (Bahman, 1348/1970), p. 90.

[a]This does not include 8,480 military personnel.

By the time of Reza Shah Pahlavi's ascendancy to the throne in 1925, Tehran had well over 210,000 inhabitants. During Reza Shah's reign, the city was physically transformed. Initially Tehran's old quarters were left intact,[38] and Reza Shah concentrated on constructing a new, modern city to the north of Tehran's old quarters. Large government buildings, wide paved streets, and squares characterized the new city. Modern amenities such as electricity were also added to the new quarters and were later extended to the older sections of the city. But as some of the population began moving north to the new city quarters, the older sections slowly deteriorated. In the post-World War II era, northward movement by the wealthier inhabitants of Tehran continued at a more rapid pace. Population of the older quarters also increased as migration from provincial areas to all parts of greater Tehran became a regular feature of the capital's life.

During the second quarter of the twentieth century, Tehran's population increased by about 4.7 times, and the city's primacy was well established (Figure 2.1). To calculate Tehran's primacy, two complementary procedures are used. The first procedure, proposed by Arnold Linsky, is to calculate the ratio of the largest to the second-largest city. A second and more comprehensive method used by Mehta is to measure that percentage of the population of the four largest cities that resides in the largest city.[39] In Linsky's study, Tehran ranked 13 among 39 metropolitan areas in 1955. In Mehta's analysis for the same year, Tehran ranked 33 among 87 urban centers. Clearly in the 1970s Tehran's primacy rank

Figure 2.1

Increase in Tehran's Population: 1910-1976
(Semilogarithmic Scale)

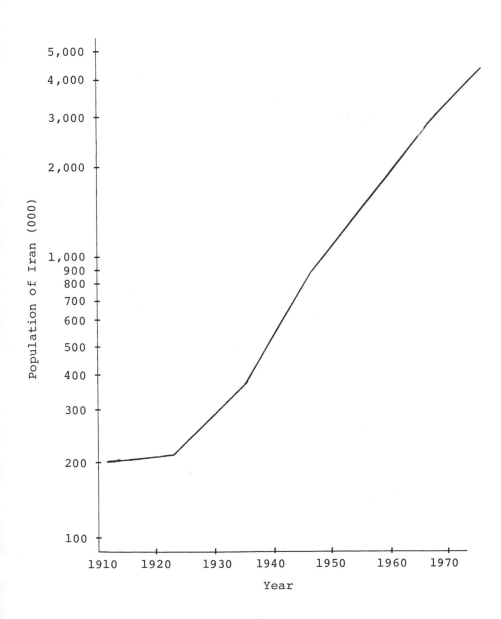

Table 2.7

Changes in Tehran's Primacy: 1900-1976

Year	Primacy (Linsky's Method)	Primacy (Mehta's Method)
1900	1.0	34.7
1946	3.2	57.3
1956	5.2	65.7
1966	6.4	68.7
1976	6.6	69.8

would be substantially higher. Table 2.7 reports changes in Tehran's primacy based on these two procedures. The results of both methods confirm the continued growth of Tehran's primacy and dominance over other cities. Compared with other major primate cities of the Middle East, Tehran shows a higher primacy value (Table 2.8). This is even true of Cairo, which has been recognized for some time as the dominant city of Egypt. This is due to the fact that Cairo has to compete with Alexandria, whereas in the case of Tehran no major competitor exists any longer. Isfahan, Mashhad, and Tabriz are all much smaller than Tehran and do not enjoy the capital's preeminence (Table 2.9)

Table 2.8

Primacy Value for Major Middle Eastern Cities

City[a]	Primacy Value (Linsky)	Primacy Value (Mehta)
Baghdad	4.7	66.5
Cairo	2.5	62.1
Damascus	1.3	46.3
Istanbul	1.6	49.3
Tehran	6.6	69.8

SOURCE: United Nations, Demographic Yearbook, 1976.

[a]Population figures are based on the latest available statistics: Iraq (1965), Egypt (1974), Syria (1975), Turkey (1973), Iran (1976).

Table 2.9

Population of Ten Largest Cities as Percentage
of Tehran's Population: 1956-1976

City	1956	1966	1976
Tehran	100.0	100.0	100.0
Isfahan	16.8	15.5	14.9
Mashhad	16.0	15.0	14.9
Tabriz	19.1	14.8	13.3
Shiraz	11.2	9.9	9.2
Ahvaz	7.9	7.5	7.3
Abadan	14.9	10.0	6.5
Kirmanshah	8.2	6.9	6.4
Qum	6.3	4.9	5.4
Rasht	7.2	5.2	4.1

Tehran's dominance over other Iranian cities has also created an exception to the rank-size rule. According to this rule, the rank of a nation's cities should roughly conform to a descending order, in which the largest city has twice the population of the second largest, three times the population of the third largest, and so on. In the case of Iran, as in some other Middle Eastern countries, the growth of the primate city has prevented operation of the rank-size rule (Figure 2.2)--although V. F. Costello maintains that below the fifth-ranked city all countries of the Middle East, with the exception of Bahrain, conform to the rank-size relationship.[40] As Charles Issawi has pointed out, in the Middle East, as in the preindustrial West, the common pattern of size distribution is for one giant city (or in some cases two) to tower above the rest.[41] Thus aside from Tehran, the prevailing pattern is domination of Baghdad in Iraq, Beirut in Lebanon, Cairo and Alexandria in Egypt, Damascus and Aleppo in Syria, and Istanbul and Ankara in Turkey.

Brian Berry in his analysis of city-size distributions in 38 countries of the world concludes that primacy tends to occur in countries that until recently have been economically or politically dependent on an outside country. Primate cities in these areas turn out to be "the national capitals, cultural and economic centers, often the chief port, and the focus of national consciousness and feeling."[42] Most of the Middle Eastern countries with primate cities fit Berry's criterion of external political-economic dependency and his description of their primate city characteristics. Berry further finds that there is no relationship between relative economic development of countries and their city-size

Figure 2.2

Rank-Size Distribution for Twenty Largest Cities, 1976
(Full Logarithmic Scale)

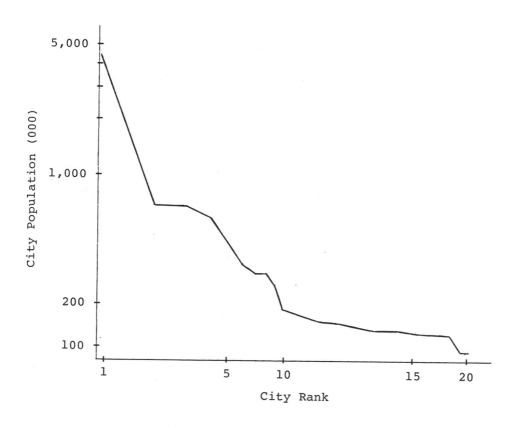

distributions.[43]   Although this is perhaps true as a broad
generalization, it is probably not an accurate statement of
the economic effects of primate city development in individual
Middle Eastern countries.   At least in the case of Iran, the
growth of Tehran as a primate city has had deleterious effects
on economic development and distribution of economic goods and
services in the rest of the nation.

The degree to which many of the desired goals of Iranian
society are concentrated in Tehran is bound to be "parasitic"
for the country as a whole.   This concentration can be seen
in practically all areas of social life.   Statistics compiled
by Marvin Zonis in the areas of education, health, communications, and economy underline Tehran's dominance in the early
1960s.[44]   For the more recent period, the following statistics
should further confirm Zonis's observations.

EDUCATION:

66.7 percent of all university students study in Tehran's
institutions of higher learning.[45]
29.6 percent of all high school students are enrolled in
Tehran's secondary schools.[46]
19 percent of all elementary school students are enrolled
in Tehran's elementary schools.[47]
31.8 percent of Iran's literate urban population lives in
Tehran.[48]

ECONOMY:

29.1 percent of all industrial establishments in Iran are
located in Tehran.[49]
46.1 percent of all large industrial establishments are
located in Tehran.[50]
36.2 percent of all persons engaged in industrial
establishments work in Tehran.[51]
82.7 percent of all companies are registered in Tehran.[52]
52.9 percent of all banking units of the 33 largest cities
are located in Tehran.[53]

HEALTH:

42.6 percent of all hospital beds are in Tehran.[54]
45.8 percent of all licensed physicians practice in Tehran.[55]
57.9 percent of all dentists practice in Tehran.[56]

COMMUNICATIONS:

24.7 percent of all cinemas are located in Tehran.[57]
54.5 percent of all telephone receivers are operating in
the Tehran census district.[58]
61.5 percent of all newspapers and periodicals are
published in Tehran.[59]

An important consequence of Tehran's rapid and unplanned
growth is the fact that the city has not been able to provide
adequate social services for its population.   Shortage of
housing units for the low-income groups is a particularly
serious problem in the capital.   In a survey of dwelling units
of Tehran in 1966, a shortage of 78,000 housing units for
low-income groups was noted (Table 2.10).   This deficiency

Table 2.10

Distribution of Families and Dwelling Units
in Four Income Groups of Tehran, 1966

Income Group	No. of Families (000)	% of Families	No. of Dwelling Units (000)	Shortage and Surplus of Dwelling Units (000)
Low income	278	44	200	-78
Low middle income	278	44	280	+ 2
Upper middle income	69	11	70	+ 1
High income	6	1	20	+14
TOTAL	631	100	570	-61

SOURCE: Iran, Economic Survey of Greater Tehran, 1966.
Adapted from Mohammed Hemassi, "Tehran in Transition: A Study
in Comparative Factorial Ecology," in The Population of Iran:
A Selection of Readings, ed. Jamshid Momeni (Honolulu: East-
West Population Institute, 1977), p. 364.

greatly increased in the 1970s as land speculation raised the
price of housing unrealistically. In addition, problems in
distribution of electricity and water, inadequate public
transportation facilities, and other such amenities have made
life for the residents of Tehran excessively difficult.
Although modern Tehran is a "heterogenetic" city in the sense
that it has developed new patterns of culture in conflict
with traditional Iranian cities, it is also "parasitic" by
virtue of its negative impact on the economic development of
the country.[60]

Migration in Iran

Some Migration Theories

Ever since the publication of E. G. Ravenstein's famous
"laws of migration" in 1885,[61] there has been much interest
in the patterns and forms of internal migration in the
countries of the world. Ravenstein's "laws" make broad
observations on the relationship between migration, on the
one hand, and several other factors such as distance, stages,
economic motives, migratory currents and countercurrents, and
urban-rural differences, on the other. Everett Lee claims
that in spite of criticisms, Ravenstein's observations "have
stood the test of time."[62] Defining migration as "a permanent

or semipermanent change of residence,"[63] Lee proceeds to develop his own theory of migration based partly on Ravenstein's laws. He states that migration involves four general factors associated with (a) the area of origin, (b) the area of destination, (c) intervening obstacles, and (d) personal factors.[64] The first three of these are presented in Figure 2.3 by pluses for forces attracting people, by minuses for forces repelling people, and by zeroes for indifferent forces. These forces are affected by a number of intervening obstacles, among which the most commonly studied is distance between the points of origin and destination. Finally, there are a variety of personal and individual factors that enter into the decision to migrate. Lee concludes his analysis of migration by proposing a number of hypotheses on the volume of migration, streams and counterstreams in migration, and characteristics of the migrants. He further maintains that "the decision to migrate . . . is never completely rational, and for some persons the rational component is much less than the irrational."[65]

After criticizing aspects of Lee's formulation, Michael Todaro proposes an economic model of migration based on the assumption that migration is primarily the product of a rational economic decision by the individual migrant. Todaro's model postulates that in spite of the high rate of urban unemployment in many developing countries, "migration proceeds in response to the urban-rural differences in expected rather than actual earnings."[66] Todaro argues that

Figure 2.3

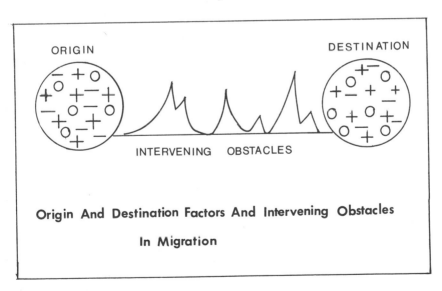

Origin And Destination Factors And Intervening Obstacles

In Migration

SOURCE: Everett Lee, "A Theory of Migration," Demography, 3 (1966), p. 50.

27

the decision to migrate to urban areas should be viewed in terms of the migrant's "permanent income" calculations. Thus, "if the migrant anticipates a relatively low probability of finding regular wage employment in the initial period but expects this probability to increase over time as he is able to broaden his urban contacts, it would still be rational for him to migrate, even though expected urban income during the initial period or periods might be lower than expected rural income."[67] What emerges from Todaro's discussion, as well as other studies of migrants, is that cityward migration is "primarily for economic reasons."[68] In the case of Iran, economic factors play a critical role in the migration decision. There are, however, some important demographic, educational, and economic characteristics of migrants that should be analyzed first.

Demographic Characteristics

Rural to urban migration is a significant factor in the recent increase in Iran's urban population. This situation, however, is not restricted to Iran alone. Todaro states that more than 50 percent of the rise in urban population of many developing countries can be explained by rural to urban migration.[69] Although there is heavy cityward migration in Iran, the overall rate of internal migration is not substantial, amounting to merely 13.8 percent in 1972 (Table 2.11). Julian Bharier's careful estimate of migration in Iran confirms the view that extensive cityward migration is of recent origin. He finds that on the basis of the "annual rates of growth of urban and total population . . . there was no significant net rural/urban migration before about 1934"[70] (Table 2.12). But there were movements of population "within both the rural and the urban areas."[71] Between 1900 and 1956, Bharier's calculations point to a total of 685,000 rural to urban migrants, accounting for 39 percent of the internal population movements for the period. For 1956-66, the net rural to urban migration was 1,680,000--a sharp increase over the previous decades. Bharier notes that this figure is equivalent to 90 percent of the total internal population movements.[72]

The pace of rural to urban migration did not slacken for the 1966-76 period. During this decade, 2,111,000 individuals migrated from the rural areas to the cities.[73] The sample census on manpower in 1972 indicated a total of 3,974,434 internal migrants in Iran. Of these, 2,121,545 (53.5%) had stated rural areas as their last place of residence before finally settling in a city. This number does not include a large percentage of step migrants who had initially departed from rural communities but had subsequently resided in another town or city before their final migration. This view is substantiated by the results of the 1976 nationwide census that indicates an annual increase of 6 percent in urban population as opposed to only 1.1 percent in rural population for the ten-year period 1966 to 1976. Rural to urban migration also varies substantially for different towns and

Table 2.11

Internal Migration: 1956-1972

Year	Migrant Population	% Migration
1956	2,081,082	10.9
1966	3,224,200	12.8
1972	3,974,434	13.8

SOURCES: Iran, Ministry of Interior, General Statistics Office, Guzarishi-i Khulasah-yi Sarshumari-yi Umumi-yi Kishvar, Volume II, November, 1956; Iran, Plan Organization, Iranian Statistical Center, National Census of Population and Housing, No. 168, March, 1968; Iran, National Statistical Center, Natayij-i Amargiri-yi Niru-yi Insani, 1972.

Table 2.12

Annual (Compound) Rates of Population Growth: 1900-1970

Period	Urban	Rural	Total
1900-26	0.08	0.08	0.08
1927-34	1.50	1.50	1.50
1935-40	2.30	1.30	1.50
1941-56	4.40	1.40	2.20
1956-70	5.30	1.70	2.90

SOURCE: Julian Bharier, Economic Development in Iran: 1900-1970 (London: Oxford University Press, 1971), p. 28.

cities of Iranian provinces, ranging from a low of 3.3 percent for migrants from Simnan to a high of 71.3 percent for East Azerbaijan (Table 2.13). The migrants tend to be equally divided between males and females. However, males most frequently migrant between the ages of twenty and twenty-four, whereas female migration is most commonly at the higher age level of thirty-five to thirty-nine.[74]

A few leading cities, and particularly Tehran, have absorbed a large segment of rural migrants. Tehran's selection as the capital in 1786 resulted in a rapid influx of population from other parts of the country. The first census of Tehran in 1884 reported only 26.6 percent native Tehranis.[75] In the modern era Tehran has continued to attract a large number of migrants. Bharier notes that between 1900 and 1956, 60 percent of all internal movements of population was accounted for by migration to Tehran.[76] In the following ten years Tehran absorbed 38 percent of all migrants.[77] In 1966 about 49 percent of Tehran's population was of migrant origin. By the 1970s the number of migrants living in Tehran exceeded 50 percent.

Educational Characteristics

Most of the studies of rural to urban migration in the developing countries report a strong relationship between educational attainment and migration.[78] In Iran the largest single group (43%) of cityward migrants in 1972 consisted of migrants without any education. Nevertheless it is important to note that more than one half of these migrants did have some literacy. Since only about 20 percent of Iran's rural population can read and write, this finding tends to support the basic association between literacy and migration.

The great majority of rural migrants in Iran are composed of landless peasants and farm laborers. The primary force for their migration is the "push" factors at the point of origin and the increasing difficulty of maintaining a subsistence life in the rural areas of the country. For these peasants and farmers, economic considerations--push factors in the village and the hope for higher expected income in the city--are the dominant reasons for migration to the urban centers. The available census data repeatedly confirm the central importance of economic factors in cityward migration. In 1972, for example, 71.6 percent of the principal migrants residing in urban areas stated that they migrated either to seek work or a better job.[79] Since this percentage also includes the intercity migrants, the actual ratio for the rural to urban migrants would be even higher. Therefore, the findings of Todaro and others emphasizing the primacy of economic reasons as causes of cityward migration seem to be confirmed.

Table 2.13

Number and Percentage of Rural to Urban
Migration of Urban Residents, 1972

Provincial Point of Origin in Migration	Number of Internal Migrants	Number of Rural to Urban Migrants	% of Rural to Urban Migration
Central	1,803,657	841,254	46.6
Gilan and Zanjan	94,821	60,347	63.6
Mazandaran	109,873	50,543	46.0
East Azerbaijan	132,115	85,368	64.6
West Azerbaijan	60,149	42,940	71.3
Kirmanshahan	112,246	62,475	55.6
Khuzistan	204,780	24,378	11.9
Fars	107,864	57,686	53.4
Kirman	41,943	26,964	64.2
Khurasan	204,083	114,089	55.9
Isfahan and Yazd	138,505	45,290	32.6
Sistan and Baluchistan	27,985	6,176	22.0
Kurdistan	27,549	11,551	41.9
Hamadan	48,173	32,770	68.0
Chahar Mahal and Bakhtiyari	9,269	3,205	34.5
Luristan	44,823	20,157	44.9
Ilam and Pushtkuh	2,163	372	17.1
Buyir Ahmadi and Kahkiluyih	11,183	2,186	19.5
Sahili and Bushihr	18,694	8,257	44.1
Simnan	8,843	297	3.3

SOURCE: Adapted from Iran, National Statistical Center, Natayij-i Amargiri-yi Niru-yi Insani, 1972.

CHAPTER III

VILLAGE LIFE AND FLIGHT TO THE CITY

Agriculture has traditionally made a significant contribution to Iran's economy. Although this contribution has gradually declined over the years, as late as 1959 the agricultural sector comprised 33 percent of the Gross National Product. With the onset of the land reform program of 1962 and the ensuing problems in Iranian agriculture, the sectoral contribution of agriculture declined to 23 percent by 1968. The oil boom of 1973 and the emphasis on massive public expenditure in urban areas further aggravated the agricultural decline. Indeed, by 1976 agriculture contributed a mere 9.4 percent to the Gross National Product.[1] An important consequence of this demise of agriculture has been the severe dislocations in the countryside and the increasing impoverishment of the poor peasantry.

Before the implementation of the land reform program, the Iranian peasantry was divided into three broad classes of rich, middle, and poor peasants. The rich peasants were capitalist farmers whose ownership of land was based on the exploitation of wage labor and their own frequent participation in farmwork. The middle peasants were the independent smallholders who owned and cultivated their land with the help of family labor. The poor peasants were the sharecroppers, farm laborers, and agricultural proletariat who cultivated the land that belonged, for the most part, to the absentee landlord.[2] Towering above this classification were the large landowners composed of the crown (saltanat), the state (khalisih), the religious foundations (waqf), large landowners ('umdih malik), and smaller landowners (khurdih malik). In contrast to the European experience, the large landowners generally did not live in the country and were mostly town and city residents. This fact has prompted Ann Lambton to state that in Iran "land ownership had always, to some extent, been an urban phenomenon."[3] The absence of the landlords from the rural areas meant that cultivation of their lands had to be conducted and supervised by a group of resident villagers who constituted the bulk of Iran's rich peasantry. The rich peasantry generally consisted of the village headmen (kadkhuda), the bailiffs (mubashir) who administered the absentee landlords' farmland, and the oxen owners (gavband) who leased plow animals.

On the basis of the available information, it is evident that the substantial majority of the Iranian peasantry belonged to the class of poor peasants. Rich peasants constituted a small portion of the peasantry--although because of ties to the landlord, their power in the village was significantly higher than their number would imply. Owing to a host of geographic and other factors, the size of the

32

middle peasantry and its contribution to the village economy remained minimal, the only exception being the middle peasantry in certain northern provinces.[4] The vast majority of the Iranian peasants were poor, exploited, and dependent on the absentee landlords for their livelihood.

These masses of poor peasants were divided into two groups. The first was the sharecropping peasant who was given the right to cultivate (nasaq) portions of the land owned by the landlords for a specified or unspecified time on the basis of either written or oral contracts.[5] These peasants joined in production teams of four to sixteen men (bunih) in order to cultivate the landlords' property.[6] The extent of the peasants' contribution to the usual five factors of agricultural production in Iran--land, water, labor, seed, and plow animals--determined their share in the final distribution of the harvest crops.[7]

The second group was composed of the agricultural proletariat. These laborers owned neither land nor the rights to cultivate another's property. They were hired to perform agricultural labor during the peak farming seasons and survived on their meager income by doing farmwork and related tasks. The sharecropping peasants often referred to the agricultural proletariat and nonfarming villagers as khwushnishin (happy squatter). This classification is misleading, however, since it includes the three distinct and varied income groups of the agricultural proletariat, the nonagricultural workers (blacksmith, coppersmith, carpenter, shoemaker, etc.), and the comparatively well off rural bourgeoisie (shopkeepers, merchants, moneylenders, etc.).[8] In the early 1960s, the agricultural proletariat constituted more than 80 percent of the khwushnishin population and one third of Iran's total rural population.[9] They were by far the most destitute of Iran's poor peasantry, barely managing minimal subsistence. The land reform program attempted to deal with the plight of the peasantry by redistributing the landlords' estates among the peasant cultivators.

The Land Reform Program

The genesis of the land reform program of Muhammad Reza Shah Pahlavi can be seen in his edict of January 1951 in which he proposed the distribution of crown lands among the peasants. During the next few years sporadic attempts were made to achieve the goals of this edict.[10] In 1952 Muhammad Musaddiq's National Front government put forth a program of agricultural reform that limited the landowner's profits and required him "to pay 20 percent of his profits back to the village."[11] With Musaddiq's fall, his decrees on agricultural reform were abrogated, although minor laws retaining features of the original reforms were later passed by the parliament.[12] The first concerted effort to inaugurate a comprehensive land reform program did not take place until 1960, when both the Assembly and the Senate passed a land reform law. This law was conceived partly under pressure from the American government, which was concerned about instability in the Middle East, especially in the wake of the Iraqi revolution of 1958 and fears of possible similar mass uprisings in Iran. The Americans hoped that land reform would stabilize the countryside and prevent the development of major pressures from below. The law, however, was "ill-conceived and badly drafted."[13] It was also opposed by the Iranian religious hierarchy for being contrary to Islamic law.

The failure of the 1960 law, coupled with extensive economic problems and political discontents, prompted the American government to demand agrarian reform as a condition for financial assistance to Iran. The result was the amended land reform law of 1962 and its subsequent additional articles of January 1963. The government of Prime Minister Ali Amini was entrusted with full implementation of the provisions of the new amended land reform program. The new law limited each landlord to one village. The remaining villages were purchased by the government for distribution to the peasants. The landlords were to be paid in several installments on the basis of land valuation determined by previous tax payments.

Corollary to the land reform program, attempts were made to establish rural cooperative societies, joint-stock corporations, and large agribusiness farms in certain designated areas. The rural cooperative societies date back to 1955, with modifications instituted in their operations in 1962. Membership in the cooperatives was open to peasants and those engaged in agriculture who purchased one or more shares in the societies of their locality.[14] These societies were charged with a variety of functions, including provision of agricultural implements, machinery, and primary necessities; purchase, storage, exchange, transport, and sale of the members' produce; and granting of loans, credits, and acceptance of deposits.[15] Joint-stock corporations were created as part of the Fourth Development Plan (1968-72) to allow smallholding farmers to pool their lands and resources under supervision and financial assistance of the government.[16] The farmers' shares in the resources were apportioned according to their land value and other contributions to the agricultural production. The agribusiness complexes were established in the early 1970s as part of the government's efforts to set up large and modern agro-industrial organi- zations. These highly mechanized agricultural operations were financed by joint private, public, and foreign interests in areas where fertile soil and water supply were available.[17] These operations were eventually linked to a plan to create a series of "poles of development" in order to tap maximum agricultural benefits from the consolidated lands.

Failure of Land Reform

The land reform program was conceived with both political and economic objectives in mind. Political considerations,

34

however, were the primary aims of the program. By the
mid-1970s it was evident that land reform had essentially
failed to achieve either its economic or its political
objectives. The economic failure was particularly noteworthy,
since it signaled the demise of Iranian agriculture and
created many political problems in its wake. In terms of
its political aspects, the land reform program had at least
two aims: (1) to destroy the power base of the major landowning families and thus neutralize a potential source of
opposition to the regime; and (2) to gain the support and
allegiance of the peasants and hence forestall a revolution
in the countryside. The first aim was achieved in the sense
that the landowning families can no longer use their rural
support in a potential confrontation with the regime. The
power of the ruling families, however, has not been totally
destroyed, since many of the former large landowners
concentrated their wealth in economic, commercial, and
business activities in the urban centers. Although these
commercial activities are regulated by the government, this
new form of concentration of wealth continues to provide the
former landowning classes with some potential leverage
vis-à-vis the government. But this leverage is of
comparatively little value, since the new owners of business
enterprises nowhere exercise the same degree of control over
the workers and employees as they did over the peasants and
villagers as landowners. Moreover, the government has made
some attempts to win the allegiance of the workers through
promises of profit sharing and other, similar ventures.

The second political objective of the land reform
program faced important difficulties. The major reason is
the fact that only one group of the poor peasantry--the former
sharecroppers--received land as part of the redistribution
program. The agricultural laborers and village proletariat,
who had previously enjoyed no cultivating rights, were left
out of the plan. This not only exacerbated the existing
intraclass tensions between the two groups but also resulted
in a rapid deterioration of economic life of the already
dispossessed agricultural proletariat.[18] Since the
agricultural proletariat included a large portion of the
Iranian peasantry, there was no possible way for the regime
to gain the support of a broad spectrum of the peasants.
In fact, the majority of the poor rural migrants who went to
to the principal cities of Iran came from among those
agricultural laborers who were now pushed off the land.

The Shah's regime was somewhat more successful with the
former sharecroppers who received some land. However, even
this limited success was at best a mixed blessing for the
regime. Although the government succeeded in making the
peasants conscious of their exploitation by the landlords,
it did not fare as well in channeling this consciousness into
clear support for the Shah. The peasants were made aware
of the land reform law by extensive government propaganda
efforts. As K. S. McLachlan points out, during the early
stages of land reform "all local [radio] stations in Iran
maintained a close coverage of land reform activities for

35

the benefit of the rural population and ensured that the official government view was widely understood."[19] There were several minor manifestations of this emerging peasant political consciousness. In Fars, for example, there were a few attempts by the peasants "to seize landlord property outside the terms of law."[20] Along the same lines, Ann Lambton reports that in her visit to a village in Azerbaijan she asked a peasant "whether the village had been transferred [to the peasants] and if not to whom it belonged. He replied, 'Our landowner has died!'"[21] Lambton notes that:

> This was, perhaps typical of the feeling abroad in many areas that the landowner as such would shortly disappear, if he had not already done so. This feeling was encouraged by notices such as "the land belongs to the person who cultivates it" which were prominently displayed in the land reform offices.[22]

The rise of political consciousness among the peasants was also evident in the activities of the peasants during the government-sponsored Congress of Rural Cooperatives in January 1963 in Tehran. About 4,700 delegates, mostly officers of the rural cooperative societies from different parts of the country, were brought together for the first time. As Lambton notes, these delegates felt that "they were no longer isolated, and experienced a sense of unity and strength."[23]

One of the chief organizers of the land reform program, Minister of Agriculture Hasan Arsanjani, was the primary force of this gathering. The congress was one of Arsanjani's most notable triumphs, but paradoxically it also caused his downfall. After many meetings and speeches, the orderly congress unanimously approved eight resolutions, the last of which thanked Arsanjani for his "selfless effort and sacrifice" on behalf of the farmers.[24] Arsanjani's popularity among the delegates and his growing identification with the peasants alarmed the regime. It is reported that during a field trip of social scientists from the University of Tehran in 1966, a number of villagers were found "who knew very little about the Shah of Iran but were very familiar with the name Arsanjani."[25] The Shah would not tolerate this new center of power even though Arsanjani was identified with the regime. Soon after the congress adjourned, Arsanjani was relieved as the minister of agriculture and appointed ambassador to Rome, far away from the rural areas of Iran and the peasants.[26] The crucial factor in Arsanjani's downfall was his failure to fully channel the peasants' political support directly to the Shah. Although at least portions of the peasantry were now politically mobilized, the Shah did not turn out to be the sole beneficiary of this development.

Another important feature of the land reform program concerned the specific relationship and form of contact between the peasants and the government. The elimination of large landowners destroyed the intermediary between the two groups. Before land reform, peasant demands focused on the landowners who were expected to respond to their economic,

social, and individual demands. If the peasants were
destitute or if the crops did not reach the expected level
of production, it was the landowner who had to satisfy or
pacify the peasants in one way or another. The government
was not directly involved in these matters. With the
imposition of land reform, the government became the sole
source for satisfying the peasants' needs and demands. As
Hossein Mahdavy observes, "now there will be no one except
the government to blame for the mismanagement of rural
affairs."[27] The economic problems that were soon to beset
Iranian agriculture made the significance of this problem all
too apparent to the regime.

All three major economic attempts to make land reform a
success--rural cooperative societies, joint-stock corporations, and large agribusiness farms--experienced varying
degrees of failure. Even the organization of rural
cooperatives, despite its early promise, did not meet
expectations. In the early stages of land reform, development
and expansion of rural cooperative societies received top
priority. By 1968, "8,652 societies with a membership of
1,105,402 persons serving some 20,803 villages had been
established."[28] The government, however, felt that it was
best to channel financial and technical services through a
smaller number of cooperative societies.[29] The societies
were consolidated, and their total number was decreased to
one third of the 1968 figure by the end of the next decade.

The trend toward centralization and the domination of
these societies by the newly created Ministry of Land Reform
and Rural Cooperatives created bureaucratic and managerial
problems in the operation of the cooperatives. As Marvin
Weinbaum indicates, most cooperatives were "too poorly funded,
their credit terms too restrictive, and the prices paid to
farmers too low to encourage expanded production or to relieve
the farmer of traditional dependence on non-institutional
moneylenders."[30] In a survey by the Office of Regional
Studies, it was found that 32 percent of the 339 cases
surveyed had obtained loans from noninstitutional moneylenders
at interest rates generally exceeding 25 percent.[31] Many
cooperative members felt that they had no choice other than
to depend on these high-interest loans, since the societies
either did not provide them with sufficient funds or their
loan requests were not granted quickly enough by the unwieldy
bureaucracy of the cooperatives.[32]

The cooperative societies also suffered from local
mismanagement and the resultant clumsy decision-making
process. Those selected as local managers of the cooperatives
were usually the more prosperous farmers who frequently
manipulated decision making to their own advantage and
economic benefit.[33] The self-serving actions of the managers
turned out to be damaging for the long-range success of the
cooperatives, especially since other members played a small
part in the societies' decisions.[34] Surveys conducted by
different outside agencies among Iranian cooperative societies
have frequently noted that "the relationship between members
and leaders was not characterized by equality and

responsiveness."[35]   It was also not uncommon to find
cooperative members who were unaware of the principles and
purposes of these societies.[36]   In terms of both internal and
external operations, the cooperative societies fell far short
of their avowed goals.

During the third and fourth stages of land reform,
efforts were made to introduce farm corporations and
production cooperatives. The procedure was for the government
to select suitable villages and to persuade the small
landholders to establish joint-stock corporations under
official management and supervision. The peasants were
expected to exchange their land titles for shares in the
corporation. The establishment of farm corporations, as
M. A. Katouzian observes, was a radical move.

> First, it meant that for the first time in history
> the boundary of the Persian village as a complete
> and integrated social and economic unit was to be
> broken; for, typically, corporations included more
> than one village. Secondly, it converted the
> ownership of land into the ownership of paper
> shares. Thirdly, it paved the way for concentra-
> tion of share ownership, since it would be only a
> matter of time before small shareholders began to
> sell to the large ones. Hence, a reform policy
> which had begun with the express purpose of
> breaking up large ownership in land was--in a few
> years--converted into one which favoured concen-
> tration. Fourthly, it made absenteeism once again
> possible. The large shareholder could now afford
> to live in the nearby town making money, while the
> army of landless peasants (unaffected by the terms
> of the Reform) would labour for cultivation.
> Fifthly, it made it easier for the government
> departments to extend their control over productive
> activity and rural life in general. For, in spite
> of the usual constitutional trimmings--shareholders'
> meetings, board of governors, etc.--the corporations
> are run by urban bureaucrats appointed by the
> state.[37]

The farm corporations, similar to other agricultural
actions of the government, were faced with "poorly paid,
poorly trained supervisory personnel and chronic underfinancing."[38]   Furthermore, the fact that by 1976 there were
only 85 farm corporations in existence--to use Weinbaum's
terms--was "hardly a success story."[39]   As Table 3.1 indicates
indicates, membership in rural cooperatives remained the
predominant form of agricultural operation. Farm corporations
included only about 1 percent of total peasant households.
Ironically, however, distribution of farm capital was heavily
on the side of corporations (Table 3.2). The average
household in a corporation had 400 times more capital than
its cooperative counterpart.[40]

The production cooperatives did not fare much better.
They differed from farm corporations by the fact that the
farmers were allowed to retain their land titles. The

Table 3.1

Distribution of Farm Corporations and
Rural Cooperatives, 1976

	No. of Units	Membership	% of Total
Rural Cooperatives	2,858	2,685,000 (households)	98.8
Rural Cooperative Unions	144	2,846 (co-op units)	–
Farm Corporations	85	32,506	1.2

SOURCE: Iran, Bank Markazi, Annual Report and Balance
Sheet, 1976.   Reported in M. A. Katouzian, "Oil Versus
Agriculture: A Case of Dual Resource Depletion in Iran,"
Journal of Peasant Studies, 5 (April, 1978), p. 360.

Table 3.2

Distribution of Farm Capital by Sector, 1976
(thousand rials)

	Total	Per Unit	Per Member
Corporations	2,883,000	34,000	800
Cooperatives	5,690,000	2,000	2

SOURCE: Iran, Bank Markazi, Annual Report and Balance
Sheet, 1976.   Reported in M. A. Katouzian, "Oil Versus
Agriculture: A Case of Dual Resource Depletion in Iran,"
Journal of Peasant Studies, 5 (April, 1978), p. 360.

production cooperatives were also "less centrally controlled" and emphasized "the personal initiative of the individual farmer."[41] Actual implementation of the plan was slow. By 1977, 181 villages with a total population of 88,000 were affected.[42] Production cooperatives suffered even more than the farm corporations from underfinancing and had to grapple with the problem of lesser economic incentives.[43]

The final agricultural reform plan and the showpiece of the government was to be a group of large agro-industrial complexes known as agribusinesses. Several such complexes were established in localities where modern irrigation was made possible by either dam construction or a system of deep wells. The land affected in the designated agribusiness farm areas was purchased from the peasant owners, who were then relocated in nearby housing settlements constructed especially for them. The peasants received "administrative prices" for their land and were charged for the cost of the new housing units.[44] The consequences of resettlement for the peasants were dramatic. As Katouzian notes:

> The peasant households lost their lands, their homes, their cultural and sociological entities, etc., by one stroke. They were turned into landless wage labourers enabled to scratch a living by providing (part-time) wage labour for the company. The cost to the peasants cannot be exaggerated, because in addition to all the other material and psychological losses, they now had to purchase their means of subsistence in the market.[45]

The total number of peasants affected by this policy is not yet clear. It is known, however, that in the Dez Dam region of the Khuzistan Province alone, 55,000 peasants were made landless by the agribusiness operations.[46] The situation was further aggravated when the complexes failed to reach most production targets and threats of bankruptcy were imminent for some of them.[47] A combination of farming methods not suited for the region, poor management, inadequate financial support, and a labor force with limited incentives is often cited as the primary reason for the grave problems of the agribusinesses. Whatever the relative influence of these factors may be, it is by now apparent that agribusiness complexes essentially failed. Even the government officially viewed this agricultural policy as "having been misconceived."[48]

An additional factor contributing to the dismal performance of Iranian agriculture has been the uneven distribution of oil revenues and public expenditures among different sectors of the economy. In the Fourth Plan (1968-72), the government adopted an unbalanced growth strategy where highest priorities were placed on services and industry with agriculture receiving only 5.7 percent of public expenditures.[49] The plan succeeded in attaining or surpassing most of its growth-rate targets. In the area of agriculture, however, it failed to meet the planned growth-rate goal of 4.4 percent. The real achieved growth rate was only 3.9 percent, substantially lower than the achieved growth

rate for any other sector.[50]   The Fifth Plan (1974-78) placed
greater emphasis on agriculture by projecting a 7 percent
annual growth rate and allocating 5.8 percent more funds to
it than the previous plan had.[51]   But the government once
again failed to attain its goals in agriculture.   In fact, by
1974 land productivity for wheat and barley had not reached
its 1967 level.[52]   Assuming Oddvar Aresvik is correct when he
points out that "wheat accounts for 60 percent of the total
cropped acreage in Iran,"[53] then the gravity of low
agricultural productivity must indeed be clear.

The government's short-run response to insufficient
agricultural productivity and the great consumer demand for
food supplies in the urban areas was to use portions of the
oil revenues to import extensive agricultural material from
abroad.   Since the oil revenues were plentiful, the pressures
to redress the structural problems of agriculture were not
immediately felt.   The damage to the basic fabric of the
nation's agriculture, however, was bound to become apparent
shortly.   Although oil revenues provided sufficient income to
satisfy consumer demands for the time being, the situation
could not continue indefinitely.   This problem prompted at
least one observer to ponder the fate of the Iranian economy
when oil is also depleted.[54]

The net result of the failure in agricultural planning
and policy was to greatly increase the marginality of large
segments of the rural population.   The basic land reform law
did nothing to improve the living conditions of the
agricultural laborers.   In the words of Nikki Keddie, the
laboring class was "given no protection--no minimum wage, no
unemployment relief, no gleaning rights on the now-private
fields, and no land."[55]   Steady employment, which had always
been a problem for them, became well-nigh impossible under
new land distribution arrangements.   The new peasant
cultivators, in contrast to the former landlords, preferred
using their own family labor rather than hiring outside
agricultural workers.[56]   Moreover, the spread of agricultural
mechanization, which was designed to increase labor productivity, had the inevitable side effect of reducing the number
of villagers needed for farmwork.[57]   In addition, large
modern agricultural enterprises, such as the agribusiness
complexes, were able to "employ only between 40 and 50 percent
of the economically active population of the areas" they
covered.[58]   Since much of the labor in agribusiness was
recruited from among the peasants, whose land had been
purchased by these companies, the employment prospects for
other agricultural workers were hardly forthcoming.

It is, therefore, not surprising that in a survey of
three villages in the Fars Province in 1967, Ismail Ajami
discovered widespread social alienation among the agricultural
proletariat.   He reports that 66 percent of the agricultural
workers in the sample expressed extensive alienation as
compared with 27.9 percent of the new landowning farmers.
Moreover, only 11.5 percent of the agricultural workers were
satisfied with their jobs.   Ajami attributes the alienation
and job dissatisfaction of the agricultural proletariat to

41

the fact that the land reform program did not distribute any land among them.[59]

The agricultural laborers found themselves in a situation of growing destitution. Unemployment or underemployment became even more of a common feature in their lives. Official statistics on the increase in agricultural employment between 1956 and 1966 point to an annual rate of only about 1 percent.[60] As the International Labour Office report on "Employment and Income Policies for Iran" notes, "there are indications of complete stagnation since 1966."[61] Statistics compiled by the Iranian government for 1971 indicate a rural unemployment rate of 13.9 percent for the economically active population.[62] Hence, pressures to leave the rural areas for the cities--where at least from the distance subsistence life seemed possible--increased daily. In a classic case of push factors at the point of origin, the Iranian agricultural proletariat migrated in droves to cities far and near.

Migration was not restricted to the agricultural proletariat alone. Other groups of the landless khwushnishin population, particularly those involved in the rapidly declining handicraft and nonfarming occupations, joined the migratory movements. Segments of the cultivating peasantry, whose land was either purchased by the agribusiness companies or exchanged for paper shares in farm corporations, found it more congenial to make the move to the city. For even some of the new peasant farmers and middle-sized farm operators who remained behind, the uncertainty about their land titles created a sense of insecurity and contributed to a slow but steady flight from the countryside.[63]

Attraction of the City

Aside from the basic push factors due to the multifaceted problems in agriculture, a number of other reasons have contributed to the peasants' decision to migrate to the cities. Most important has been the wide gap and perceived differences between rural and urban incomes. In 1959 the ratio of urban to rural income per head was estimated as 4.6 to 1. This ratio increased to 4.7 to 1 by 1969 and increased in the later years.[64] According to official reports, in 1972 the average earned income per day from agricultural work was only $1.40 for male and 74 cents for female laborers.[65] An unskilled construction worker in the urban areas for the same year earned several times this amount. On the basis of this fact, some agricultural workers decided to become part of the urban rather than the rural proletariat. The expansion in urban construction during the mid-1970s absorbed a portion of the unskilled rural migrants and probably contributed to the continuing influx of rural workers to the city. Not every rural migrant, however, was able to secure the usual temporary employment in the construction field. For those who obtained temporary work, the danger of unemployment was always present. The damaging effects of unemployment for some and potential unemployment

for others perpetuated the poor migrants' insecure position.[66]
Their marginal life on the fringes of society was not really
changed by their move to the city--it was merely transplanted
from one environment to another.

It is sometimes pointed out that migrants are attracted
to the city because it provides them with amenities--such as
piped drinking water, electricity, health centers, schools--
not usually found as easily in the countryside.[67] Or it is
stated that rural residents find the "bright lights" of the
city "irresistible," simply because of "the excitement of
being where the action is."[68] It is abundantly clear that
neither the city amenities nor the "bright lights" theory has
been a significant factor in the Iranian poor peasantry's
migration to the urban centers. Urban amenities are far from
adequate in Tehran or in other major Iranian cities and are
practically nonexistent in those areas of the city where the
migrants reside. The various surveys of the poor peasantry's
reasons for migration have not so far unearthed a "bright
lights" explanation.

A more plausible explanation contributing to cityward
migration is the increase in the degree of education in the
countryside. As Paul Bairoch points out, "this correlation
between educational level and the tendency to migrate, and in
particular to migrate to the town, emerges from most of the
studies on the causes of migration in the Third World."[69]
Although as late as 1971 only 20.4 percent of Iran's rural
population six years and older could read and write, this was
an increase of 35 percent over the 1966 figure. For those
who receive education, there is a greater chance of leaving
the land for the city. A side effect of this development, as
the International Labour Office report on Iran notes, "is
that education transforms disguised unemployment and
under-employment into open unemployment."[70] The fact that
education is restricted almost completely to the primary level
has little bearing on the tendency to leave rural society.
The relationship between educational attainment and migration
is further documented in a study of the effectiveness of a
joint 1967 United Nations-Iranian Government program, which
was designed to include technical agricultural education in
certain adult literacy classes in selected rural areas of
Iran. It was discovered that 64 percent of those who
completed the program wanted to change their employment from
agriculture to occupations that necessitated migration to
cities. A control group of farmers in the same area, who had
received a nontechnical primary education, still found
43 percent wanting to change jobs and migrate to industrial
cities.[71] It is likely that the current steady expansion in
rural literacy will result in an increase in the rates of
cityward migration among the Iranian peasants.

A Sample of the Migrant Poor

A stratified random sample of 224 poor migrants from
the rural areas to Tehran, administered in the summer of 1977

43

by the author, confirms the preceding observations on the importance of push factors in the decision to migrate. The survey, conducted among male heads of households (with an average age of thirty-five years), indicates that nearly 85 percent left the villages due to unsatisfactory employment and inadequate income. Economic hardship brought about by the basic structural problems of Iranian agriculture compelled these peasants to go to Tehran to search for better work and higher pay.[72] If there was any selectivity involved, it concerned the extent of educational attainment of this particular sample--66 percent literacy confined primarily to the elementary level--compared with the rural literacy rate of 20 percent in Iran.[73] Moreover, the group's literacy was substantially higher than that of their nonmigrant fathers (less than 10%). This tends to support previously reported research findings stressing the relationship between literacy and migration. It is reasonable to conclude that whereas push factors in the form of economic hardship are primary forces of migration for the peasants, it is likely that those who are literate will be more prone to make the decision to migrate than those who are illiterate.

In a study of migratory patterns in Iran, Mohammad Hemmasi claims that "distance seems to be the best explanatory variable of migration."[74] He justifies this observation by references to the vastness of Iran, its difficult terrain, and the underdeveloped transportation system. Although remarks about Iran's rugged terrain and its other features are basically valid, distance was found to have no obvious effect on migration in my sample of heads of households. They came from rural areas far and near and were not affected in any discernible way by their distance from the capital.[75]

The overwhelming majority of these migrants (about three fourths) left their rural villages for immediate settlement in Tehran. They arrived in the city with no significant previous urban experience. Recent empirical research among migrants in Istanbul and Rio de Janeiro further confirms the view that step migration from village to town to city is not a common pattern with the migrant poor.[76] As is the case with the migrants in Mexico City and Rio de Janeiro,[77] my sample of Iranian migrants indicates a tendency to migrate with the family. Those who migrated alone initially made arrangements for their families to join them as soon as they were reasonably settled in Tehran. The idea of migrants as "solitary travelers" is not generally applicable to the Iranian case.

Most of these migrants had relatives and friends who were already settled in various corners of Tehran. They could, therefore, easily learn about their city of destination through prior communication with urban cousins.[78] The sample demonstrates that relatives and friends were the most important sources of information on employment opportunities in Tehran (Table 3.3). The same relatives and friends were instrumental in securing employment for 67.6 percent of the migrants after their arrival in the capital.

44

Table 3.3

Migrants' Sources of Information and Assistance in Securing Employment
(N = 224)

Source	Employment Information (%)	Employment Assistance (%)
Relatives and friends	74.0	67.6
Personal search	16.9	25.6
Government	–	3.2
Mass media	3.2	–
Other	5.9	3.6

This group of poor migrants in Tehran represents a much larger population who, because of the dislocations in Iranian agriculture, have fled from the land to seek a better life in the city. Arriving with great hopes and aspirations, they expect to improve their lot and economic position. They will soon come to realize that their new urban life is not an escape from marginality but indeed a perpetuation of their struggle for subsistence.

CHAPTER IV

THE MIGRANT POOR IN THE CITY

Residential Patterns

Characterization of residential areas inhabited by the migrant poor as squatter settlements, shanty towns, or slums raises certain definitional difficulties. All those who have studied low-income urban groups in different parts of the developing world have had to grapple with this problem. John Turner, for example, believes that the phrase "autonomous urban settlement" may be a more apt term than the commonly used squatter settlement.[1] Other terms such as "transitional," "uncontrolled," "sub-integrated," "marginal," "nonplanned," "provisional," "spontaneous," and "unconventional" have also been used in the literature.[2] Sometimes local terms such as barriada, favela, sharifa, or gecekondu are employed to refer to the same phenomenon. In order to avoid unnecessary debates on terminology and typology, the United Nations Conference on Human Settlements proposed the phrase "slums and squatter settlements" as a "familiar shorthand to describe areas of relatively permanent housing which, in appearance at least, are poor, underserviced, overcrowded and dilapidated."[3] This phrase is to be used, the United Nations Conference suggests, to reduce the expanding plethora of terms describing "various types of urban settlements."[4]

The phrase "slums and squatter settlements" is probably a reasonable description of the residential compounds of the migrant poor in Tehran. Squatting, defined as "forcible preemption of land by landless and homeless people,"[5] is limited to only a portion of Tehran's migrant poor. There are many poor migrants who are not squatters and reside in rented or owned dwelling units in low-income communities in Tehran. Most of these communities can be characterized as slums by common standards. They resemble the traditional core-city slumlord tenements found in many urban centers throughout the world. There are, however, some low-income communities that are not, strictly speaking, slums. These communities have made the transition to a relatively higher income category and are for the most part homes to the fully employed and regular wage-earning migrants. Nevertheless, the low-income level of these migrants at the bottom one fourth of the urban population still places them among the migrant poor. They also share with their slum-dwelling neighbors a marginal life characterized by low income, insecure tenure, and inadequacy or absence of basic urban services. But what differentiates this last group from other poor migrants is that they have secured regular wage-earning occupations and have become what Turner calls "consolidators."[6]

46

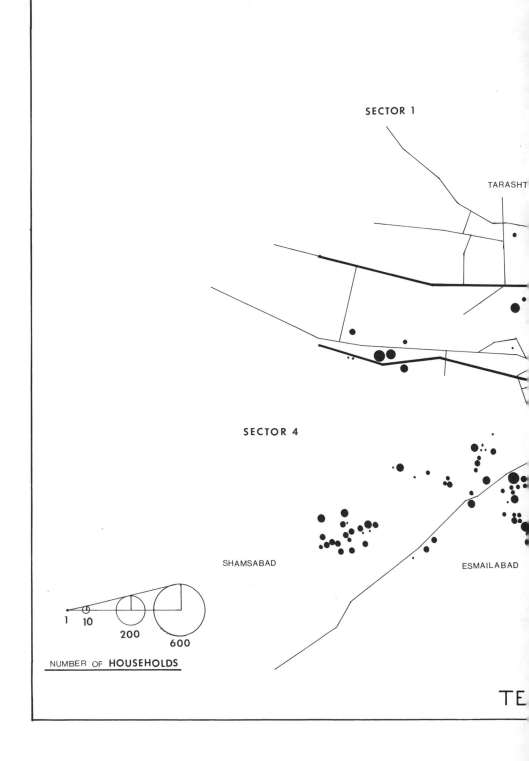

SECTOR 1

TARASHT

SECTOR 4

SHAMSABAD

ESMAILABAD

1 10
200
600

NUMBER OF **HOUSEHOLDS**

TE

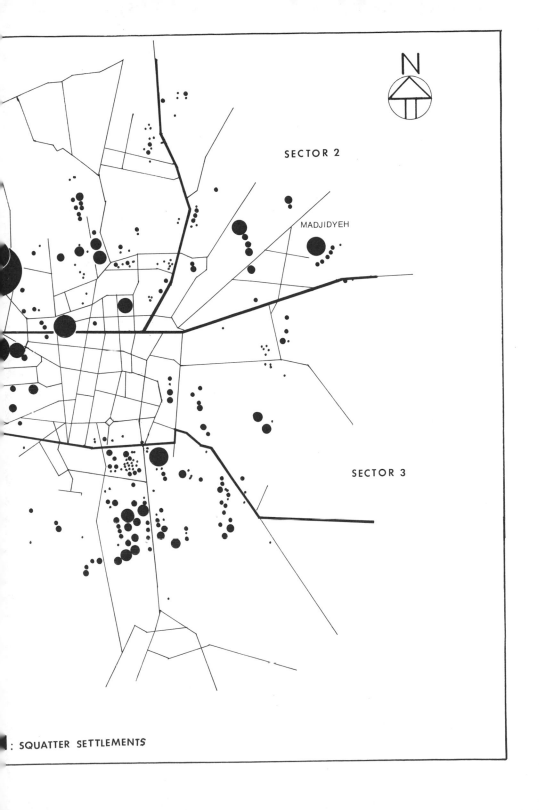

SECTOR 2

MADJIDYEH

SECTOR 3

: SQUATTER SETTLEMENTS

Low-income migrants in Tehran are settled in a large
variety of dwelling units in most sections of the city. The
largest concentration of migrant poor is in the peripheries
of Greater Tehran, particularly in its southern sections. A
survey of Tehran's squatter settlements was undertaken in 1972
by the Institute for Social Research of Tehran University.[7]
The survey was confined strictly to the squatters and hence
excluded substantial groups of the migrant poor in the slums
and nonsquatting areas of Tehran. For purposes of identifying
the squatter settlements, Tehran was divided into four major
geographical sections (see attached map based on map prepared
by the Institute for Social Research). The survey discovered
428 settlement units with 3,780 households (Table 4.1). The
highest concentration of the settlements was in South Tehran,
which accounted for over 61 percent of the units.

The overconcentration of squatters and other poor
migrants in South Tehran is not surprising to anyone who has
visited the city. When Tehran expanded in population and
increased in area, the well-to-do classes moved northward.
This movement of the dominant classes and their wealth to the
northern sections of the city is clearly reflected in the
topography and physical appearance of Tehran. As one leaves

Table 4.1

Squatter Settlement Units of Tehran by
Household Size and Area

Units	Northwest		Northeast		Central		South		Total	
	No.	%	No.	%	No.	%	No.	%	No.	%
1-4 households	59	24.2	19	7.8	35	14.3	131	53.7	244	57.0
5-9 "	4	4.0	6	5.9	9	8.9	82	81.2	101	23.5
10-14 "	6	16.2	1	2.7	3	8.1	27	73.0	37	8.6
15-19 "	2	9.1	2	9.1	4	18.2	14	63.6	22	5.1
20-29 "	1	12.5	-	-	3	37.5	4	50.0	8	1.9
30-39 "	-	-	-	-	1	50.0	1	50.0	2	0.5
40-49 "	2	66.7	-	-	-	-	1	33.3	3	0.7
50-59 "	1	50.0	1	50.0	-	-	-	-	2	0.5
60-79 "	1	50.0	1	50.0	-	-	-	-	2	0.5
80-99 "	-	-	-	-	-	-	1	100.0	1	0.2
100-199 "	1	50.0	-	-	1	50.0	-	-	2	0.5
200 or more "	2	100.0	-	-	-	-	-	-	2	0.5
Unspecified	-	-	-	-	-	-	2	100.0	2	0.5
TOTAL UNITS	79	18.5	30	7.0	56	13.1	263	61.4	428	100.0

the southern sections and moves gradually to central and
northern parts, the streets become wider and less congested,
the shrubbery and trees become more frequent, and a very
different style of architecture and life meets the eye. It
is as if the city is divided into the dusty and gray southern
poor and the green and opulent northern rich. There are
perhaps not many other cities where the contrast between the
extreme poverty of the south and extensive wealth of the north
is so vividly documented.

The living quarters and housing arrangements of the
migrant squatters further attest their poverty and marginal
life. When surveyed in 1972, the squatters were living in
shelters made of a wide variety of materials, which included,
among others, tents (12.4%), makeshift rooms in the brick
kilns (41.6%), and hovels (40.9%). Brick kiln shelters were
restricted to the squatters of South Tehran only (Tables 4.2,
4.3). The kilns are not permitted to operate in central and
northern sections of the city. It may be difficult to grasp
the fact that many of the squatters actually lived in
functioning kilns that were routinely manufacturing large
numbers of bricks.

The squatters' security of tenure was no better than
their living quarters; 68.1 percent of the households and
58.2 percent of the units had made no legal arrangements for
their stay on the property and were thus potentially subject
to the whims of those who owned the land. Another 26.5
percent of the units had obtained either the owners'
permission or the consent of the brick kiln supervisors for
their stay. Only 2.3 percent of the units (134 households)
could be classified as squatter tenancy; that is, they were
made up of households that did not own their shacks but paid
rent to other squatters.[8] Although no definitive figures can
be given, it appears that squatter tenancy is on the rise in
Tehran. In a recent report, some newly arrived migrant
squatters in North Tehran frequently complained that in
addition to paying 17 dollars monthly rent to the owner,
they had to pay 400 dollars for the right to live in a shack
that was already constructed.[9] It is apparent, however,
that the more prevalent type of squatting in Tehran is, to
use Charles Abrams's term, the owner-squatter.[10] These are
squatters who own their shacks or tents but have no legal
title to the land.

Although illegal seizure or forcible preemption of land
is the most common form of squatting in Tehran, prearranged
and organized large-scale land invasion is rarely practiced
among the squatters. Seizure of land is done gradually in
cooperation with a small group of family members and cohorts.
Participation in organized and massive land invasion, not so
infrequent in Latin America, is generally uncommon among
Tehran squatters.[11] This may have important implications for
later political participation of the migrant squatters, since
they do not normally experience the particular form of
political involvement and group solidarity that is exhibited
in large-scale invasion and defense of preempted land.

Table 4.2

Squatter Settlements of Tehran by Dwelling Type and Area

Dwelling Type	North-west	North-east	Central	South	Total No.	Total %
Tent	2	9	23	19	53	12.4
Cavelike dwelling	1	-	-	9	10	2.3
Shack/Hovel	76	21	32	46	175	40.9
Burial site	-	-	1	-	1	0.2
Basement	-	-	-	2	2	0.5
Nonfunctioning brick kiln	-	-	-	29	29	6.8
Active and inactive brick kiln	-	-	-	149	149	34.8
Other makeshift shack	-	-	-	7	7	1.6
Hut	-	-	-	2	2	0.5
TOTAL UNITS	79	30	56	263	428	100.0

Table 4.3

Squatter Households of Tehran by Dwelling Type and Area

Dwelling Type	North-west	North-east	Central	South	Total No.	Total %
Tent	2	117	151	99	369	9.8
Cavelike dwelling	2	-	-	11	13	0.3
Shack/Hovel	1,369	122	360	230	2,081	55.1
Burial site	-	-	11	-	11	0.3
Basement	-	-	-	2	2	0.05
Nonfunctioning brick kiln	-	-	-	278	278	7.3
Active and inactive brick kiln	-	-	-	966	966	25.6
Other makeshift shack	-	-	-	57	57	1.5
Hut	-	-	-	3	3	0.05
TOTAL HOUSEHOLDS	1,373	239	522	1,646	3,780	100.0

The squatter settlements of Tehran tend to be smaller and more scattered than their counterparts in Latin America and other parts of the world. As Table 4.1 indicates, the predominant size of Tehran's squatter units in 1972 was between 1 and 9 households, although there were units composed of as many as 600 households. The most startling fact about these squatter settlements is that 193 units, or 45 percent, were built in the five years preceding the survey. In 1971 alone 87 new units (20.3%) were added to Tehran's squatter settlements. The rapid growth of Tehran has apparently resulted in as rapid a growth in its shanty towns. Of the rest, 120 units (28%) were set up between 5 and 14 years ago. Another 86 units (20%) were built between 15 and 29 years ago. Only 14 units or slightly over 3 percent date back 30 years or more (Table 4.4).

For the nonsquatting migrant poor of Tehran, housing continues to present major problems. In my 1977 survey, only about 18 percent of the migrants owned their dwelling units. There was an average distribution of three persons per room in these units, and many of them lacked basic urban services such as piped water or electricity. The joy of ownership was further mitigated by the fact that practically all the owners had incurred heavy debts in order to be able to make their purchases. The migrants frequently expressed strong apprehension about their ability to pay back the loans.

The majority of the nonsquatting poor migrants reside in rented rooms. The exponential rise in the price of real estate and housing in Tehran in the mid-1970s effectively eliminated any realistic possibility of home ownership for the migrants. For most, even the hope of purchasing a single room in the future has become a distant dream.

In the fall and winter of 1974-75, I made several visits to two poor migrant compounds located in the southern section of Tehran in an area known as Javadiyih. Each compound consisted of an old mud-brick caravansary that housed about 40 migrant households. The average household had six members in the one-room shelter. The first caravansary had no running water, no faucets, and no electricity. The few outhouses were shared by all inhabitants. Cooking was done inside the rooms, and water had to be brought in with buckets from a public spigot two blocks away. The second caravansary was less dilapidated and provided the residents with a communal water faucet and an electric light bulb in the yard. Although compared with the squatters these migrants have better living arrangements, they still suffer the worst urban ills. They face an untold number of problems in the areas of health, nutrition, employment, schooling, and the like. The average length of stay for the households in these compounds was seven years. Clearly, the difficulty of moving out of the compounds is immense; and the migrants are doomed, at least for the time being, to continue their subsistence life in the caravansaries.

The owner of the two compounds was a rapacious businessman who was making substantial profits from his operations. Bilking the migrant poor as part of

Table 4.4

Length of Establishment of Units of Squatter
Settlements of Tehran by Area

Length of Stay	North-west	North-east	Central	South	Total No.	%
Less than 1 year	8	5	13	61	87	20.3
1-less than 2 years	-	3	3	21	27	6.3
2-less than 3 years	4	2	4	25	35	8.1
3-less than 4 years	1	4	3	25	33	7.7
4-less than 5 years	2	-	1	8	11	2.6
5-9 years	20	4	6	37	67	15.7
10-14 years	13	4	8	28	53	12.4
15-19 years	14	3	6	19	42	9.8
20-29 years	16	2	10	16	44	10.3
30 years or more	1	-	1	12	14	3.3
Unspecified	-	3	1	11	15	3.5
TOTAL UNITS	79	30	56	263	428	100.0

entrepreneurial activity is not restricted to this particular
owner. In my visits to other poor migrant areas of Tehran,
similar patterns of profit making were detected. In one
section of the city, several rooms were discovered with long
cloths hanging from the ceiling to the floor for partitioning
of the space. Upon questioning, it became apparent that each
partitioned area was rented by the hour to individual,
itinerant migrant laborers who had nowhere to sleep. By
paying a nominal hourly fee, the migrants were able to find
a few hours of unencumbered rest before their next attempt to
search for employment. When these migrants find temporary
employment in construction, they normally camp out at the
site, either in tents or inside the partly completed
buildings. The practice of sleeping at the construction site
is a common and widely used means of shelter for the migrant
laborers in Tehran and other Iranian cities.

It is evident that housing and security of tenure are
among the most problematic issues facing the migrant poor,
whether in the squatter settlements or in the low-income
communities of the city. Although the difficulty of
obtaining appropriate shelter in Tehran is not limited to
the poor migrants, they nevertheless carry the brunt of the
problem. Aside from their continuous daily struggle for food
and employment, the poor migrants and especially the
squatters have to engage regularly in a "desperate contest
for shelter and land."[12]

The government's role in providing low-income housing for the migrant poor has been minimal at best. Although much lip service has been paid officially to the housing plight of the poor, concrete actions in resolving the issue were not forthcoming in the Shah's regime. The only notable exception was a large housing project in South Tehran known as Kuyi Nuhum-i Aban, constructed over ten years ago. This housing project was built at the former site of an extensive squatter settlement that was destroyed by the government in 1958. Many former squatters are sheltered in individual two-room houses with both electricity and water supplied to them. There are a few other minor housing projects organized by various divisions of the government. However, considering the vast oil wealth of the country, the official performance in low-income housing has been abysmal. Those portions of oil revenues earmarked for housing were generally used to construct massive modern housing complexes that could be afforded only by the upper-middle and upper-income groups; the same applied to the housing projects built by the private sector. These ultramodern apartments have been purchased by the well-to-do, not the migrant poor.

The absence of commitment to housing construction for the poor has sometimes been rationalized by government officials and others by pointing out the alleged existence of a "culture of poverty" among the very poor as well as their resistance to living in anything but substandard shelters. Examples from Latin America--such as the Buenos Aires poor workers' "destruction" of the new apartments donated to them by Eva Perón and their return to the original settlements, or the refusal by the inhabitants of the "favelas" of Rio de Janeiro to move to the government's suburban projects[13]--have been cited as evidence for arguing against sponsored housing for the poor. In regard to Iran, two examples of such thinking are worth reporting. The first case concerns the settlement of a group of poor Kurdish refugees from Iraq in the early 1970s who lived in a section of Kuyi Nuhum-i Aban. In one of my visits to this project, I was informed that many of the refugees sold their homes at a price about equal to the cost of a tent. They subsequently purchased the tents and squatted in an area not far from their original homes.

The second case involves the image of squatters in Iran as presented in a government-sponsored publication in which the squatters were often berated for their deceitfulness and preference for a life of squalor. The author asserts that in the 1971 resettlement of a group of squatters from central Tehran to Kuyi Nuhum-i Aban, it was discovered that 20 families among the new residents had previously been provided homes at the same housing project. They had apparently sold their homes at the project and returned to their former life of squatting in a different area of Tehran.[14]

Effective arguments have been presented against the "culture of poverty" view of the Latin America migrant poor by Janice Perlman and Alejandro Portes.[15] Perlman explains the squatters' desire to continue living in the "favelas"

by pointing to several factors such as the settlements' sense
of community, no rent, and proximity to job markets. Using
Turner's distinction between the semiemployed "bridgeheader"
and the fully employed "consolidator" squatters,[16] Portes
maintains that it is the bridgeheaders who normally resist
forced resettlement. Since the bridgeheaders are not fully
employed, they naturally view occupation, not housing, as
their primary concern. This is a perfectly rational position
in light of the fact that they already have some form of
shelter in the squatter settlements. By contrast, the
consolidators with stable occupations "demand and often
force development of suburban settlements appropriate for
establishing permanent houses."[17]

The squatter settlements of Tehran include practically
no consolidators. Very few are fully employed in regular
wage-earning occupations. The wage-earning poor migrants
reside in nonsquatter, but low-income, areas of the city. As
is the case with respect to the actions of Latin American
officials, the Iranian government's meager efforts in
low-income housing were directed primarily at the squatters,
not the fully employed, consolidator wage earners.

Perhaps the two examples of resistance to government
housing can be explained. In the first instance, the nomadic
and seminomadic Kurdish refugees had opted for their
accustomed life in the tent. From their perspective, it was
probably a rational decision to exchange government houses
for tents. In the second case, the residents became aware
of the profits that could be gained from the sale of their
homes. The income obtained from the transaction was most
likely used to defray the costs of more urgently needed food
and clothing. A survey of Kuyi Nuhum-i Aban in 1966 attests
to high rates of unemployment, low income, and unskilled
occupations of the residents.[18] In other words, the majority
were not fully employed wage earners but rather were the
semiemployed bridgeheaders for whom employment was the
paramount concern.

Socioeconomic Characteristics

The occupational breakdown of the male squatter heads of
of households in the 1972 survey pointed to a concentration
of unskilled laborers in the squatter settlements. Although
the questionnaire format identified 34 percent as unskilled
workers, most other occupational categories listed can be
viewed as employment requiring no special skills (Table 4.5).
Very few held occupations with any degree of employment
security. The absence of regular wage earning and steady
employment is further documented in a study of the resettled
squatters in Kuyi Nuhum-i Aban. On 481 heads of households
living in the project, 15 percent were unemployed and
56 percent held unskilled occupations.[19]

No information was given in the 1972 survey on the
employment of female squatters. The Kuyi Nuhum-i Aban study,

Table 4.5

Occupation of Male Squatter Heads of Households in Tehran

Occupation	Number	Percent
Beggar and darvish	10	2.1
Agricultural laborer	14	2.9
Keeper of domesticated animals	19	4.0
Unskilled laborer	163	34.0
Semiskilled and skilled laborer	169	35.2
Tradesman and peddling tradesman	16	3.3
Salesman, peddler, and middleman	57	11.9
Minor office employee	2	0.4
TOTAL OCCUPATIONS	450	93.8
Unable to work	4	0.8
Unemployed	26	5.4
TOTAL RESPONDENTS	480	100.0

however, indicated a high rate of unemployment among the female residents of the project. Unemployment of women is a widespread fact in all squatter areas of Tehran. The few who find work are employed mostly in nonskilled and menial jobs on a temporary or part-time basis. This means that the meager earning of the male head of household is usually the only source of income for the whole family. In the 1966 survey of Kuyi Nuhum-i Aban, wages amounted to approximately 9 dollars per month for the average head of household. Although the oil boom of post-1973 resulted in a sizable increase in wage scales, particularly for skilled and unskilled labor, it did not noticeably improve the living conditions of the squatters. Comparable increases in the cost of living and the inflation rate mitigated the impact of the steep rise in wage scales. The rising costs of food and other basic necessities eliminated any real gains that higher wages might have brought to the squatters.

The squatters, portions of the nonsquatting migrant poor, and the lowest-income groups in Tehran have sometimes been characterized as the lumpenproletariat. Ahmad Ashraf, for example, points to three major components of the lumpenprole-tariat as unskilled laborers in the construction field, street vendors, and domestic servants. In addition, he includes the unskilled agricultural workers, load carriers, and mule drivers as well as the declassé elements of thieves, beggars, hoodlums, gamblers, and prostitutes.[20] Whether all these groups conform to Marx's view of the lumpenproletariat as "the social scum, that passively rotting mass thrown off by the lowest layers of old society"[21] is questionable. Ashraf is, however, right in pointing to the concentration of elements of the lumpenproletariat in lowest-income communities of Tehran. A report on the living and employment conditions of the lumpenproletariat in squatter settlements of South Tehran is worth noting.

> At the southwest corner of Shush Square, an unpaved, dirty street leads to a pit, the first in an area known as the South City Pits. This enormous hollow measures three hectares wide and ten meters deep. Dumped city trash, discarded scrap metal, parts of destroyed machinery, old cardboards, bones, and rotted refuse lie in the middle. Outside the pit, a row of houses, loading areas, and tea-houses meet the eye. These tea-houses cater to mostly thieves, pick-pockets, drug pushers and smugglers. The area inside the pit appears uninhabitable. But in truth, cave-like dwellings have been dug into the surrounding walls. Used cardboard and paper cover the floors. The brightest corners have been set aside for addicts who come to pursue their habits undetected. Additional shacks for the addicts have been constructed in the pit out of discarded scrap metal. Nearby, similar pits and cave-like dwellings are the homes of many more people. In a separate section, another pit is geared to a different kind of business. Here dwellings are constructed of discarded scrap metal and cardboard, or they have been dug into the ground itself and covered with the same materials. A steep path leads to the shacks' entrances, which are occasionally adorned with hanging cloths. Ownership of these shacks and holes is fiercely defended by a group of resident prostitutes. They receive their own "guests" in these dwellings or rent their "rooms" to male customers for specified times. . . . Half-way to Ray on the eastern side of the road, more prostitutes operate. Hiding behind the natural up and down formations of the landscape, they make their availability known by displaying black cloths mounted high on sticks.[22]

These are the lumpenproletariat or what Karl Marx called the "dangerous class," "living on the crumbs of society, people without a definite trade, vagabonds, gens sans feu et sans aveu."[23] They are differentiated from the nonsquatting migrant poor by occupation, income, and residence.

The occupation and income of the nonsquatting migrant poor, as determined by my 1977 sample survey in Tehran, indicated higher levels of income and occupational attainment. The average nonsquatting migrant earned 225 dollars per month and was employed in a semiskilled occupation. Approximately one half of the respondents worked in various low-level jobs in the private sector. The rest were either regular wage earners in government and public agencies or possessed certain skills (e.g., as masons, house painters) that allowed them to operate as independent workers or contractors (Table 4.6). The majority of these migrants can be classified as fully employed wage-earning consolidators. Temporary and seasonal employment was limited to only 11 percent and intermittent unemployment was reasonably low. A similar pattern emerges in a study of the nonsquatting migrant poor in a southern section of Tehran in 1972. The majority were regularly employed workers in the private sector and earned on the average about 100 dollars a month.[24]

Compared with the squatters, these migrants are better off both occupationally and in terms of their earned income. Their life, however, is not above the subsistence level. As among the squatters, it is usually only the male head of household who contributes to the family income. In my sample, a very small minority stated that either their wives or children worked. The average household income of 246 dollars per month was only slightly higher than the earnings of the typical head of household. Considering that every household had about four members, income per capita amounted to only 61 dollars monthly. This is a far cry from an adequate income necessary for essential expenses in food, clothing, housing, and medicine.

Occupational mobility is highly limited for both groups of the migrant poor. The squatters are virtually doomed to a life based on temporary and menial jobs with no realistic prospects for steady and regular employment. The evidence from the Kuyi Nuhum-i Aban study makes the case for absence of occupational mobility amply clear. Of the 103 unskilled laborers in the sample, only 15 had managed to move up to the status of semiskilled and skilled workers. There were even cases of downward occupational mobility for about half of the workers who were previously employed in skilled occupations but subsequently had to settle for unskilled jobs or for work as domestic servants (Table 4.7).

Table 4.6

Occupation of Nonsquatting Migrants in Tehran

Occupation	Number	Percent
Foreman	2	0.9
Independent worker	38	17.0
Government or public agency employee (minor civil servant)	32	14.3
Government or public agency worker/ laborer	27	12.1
Private sector wage earner	108	48.2
Unemployed, unable to work	17	7.5
TOTAL RESPONDENTS	224	100.0

Table 4.7

Occupational Mobility of Employed Residents
of Kuyi Nuhum-i Aban

Former Occupation

Present Occupation	Unemployed	Student	Housekeeper	Skilled worker	Semiskilled worker	Unskilled worker	Minor civil servant	Domestic servant	Self-employed	Agricultural worker	TOTAL
Skilled worker	44	2	3	24	3	10	2	1	7	6	102
Semiskilled worker	10	2	2	-	9	5	-	3	3	4	38
Unskilled worker	71	20	2	11	5	60	1	2	9	24	205
Minor civil servant	10	9	1	7	1	4	4	-	2	3	41
Domestic servant	51	3	52	9	2	13	8	17	4	9	168
Self-employed	11	1	-	2	4	11	-	3	19	11	62
Agricultural worker	-	-	-	-	-	-	-	-	-	-	-
TOTAL	197	37	60	53	24	103	15	26	44	57	616

The situation is not substantially better for the nonsquatting poor migrants. It can perhaps be argued that shifts from agricultural work to jobs in the industrial and service sectors are forms of occupational mobility brought about by migration. Although this may be a valid observation, it does not diminish the fact that after arrival in Tehran occupational mobility has nevertheless been visibly restricted. An assessment of the poor migrants' employment histories indicates a pattern of horizontal movement along basically similar occupations. Mobility from semiskilled to skilled jobs is not found for any significant number of the migrant poor. The relative absence of occupational or social mobility of the migrant poor can be explained partially by their low level of educational attainment. It is true that 66 percent of the nonsquatting poor migrants in my sample could read and write. However, barely 19 percent had a level of literacy beyond that of the sixth grade, and only three individuals had more than nine years of education. Their low level of educational attainment has severely limited their opportunities for occupational mobility.

In his comparative analysis of squatter settlements in Latin America, William Mangin eloquently argues that squatters make four kinds of contributions to the national economies. First, they solve their housing problems by investing in construction and land improvement when the national governments are unable to provide housing for them. Second, they contribute to the job market by transforming an unused area into a place where large numbers of occupations are made available to masses of people. The range of occupations created in the settlements and their vicinity is extensive and includes menial jobs as well as highly skilled professions. Third, small-business operations grow very rapidly within the settlements. Markets, repair shops, bars, restaurants, and other businesses proliferate in a short time. Finally, the settlements contribute to the national economies through their investment of social capital, which can be used to create a community. The communities make possible numerous investments and involve the squatters in the economic, social, and political life of the nation.[25]

Mangin's arguments are well taken as far as the Latin American squatter settlements are concerned. Practically none of his points, however, are applicable to the Iranian squatter establishments. One has to search in vain to find jobs and small businesses created in the settlements, or even a community remotely similar to the Latin American types. Clearly, the Iranian squatter settlements are also responses to the shortage of housing and shelter and indicate some investment on the part of the squatters. But this development rarely results in land improvement or capital investment beyond the absolutely minimum degree. Mangin's observations may be more relevant to certain small segments of the poor migrants in Tehran who own their rooms. These homeowning migrants are more likely to engage in activities and make investments along the lines he suggested.

The poor migrants' economic activities in the urban areas may be analyzed in the context of the dual economy model or the two sectors. The first or the "formal" sector designates economic activities centered on public agencies, capital-intensive private enterprises, hospitals, large stores, banks, hotels, and other such organizations where government regulation is reasonably high. The "informal" sector, on the other hand, consists of labor-intensive small enterprises, self-employed vendors, tradesmen, and domestic servants. The government rarely interferes in the operation of the generally self-regulating informal sector in any systematic manner.[26]

Owing to the requirements of some schooling and level of skill, entrance into the formal sector of the urban area is much more difficult for the migrant poor. Although the formal sector employs some unskilled and semiskilled workers, its absorptive capacity is considerably lower than the job demands of the urban poor. Hence the informal sector tends to develop relatively faster, partly in response to the migrants' need to somehow find a way to make a living in the city. The two sectors are, however, highly interdependent. In fact, Peter Lloyd claims that the growth of the informal sector "is the result of the development" of the formal sector.[27] This can be seen in the way the informal sector produces certain components for the formal sector's industry and provides services for the middle and affluent classes. The "invisible" unemployment or underemployment of the migrant poor, a substantial portion of whom are part of the informal sector, is rarely if ever reported in unemployment statistics of the Third World countries.

For many unskilled poor migrants a cherished goal is to be able to enter the labor market of the formal sector as regular wage earners. Although some informal sector workers are able to do well and increase their income regularly (and conversely, the "lower fringe" of the formal sector workers often do very poorly),[28] there is an underlying desire and attempt by the poor migrants to attain permanent formal sector employment.[29] Clearly, jobs in the formal sector encompass a wide range of activities with various levels of remuneration and status. But the vision of becoming a fully employed wage-earning consolidator is most attractive to the poor migrants, since it promises security and economic stability. Therefore, it is not surprising that an overwhelming number of poor migrants of Tehran also desire to make the transition and find employment in the formal sector.

Adjustments in the City

The scholarly literature on the poor migrants' adjustment to city life has generally emphasized their difficulties in coping with urban ways. It is often mentioned that because of the break with the village tradition, the new migrants are uprooted, experience social isolation, and develop a sense of anomic. Philip Hauser, for example, asserts that the migrants "must adapt to new and unfamiliar ways of making a living; a money economy; regular working hours; the absence of warm family living; large numbers of impersonal contacts with other human beings; new forms of recreation; and a quite different physical setting, often involving new kinds of housing, sanitation, traffic congestion, and noise."[30] Others stress the migrants' problems in the economic, social, and psychological spheres. But for the most part, these scholars seem to emphasize the psychological and anomic aspects of the new migrants' behavior. Bert Hoselitz, for instance, says that the migrants need to "overcome forces fostering anomie."[31] Lucian Pye stresses the psychological problems of transition from the intimate world of the village to the impersonal world of the city for the migrants and points out that "in a multitude of ways rapid urbanization can cause social, economic, and psychological divisions and tensions which, translated into the political realm, become sources of instability."[32]

Yet another group of writers takes issue with observations that emphasize the migrants' difficulties in adjusting to city life. They point out that migrants cope reasonably well with the urban ways and do not generally experience either a rupture of their traditional interpersonal life or a sense of social isolation. Thus, Oscar Lewis maintains that "peasants in Mexico City adapted to city life with far greater ease than one would have expected . . . family life remained quite stable and extended family ties increased rather than decreased."[33] Similarly, Douglas Butterworth concludes from his study of Indian migrants in Mexico City than "the substitution of secondary, contractual, Gesellschaft relationships for primary, status-based, Gemeinschaft relationships, considered to be the sine qua non of urbanization process, is not characteristic" of these migrants.[34] Janet Abu-Lughod's studies of poor migrants in Cairo also dismiss the view that the migrants suffer from anonymity or anomie. She ascertains accurately that "Middle Eastern culture places a high value on personal relationships, even at a sacrifice of privacy and internal development."[35] Abu-Lughod's observations are supported by Karen Peterson, who notes that "kin play a major role in villagers' adjustment to Cairo."[36] Hence, the notion of poor migrants, lost in a labyrinth of secondary and nonpersonal relationships in the city, is not a valid one.

It is possible to present evidence in support of both positions from different parts of the world. As Paul Doughty indicates, migrants' adjustment to city life may vary according to the strengths and weaknesses which they bring from their respective village cultures.[37] The empirical research in the Third World cities, however, is strongly supportive of the second theme: the migrants maintain an extensive network of personal relationships in the city and are not socially and psychologically isolated from their kin and friends.

The evidence from Tehran is consistent with other empirical findings. A vast majority of the poor migrants have relatives living in the city with whom they maintain regular and routine contacts. This is supplemented by visits and interactions with new friends met during the course of their urban residence. All migrants stated that they visited their friends regularly. Some 35 percent mentioned that these visits were on the average more than once a month. This applied even to friends who no longer lived in the migrants' present neighborhoods. Since change of residence is not uncommon among the migrant poor (64.1 percent had changed residence two or three times after moving to Tehran), the fact of extensive contacts with friends and relatives further proves that the migrants are not socially isolated. When asked whether they felt lonely in Tehran, 96 percent of the migrants responded negatively.

Migrants' adjustment to city life takes various forms and patterns. Kemal Karpat notes that Istanbul's migrant squatters undergo four different phases of urbanization. Initially the squatters adopt urban dress and habits as a symbolic sign of their readiness to adjust to the urban ways. Next the migrants come to make use of urban public facilities, food and clothing shops, and begin to think about building their dwelling units. The third phase involves establishment of more extensive relationships with other city people and a reevaluation of the squatters' traditional beliefs and practices. Finally, the squatters reach the phase of total identification with the city and detachment from village values.[38]

It is not always easy to observe these four distinct phases of adjustment to city life among the Iranian migrant poor. Although the first three phases are generally applicable to most migrants in different parts of the world, the final phase of full identification with city life and detachment from rural values is not a necessary outcome. Migrants may live in the city for extended periods but still adhere to the basic values and norms inculcated during their village years. Acculturation in the urban ways is a complicated process and is not only a function of time or extent of urban ties. As Ned Levine has demonstrated, the Ankara migrants' "old culture contacts" with villagers actually promoted the migrants' urban participation and acculturation.[39]

Adjustment to city life is perhaps best explained by the context of the migrants' urban community. The process of learning about urban life takes place both in the community of residence and at the place of employment. For the migrant poor, the community is a very important source of knowledge and new learning. The poor migrant communities of Tehran are extensive and heterogeneous, reflecting the vastness of the country and its social diversity. Within this heterogeneous context, limited ethnic or linguistic homogeneity can be observed. There is a tendency for migrants from a given rural area to inhabit the same low-income community.[40] This is particularly true of certain

61

Turkish-speaking migrants. The pattern, however, is not universal. The low-income migrant communities of Tehran are composed of diverse linguistic, ethnic, and geographic groups. It is also fairly routine for the Turkish-speaking migrants to pick up enough Persian in a short time to be able to communicate in the language of the majority.

The poor migrant communities of Tehran serve as the primary arenas for resocialization of the migrants into the unfamiliar ways of urban life. They make adjustments to the city possible and ease the process of transition. This is done sometimes by the migrants socializing with one another at their homes or at nearby mosques and teahouses. Much information is transmitted through these informal channels of communication. Although poor and destitute, the migrants help each other locate jobs and even provide cash advances to a needy kin or friend. While the amount of spare cash available to the poor migrants is extremely limited, 34 percent of my sample stated that they had received loans from friends or relatives. The community, therefore, is an important source of information and assistance to the migrant poor. It also helps to protect them, at least on a limited scale, from feeling lost in a large metropolis.

The pattern of mutual assistance among the poor migrants is a vital feature of marginal life in the urban community. This is essential not only to ease adjustment to the city but also to make economic survival possible. In this context, Larrisa Lomnitz's analysis of "networks of reciprocal exchange" among the shanty-town dwellers of Mexico City is highly relevant. These neighborhood networks are constituted and disbanded according to the dynamics of "the flow of reciprocal exchange of goods, services, and economically vaulable information."[41] Based on family, not individual membership, the reciprocity networks function because of the critical importance of reciprocal exchange in matters central to migration and survival in the city.[42] Reciprocity and equality of wants among members are the overriding elements of these networks and influence other aspects of economic and social life in the neighborhood. The networks, therefore, have fluctuating membership and may include nonkin and nonethnic members, depending on the requirements of economic and social survival.

The networks of reciprocal exchange exist in Iranian squatter settlements and migrant poor areas as they do in perhaps all other urban centers of the Third World. All the evidence from Latin America, Egypt, and Turkey points to the important role of these netowrks and voluntary associations in the life of migrants. In the case of Iran under the Shah's regime, however, these reciprocity networks were not generally transformed into effective secondary associations. Although neighborhood associations existed in some migrant poor parts of the city, they were rarely found among the squatters. Even the existing neighborhood associations were so tightly controlled from the top by the government that their effectiveness in expressing the neighborhoods' needs were greatly hampered. Fearful of antiregime developments in the poorer sections of the city, the Shah's government discouraged establishment of such organizations. It is, however, too easy to attribute the relative lack of voluntary associations only to the past regime's behavior. There are many factors that provide incentives to the formation of neighborhood associations that are not universally present in the Iranian migrant poor, and especially the squatter, areas. In the words of Joan Nelson, these include "the residents' commitment to stay in a neighborhood, its legal status, its physical characteristics, and the adequacy of basic services . . . the ethnic composition and class structure of the neighborhood, its size, the circumstances of its founding, and its subsequent history."[43] The strength and pervasiveness of these factors vary from one migrant poor area of Tehran to another. However, absence of sustained and effective leadership among the migrant poor was a common and readily noticeable phenomenon in the 1970s.

An important exception to this general pattern has been the intermittent activities of the Shi'i religious associations in both the squatter settlements and other migrant poor sections of the city. These associations, referred to as hay'ats, are often organized on the basis of common ethnic or geographical origin of the members and promote religious observance and celebrate major Shi'i festivals. The peak of their activities is invariably during the holy months of Muharram and Safar, particularly the first ten days of Muhurram (the Ashura period), which mourns the martyrdom of Imam Husayn in Karbala in 680 A.D. On other occasions, the hay'ats in the migrant poor areas meet on a semiregular or irregular basis in various homes of the poor and discuss common religious issues and concerns. Frequently these gatherings are led by a lower-ranking Muslim divine who listens, participates in the discussion, and provides guidance in religious matters. The local hay'ats of one migrant poor area usually have horizontal connections to other hay'ats in different parts of the city. They do, therefore, function loosely as networks of interrelated associations organized ostensibly for religious purposes.

These associations are perceived as highly significant by many of the poor migrants. As one young squatter indicated, "Nothing brings us together more than the love for Imam Husayn. My personal view is that these hay'ats have a positive aspect in uniting us and keeping us informed about each other's affairs."[44] The importance of these hay'ats as links between the Shi'i religious organization and the urban poor and their potential mobilization role during revolutionary situations will be discussed later in this book. Here it suffices to point out that despite vigorous attempts by the Shah's regime to limit and control the pervasive role of the religious institutions, the hay'at associations and other networks connecting the clergy and the poor continued to function throughout the country.

Village Relations

The migrants' decision to settle permanently in the city does not necessarily imply that all relations with the village of origin have ended. Many migrants maintain strong ties to their rural homes and make regular visits to their villages. In discussing the village relations of a group of migrants in Mexico City, Butterworth points out that "the continuance of strong ties with their 'tierra' is a striking universal characteristic among the emigrants from Tilantongo, who are unanimously and vociferously linked in spirit to their village."[45] Karpat similarly notes that many Istanbul squatters visit their villages regularly and a number "mentioned specifically that they went to visit the village for moral duzeltmek (uplift of morale)."[46] Clearly, there is an attachment to the village of origin for a substantial portion of the migrants. But there are also other reasons for village contacts. Migrants sometimes return to the village for specific periods to help in plowing family land or for harvesting fields. Some return to supervise personal property left behind. Others come to inquire about the well-being of parents and kin.

In my sample of the migrant poor in Tehran, over 91 percent said that they had relatives living in the villages. Approximately three fourths of these migrants had visited their villages either once or twice during the course of the previous year. Twenty-three percent of the migrants had minor property in the village, although only 7 percent received income from their possessions. Largely because of their own difficult financial position, a very small minority of the migrants sent money to their kin in the village (Table 4.8).

The relationship of the poor migrants in Tehran with their villages of origin raises several important issues. First, the departure of the peasants from the rural areas relieves some of the pressure on the land by removing the surplus population. The land reform program as well as the mechanization of agriculture in Iran have created an excess population in the rural parts who have no possibility of

Table 4.8

Migrants' Forms of Assistance to Village Relatives

Form of Assistance	Number	Percent
Monetary aid	8	3.6
Nonmonetary aid	9	4.0
None	194	86.6
Not applicable	13	5.8

productive employment in the near future. Hence, cityward migration can be viewed as a response to the agrarian imbalance imposed from above. From among the displaced peasants, it is probably the more innovative and enterprising who have made the initial decisions to leave. As my sample of the migrant poor has indicated, those who left had generally greater literacy than their rural compatriots who stayed behind. It is perhaps reasonable to conclude that the peasants remaining in the villages are composed of the more traditional elements of the Iranian rural society.

The second issue concerns the role of visiting migrants as informal agents of change and modernization in the villages. Although some migrants may act as modernizing agents, it would be a mistake to stress this role. As Karpat has pointed out, such agents cannot bring about important changes in the village "without the support of national programs for economic and social development and without a suitable political atmosphere."[47] It would be folly to think that sporadic visits by the destitute poor migrants in Tehran can result in substantial changes in life styles of the rural villagers. This problem is further aggravated by the fact that the cash flow to the villages from the migrants is inconsequential. The infrequency of capital flow, and its excessively limited amount, cannot affect the village economy in any realistic way. Furthermore, the migrants have repeatedly made clear that they have no intention to return for permanent settlement in their villages. Well over 92 percent of my sample emphatically stated that they had no desire or plan to return. When pressed for reasons, three fourths of the migrants said that unsatisfactory employment or inadequate income in the villages mitigated against their eventual return. Thus, although the migrants maintain their ties with their villages, they are either not in a position or do not desire to commit capital and resources to transform rural society.

Tabriz Migrants

Cityward migration by the poor peasantry is not limited to Tehran. All major urban centers of Iran, and many of the country's medium-sized cities, are faced with similar situations. Tehran has received the lion's share of the migrant population and the many problems associated with resettlement of a massive number of rural migrants. Other cities have had to deal with the same problem but on a reduced scale. A recent study of the migrant poor in Tabriz, the nation's fourth-largest city, sheds some light on the socioeconomic characteristics of the migrants.[48] At least in terms of these characteristics, the nonsquatting Tabriz migrants are not that different from their counterparts in Tehran.

The survey was conducted among 1,123 migrants, nearly 80 percent of whom were village born. The most notable difference between Tabriz and Tehran migrants was the point of origin in migration of the two respective groups. Tehran migrants came from all parts of the country with basically no regard to distance, ethnic, or linguistic factors. In Tabriz, 96 percent of the migrants were originally from other parts of either West or East Azerbaijan. Very few non-Azerbaijanis had decided to migrate to the area's most important urban center. This is probably explained best by linguistic factors. Since Tabriz and Azerbaijan are Turkish-speaking areas, the attraction of Tabriz is restricted primarily to those who speak Turkish as their mother tongue. Non-Turkish-speaking migrants would as easily depart for Tehran or other Persian-speaking cities. Whereas Tehran attracts all the various linguistic and ethnic groups, Tabriz's appeal is primarily regional and confined to the area's linguistic minority.

Literacy was low among the Tabriz migrants. Only 41 percent of the heads of households and 31 percent of their spouses were able to read and write. The average monthly income of the head of household was approximately 230 dollars. Most migrants were regular wage earners in construction, industry, or commerce. Excluding the secondary migrants, 63 percent of the sample had migrated because of low income, unemployment, or work-related problems. Tabriz was selected as the point of destination mostly because the migrants had hoped to secure higher pay or better employment in the city. The length of time spent in finding employment ranged from one week for a few to over two years for some. The migrants found jobs through a variety of channels and sources (Table 4.9). Previous temporary visits to Tabriz was the single most effective method of finding employment. More than half of the migrants had secured their jobs by personally coming to Tabriz for a few days at a time to evaluate the prospects. Since their villages are mostly located in the same province as the city of Tabriz, these temporary stays did not require extensive travel or expense. Another 26 percent mentioned that relatives and friends were their primary sources of information in their job search.

The overwhelming majority of the migrants stated that their income expectation in Tabriz was either met or exceeded. Judging by their average monthly incomes, it is clear that the expectations were low. Nevertheless, the fact that the expectations had materialized probably contributed to the migrants' desire and intention to remain in Tabriz. It is also interesting to note that 82 percent of those who had prior temporary urban experience in Tabriz or had found employment through help from friends and relatives realized or exceeded their income expectations after settlement in the city. These experiences and contacts had given the migrants a realistic sense of what to expect in Tabriz.

The Tabriz poor migrants, then, are largely similar to poor migrants in Tehran. They share related socioeconomic problems in housing, employment, and income, and lead insecure lives on the margin of urban society. They also share these characteristics with many more poor migrants in other cities and towns of the country. Such problems and issues presented by the migrant poor are clearly among the most important and basic challenges confronting urban Iran.

Table 4.9

Employment Information Source of Economically Active
Migrant Heads of Households and Income Expectation
in Tabriz at the Time of Migration

Income Expectation

Information Source	More than expected	Less than expected	Equal to expectation	Not stated	Total
Friends and relatives in Tabriz	27	42	142	-	211
Previous temporary visits	91	92	248	4	435
Mass media	-	1	4	-	5
Personal inquiry	4	18	46	-	68
Other sources	2	6	16	3	27
None	6	9	29	-	44
Not stated	-	3	1	9	13
TOTAL	130	171	486	16	803

Chapter V

POLITICS IN THE CITY

Urbanization and Participation

The relationship between urbanization and political
participation has long been a subject of debate among
political theorists. Many have argued that increased
urbanization leads to higher levels of participation in the
political system. These theorists maintain that cityward
migration and urban residence result in greater exposure to
modern life and bring about more extensive participation.
In one of the earliest formulations of this relationship,
Daniel Lerner states that "it is the transfer of population
from scattered hinterlands to urban centers that stimulates
the needs and provides the conditions needed for 'take-off'
toward widespread participation."[1] Lerner's theory of
modernization posits a developmental sequence beginning with
urbanization and leading to greater levels of literacy; mass
media participation; and finally, political participation.
Urbanization is the key variable and "a necessary condition
of modernization"[2] in Lerner's theory, for, as he argues,
"it is with urbanization that the modernizing process
historically has begun in Western societies."[3] Aside from
his own application of this theory to the Middle East,
Lerner's theory (or aspects of it) has been tested and
applied in a variety of contexts and places. In more recent
years, findings by Donald McCrone and Charles Cnudde based
on data from a large group of nations have corroborated
Lerner's theory.[4] Gilbert Winham in a study of the United
States over a long period of time also essentially confirms
Lerner's theory, although he introduces some minor modifications.[5]

Another major view that links urbanization to
participation is Karl Deutsch's concept of social mobilization. Social mobilization was originally conceived as a
process initiated primarily by urbanization,[6] but later this
concept was expanded to include other variables. In his
later writing, Deutsch delineates social mobilization more
precisely and defines it "as the process in which major
clusters of old social, economic, and psychological
commitments are eroded or broken, and people become available
for new patterns of socialization and behavior."[7]
Urbanization, however, continues to play a critical role in
this development. The effect of social mobilization is to
unleash social forces and expand the politicized strata of
the population.[8] This process broadens political participation that, as Deutsch notes, "may express itself informally
through greater number of people taking part in crowds and
riots, in meetings and demonstrations, in strikes and

uprisings, or less dramatically, as members of a growing audience for political communications, written or by radio, or finally as members of a growing host of organizations."[9]

Deutsch's discussion of social mobilization posits a direct relationship between social mobilization and political participation. Political participation is defined broadly, along the lines set by Gabriel Almond, as the pressures from the politicized population for shares in the decision-making structure of the political system. Hence, participants can be defined as "those individuals who are oriented to the input structure and processes, and engage in, or view them themselves as potentially engaging in, the articulation of demands and the making of decisions."[10]

Although many scholars have argued in favor of linking urbanization and political participation, recent empirical research conducted mostly in the Third World cities rejects a necessary association between the two. Wayne Cornelius, for example, finds the assumption of high urban politicization as a result of migration to Mexico City untenable.[11] Clifford Kaufman's study of Mexico City confirms that "urbanization (urban residence), as a single factor, appears to explain little of the variations in individual political orientation and behavior."[12] Similarly, in their cross-national study of five Western and non-Western countries, David Cameron and his associates conclude that "urbanization when isolated from other dimensions, is not positively associated with participation."[13] And finally, further analysis by Norman Nie, Bingham Powell, and Kenneth Prewitt of survey data collected in Germany, Italy, Mexico, the United States, and the United Kingdom points to the absence of any consistent relationship between urbanization and political participation. The authors explain that when nations develop economically, there is an increase in the proportion of both urban residents and political participants. "However, the ecological correlation between urbanization and mass political partici-pation is spurious, as indicated by the absence of relationship between urban residence and participation within each nation."[14]

Clearly, the relationship between urbanization and political participation is complex. In some cases, urbanization would seem to be associated with increased participation. But in other cases, urbanization does not in any significant way explain greater political participation by different groups. The critical link in this relationship is a host of variables other than urbanization--such as education, income, and mass media participation--that may be better predictors of participation. Increased urbanization when not accompanied by higher literacy, media involvement, organizational activity, and other such factors is unlikely to find expression in greater political participation. This is generally the situation with the migrant poor in Tehran and other Iranian cities. The migrants have simply changed their residence from a rural to an urban locality without necessarily and concomitantly becoming more involved in those aspects of urban life that normally increase political

participation. Moreover, prior to migration and while in
the village, the migrants' participation and involvement in
politics has been extremely limited.

Political Involvement before Migration

The involvement of Iranian peasants in politics has gone
through two phases in modern times--before and after land
reform. Although political awareness and involvement
increased somewhat as peasants moved from one phase to
another, in neither period can any regular, persistent, or
widespread political activities be observed. The Iranian
peasants have remained essentially passive and noninvolved in
politics partly because the usual factors that lead to greater
political participation have been slow in reaching the
villagers. The peasants' levels of literacy, income, and
their participation in mass media, especially in the written
form, have continued to be low. Their partial insulation
from the outside world and their disenfranchised position in
the village economy have effectively prevented any regular
involvement in politics.

Before the era of land reform, the peasants suffered
from almost complete economic and social dependency on the
absentee landlords. The peasants' economic burdens and their
reliance on the landlords for their livelihood allowed the
landlords to demand and dictate all forms of political action.
As Ervand Abrahamian states, "in such an environment,
political action occurred only when ordered by the khans and
landlords."[15] Thus, in election times when peasants' votes
were needed, the landlords mobilized their peasants for
political action. This was the extent and range of peasants'
political participation. Occasionally, there were sporadic
clashes and even opposition was expressed to a particular
landlord, but these incidents were rare and clashes mostly
concerned disputes over irrigation rights among villagers.

In the land reform period, some segments of the peasantry
were politicized as a result of the government's efforts to
gain the peasants' support against the landlords. Furthermore, those peasants who received land were organized in
various cooperative and organizational arrangements.
Corollary programs such as the Houses of Justice, Literacy
and Health Corps, as well as other, similar agencies were
geared to make the peasants conscious supporters of the
regime. Most of these efforts, however, were largely
unsuccessful. Nevertheless, they created an environment
where the peasants did not feel as isolated from the outside
world as they had before. Yet, because of the restricted
impact of these actions and the fact that a substantial
number of peasants were forced off the land, the newly
created environment did not result in any discernible
increases in political participation for the masses of
Iranian poor peasants. Voting in times of election, however,
remained relatively constant and, on a percentage basis,
higher than one would expect.[16] The only difference between

voting before and after land reform was the fact that in one instance it was ordered by the landlord; in the other, it was dictated by the government.

The migrant poor, therefore, did not enter the urban world with any significant prior political involvement and participation. Their village life did not generally relate to politics and their occasional participation in voting was controlled and ordered by more powerful forces. As villagers, they were subjected to a political culture that emphasized their marginality and dispensability. Hence, their attitudes and views about politics were predicated on the absence of any strong sense of political efficacy. Upon arriving in the city, the migrants brought with them village views and attitudes about politics and its seeming irrelevance to their daily lives.

Political Involvement after Migration

The poor migrants in Tehran are not involved actively as a group in the politics of the city. Their primary preoccupation is to make ends meet in a costly city with inadequate housing, transportation, and social services. Moreover, the level of migrants' political awareness and organizational involvement (factors that promote political participation) is low. National politics has generally no salience for them. It becomes important only if it dramatically affects their lives. Under normal circumstances, the migrants' involvement in politics is minimal and, for many of them, is nonexistent. The migrant poor, however, can be politicized during unusual situations. There is, for instance, some evidence pointing to the migrants' partici- pation in the 1978-79 antiregime demonstrations and riots in Tehran. These were, of course, revolutionary times, and antiregime activism involved virtually all groups, segments, and classes of Iranian society. Before discussing the migrants' role in the recent turmoil, their relationship to politics in normal and nonrevolutionary circumstances should be analyzed.

Political Awareness

The migrants' knowledge and awareness of politics is generally low. In my survey of the migrant poor, an attempt was made to gauge the extent of migrants' political cognition. Because of the government's sensitivity to this kind of research, questions dealing with politics had to be simplified and made to appear "nonthreatening" to the regime. Five items on the questionnaire asking basic, simple questions of political knowledge were used to construct a summative index of political awareness. These responses were transformed into a scale of political cognition consisting of low, medium, and high levels for the group as a whole. On the basis of this procedure, the migrants' level of political awareness was correlated with other variables.

It soon became apparent that educational attainment
was a key determining factor leading to greater political
awareness. This relationship was substantiated by a Pearson's
R coefficient of 0.62 for 221 respondents. The migrants with
greater education were also prone to give an accurate response
to the ostensibly more difficult questions. It was primarily
the migrants with education beyond the sixth grade who
responded correctly to the question about the duties of the
Iranian parliament. For the illiterate or semiliterate
migrants, the question made little sense; this group was
also unable to identify the current mayor of Tehran.

The better-educated migrants were more likely to listen
to the news program on national radio than others. Although
84 percent of all respondents listened to the radio, only
29 percent regularly followed news. For the majority of the
migrants, media participation consisted of tuning in to radio
broadcasts of Persian music and songs, stories, and athletic
events. Thus, although there is extensive media participation
by the migrants as a whole, only the more literate portion
shows an interest in news about politics and public affairs.
Listening to the news on the radio and the political awareness
index were associated with a Pearson's R coefficient of 0.48
(and a Gamma of 0.72) for the 219 respondents. This
relationship is clearly selective and is partly mediated by
the migrants' educational attainment. The effect of mass
media participation in raising the level of political
awareness has to be viewed with caution. Two factors are
significant in this relationship. First, the contents of
programs listened to on radio or watched on television are
probably more important in explaining greater political
awareness than the fact of media participation alone. If no
explicit or implicit political knowledge is imparted in the
observed programs, there can be no expectation of increased
political cognition as a result. Second, media participation
through written forms (reading of newspapers and periodicals)
may be a more critical channel for increasing political
awareness. The proportion of news and political reporting is
substantially higher in newspapers and weeklies than in either
radio or television. Regular participation in written mass
media is more likely to be a better predictor of greater
political awareness. It is, therefore, important to note
that practically none of the poor migrants in Tehran
regularly read newspapers or periodicals.

The relationship between the migrants' income and their
political awareness was also examined. This relationship was
moderately sustained by a Pearson's R coefficient of 0.31 for
208 respondents (Table 5.1). The correlation can be explained
by the fact that generally it was the better educated groups
who also had higher incomes. Length of stay in Tehran was
found to have no significant relationship to the index of
political awareness. Controlling for education, there was
again no significant association between urbanization (length
of urban residence) and the individual items on the political
awareness index. It follows that unless there is some degree
of political cognition, the chances for political participation are at best minimal.

Table 5.1

Correlations (Pearson's R) of Education, News Consumption,
and Income with Political Awareness[a]
($\underline{n}$ = 208-221)

Index	Education	News Consumption	Income
Political awareness	0.62	0.48	0.31

[a]All correlations are significant at least at the 0.005
level.

To further analyze the migrants' political awareness and
behavior, a summative index of socioeconomic status consisting
of education, income, ownership of the dwelling unit, and
level of occupational skill was constructed. The index was
then categorized into high, medium, and low levels and
correlated with the political awareness index. The hypothesis
that higher socioeconomic status is correlated with a higher
degree of political awareness was sustained with a Pearson's
$\underline{R}$ coefficient of 0.44 (significant at the 0.005 level for
$\underline{n}$ = 222). The migrants' length of stay in Tehran was not an
important factor leading to higher socioeconomic status
(Pearson's $\underline{R}$ of 0.20). Controlling for age, the effect of
urban residence on socioeconomic status was further reduced.

What emerges from this discussion of the migrants'
political awareness is the importance of a few key variables
responsible for greater political cognition. The most
critical of these is the level of educational attainment.
The migrants with greater education were consistently the
most politically aware of their group. The crucial importance
of education is also very clear to the migrants themselves.
Almost without exception, the migrants perceived education as
a key determinant for economic advancement and social
mobility. They often explain a lesser degree of achievement
in life by referring to their low or inadequate literacy.

Organizational Affiliation

The absence of secondary and voluntary associations for
the migrant poor in Tehran has deleteriously affected the
opportunity for political action by the migrants. As Deutsch
states, "while many of these organizations are ostensibly
non-political, such as improvement societies, study circles,
singing clubs, gymnastic societies, agricultural and
commercial associations, fraternal orders, workmen's benefit
societies, and the like, they nevertheless tend to acquire a
political tinge, particularly in countries where more open
outlets for political activities are not available."[17]
Clearly such associations cannot acquire a political tinge

73

when they are essentially nonexistent in the first place.
Voluntary associations in Iran similar to those of the Latin
American urban squatters, if and when developed fully, may
turn out to be an important arena for making the migrant poor
more involved politically. Organizational membership--to use
the words of Nie, Powell, and Prewitt--"could be a political
resource for the lower classes."[18] These organizations can
serve as important agents for the migrants' political
socialization and later political action.

The migrants also are not, for the most part, affiliated
with organized political parties. Only 14 individuals (about
6%) belonged to the government-sponsored Rastakhiz-i Iran
(Resurrection of Iran) party. This noninvolvement in
political parties is particularly interesting since in 1975
all existing parties were abolished by the government and a
single "mass" party was created in their place by the Shah.
As part of this process, efforts were made to increase party
membership by all groups. However, fully two years after the
establishment of the Rastakhiz-i Iran party, the great masses
of migrants had not joined the organization. This lack of
participation by the migrants was not related to the decision
of many members of the intelligentsia who, as an act of
protest, refused to join the party. The migrants did not
become party members simply because such activities were
beyond their daily and routine concerns. Furthermore,
probably no government agent asked or pressured them to join
the party, because their participation was viewed to be
immaterial to the success or failure of the organization.[19]
There was no significant association between the migrants'
length of stay in Tehran and their political party
affiliation. Controlling for education, urbanization failed
to explain political participation by the migrants as
measured by voting at elections.

Forms of Political Participation

The low level of migrants' political awareness,
organizational affiliation, and political participation can
be explained partly by their socialization experience. The
usual agents of political socialization such as family,
school, mass media, and workplace have rarely imparted any
important degree of political knowledge to the migrants.
Limited or nonexistent schooling in a controlled and
restricted rural family environment is not conducive to
modern political learning. Participation in mass media is
confined mostly to nonnews programs on radio. The workplace,
which can be an important arena for political socialization,
has limited relevance for a good portion of the migrant poor.
The overwhelming majority of squatting migrants are employed
in a wide variety of temporary menial jobs or are unemployed.
Many of the nonsquatting poor migrants are employed in
semiskilled small workplaces where the extent of contact with
fellow workers is not substantial. The only exception to

74

this pattern is the situation of fully employed migrants in factories and large industrial operations.

Another factor that has influenced migrants' political participation has been the Iranian government's attitude about citizen participation in politics. The Shah's regime was wary of any form of political involvement that was not organized and controlled by its agents. The regime's political apparatus for citizen participation, such as the Rastakhiz-i Iran party, was centralized and its operation dictated from above. There was, therefore, not much opportunity, except in highly controlled situations, for conventional political participation. The squatting migrants practically never voted in parliamentary or city council elections. They were left out completely even from the controlled and sanctioned elections. Many of the nonsquatting migrants, however, were coerced by the regime to vote for approved government slates. This explains why approximately 70 percent of my sample of nonsquatting migrant poor had voted at least once in the elections since arriving in Tehran. The migrants' participation in this form of electoral politics was a mere mechanical act of confirming the officially sanctioned choices, without knowing who they were, under regime supervision. If they were not physically brought by government agents to the polling stations, they would not have participated in voting.

Second Generation Hypothesis

It is sometimes argued that the second-generation migrants--sons and daughters of the migrant poor who are born or reared in the city--are more politically aware and active than their parents. Because of their urban socialization experience and absorption of "goals and aspirations of the city,"[20] second-generation migrants are considered more likely to be politically conscious and to engage in political action. A few observers have even predicted radical and violent behavior by the second generation if their aspirations and demands are not met by the political system. Samuel Huntington, in a frequently quoted passage, states: "In Asia and Latin America, as well as North America, urban violence, political and criminal, is due to rise as the proportion of natives to immigrants in the city rises. At some point, the slums of Rio and Lima, of Lagos and Saigon, like those of Harlem and Watts, are likely to be swept by social violence, as the children of the city demand the rewards of the city."[21]

In order to assess the validity of the second generation hypothesis, at least in terms of levels of political awareness, two different groups of young male and female second-generation migrant poor in Tehran were selected for study.[22] The results gave mixed support, differentiated along sex lines, to the argument. Since both groups lived in the same poor area of Tehran known as Javadiyih, the comparison of the two provided interesting insights. The first group consisted of 60 young women who lived with their migrant parents in the area. Although most of them could read and write, their literacy level was low, with 87 percent having six years of education or less. The second group was made up of 42 male students enrolled in the twelfth grade of the area's public high school. They, too, lived with their migrant parents in the neighborhood or its immediate vicinity.

The female second-generation migrants were similar to their parents along different dimensions of social and political consciousness. Their knowledge of political issues and personalities was very limited. They were among the least politically aware groups that I encountered in the nonsquatting migrant sections of Tehran. They led a highly restricted social life that was primarily confined to helping at home and occasionally visiting a friend in the neighborhood. The overwhelming majority had never traveled to any other part of Tehran. A few were receiving training in sewing and dressmaking at a center operated by the Tehran College of Social Work. Almost none of them expected to be gainfully employed after completing the training period. They thought their new skills would be used for making clothes for the family after they married. Therefore, the fact that these women were second-generation migrants had no effect on their social and political awareness and the potential for greater political participation.

The situation, however, was dramatically different with the male high school students. These were politically aware and reasonably knowledgeable about the most important national political events and issues. Their political consciousness and sensitivity was in sharp contrast to that of the female second-generation migrants. Some of them thought I was an agent of the Iranian government, and hence geared their responses to my questions according to what they considered to be the official and pleasing answers. One student in particular showed excessive zeal, giving the "party line" on almost every question and using long and flowery expressions in his responses.

None of these students worked part-time during the school year or in the summer months. Lack of time or too much schoolwork were frequently cited as their reasons for not working. Their leisure or vacation time was spent with peers in the streets, not only in their neighborhood, but also in other parts of Tehran. The students all hoped for and expected to obtain "respectable" jobs upon completing their last year of high school.

The contrast between these two groups of second-generation migrants raises an important question about the universal validity of the second generation hypothesis. It is apparent that the simple fact that a migrant is a second-generation one is not necessarily equated with an increase in level of political awareness and participation. Although some second-generation migrants are politically aware and active, others are not. The explanation for the variation probably lies in the type and form of socialization with different migrants experience.

Significant differences separate the two samples of second-generation migrants in Tehran. First, socialization through the educational system was limited for the female group. Most had no regular schooling beyond the first few years of the elementary level. The male group, however, had the full benefit of secondary school socialization experience. This is important because Iranian high schools have always been among the most significant arenas for political learning and activism. This particular high school was no exception to the basic norm. Second, family socialization experience tends to be different for boys and girls in most segments of Iranian society, especially among the lower classes. The girls in the sample were prepared for life differently than the boys. They were essentially confined to a restricted personal and social life centered around the immediate family and neighborhood. The boys, however, experienced a social life that allowed them to absorb the "goals and aspirations of the city." They all had expectations of "respectable" jobs and aspirations for a future that would be substantially better than their parents' achievements. If the hopes and goals of this group are thwarted, then Huntington's prediction of their radicalism and social violence could be one outcome.

Political Demand Making

A possible form of political participation by the migrant poor is through political demand making. Political demand making is defined in Cornelius's terms as "individual or collective activities aimed at extracting certain types of benefits from the political system by influencing the decisions of incumbent government officials."[23] The process of demand making involves a few distinct stages. These are: "existence of objectively defined needs → perception of needs as requiring ameliorative action → perception of needs as susceptible to satisfaction through government action → perception of channel for influencing government → political demand-making."[24] Political demand making is an important link between the migrant poor and the political system. It is differentiated, as Cornelius States, "from political activity intended to influence government resource allocation by replacing or retaining the incumbent authorities (e.g., electoral participation) or by overthrowing or restructuring the political system (e.g., through violent revolution)."[25] Political demand making is a conventional mode of participation whereby explicit needs of the migrants are presented to the political system with the hope that positive responses will be forthcoming from the officials.

The most obvious needs, as seen by the migrant poor in several different surveys in Tehran, concerned a number of socioeconomic factors, such as security of tenure, improvement of living conditions, and better employment opportunities. Security of tenure is the single most

important need that is expressed frequently by the migrants.
This is not restricted only to the squatters and other
nonhomeowning migrants. Even those who own their dwelling
units expressed fears of losing their homes because of
inability to pay back debt incurred for their purchases.
Others complained about their problems in sharing two-room
houses that were bought in partnership with other families.
In a survey of a migrant poor area known as Khazanih-yi
Fallah, 78 percent of the residents were reported to own their
homes. However, 46 percent of these houses had only one room
and another 45 percent two rooms. The typical family in this
area had between 6 and 7 resident members.[26] These migrants
were similar to the majority of homeowning poor migrants in
other parts of Tehran who normally live with large families
in one or two rooms. It is apparent that legal title to a
dwelling unit does not eliminate housing problems.

The residents of Kuyi Nuhum-i Aban who already lived in
government-built projects, and thus did not face security of
tenure as an immediate problem, expressed three other
categories of need.[27] These concerns were related to
(1) improvement of their dwelling units, (2) service
facilities in the settlements, and (3) general social needs
(Tables 5.2, 5.3, 5.4). For these migrants, perceived needs
had now assumed a pronounced community-related character.
Although individual needs, such as better employment, remained
central to the migrants, there was also a distinct preoccupation with needs that concerned the community as a whole.

In my follow-up survey in 1974 in Kuyi Nuhum-i Aban, it
became apparent that a sizable segment of those questioned
expected some government action to ameliorate their pressing
community-related problems. This contrasted with the
reactions of other migrants in non-government-constructed
projects where such expectations were generally not conveyed
to the interviewer. In Kuyi Nuhum-i Aban needs were expressed

Table 5.2

Migrants' Needs in Dwelling Units of
Kuyi Nuhum-i Aban

Type of Need	Percent
Pool[a]	30
Closet, shelf, space heater	27
Roof for bathroom	13
Sink apart from kitchen	12
Other	18

[a]Pool is not for swimming purposes but is used mainly
for washing.

Table 5.3

Migrants' Needs for Service Facilities in
Kuyi Nuhum-i Aban

Type of Need	Percent
Public bathhouse	37
Butcher shop	31
Bakery	15
Grocery	9
Other	8

Table 5.4

Migrants' General and Social Needs in
Kuyi Nuhum-i Aban

Type of Need	Percent
Health facilities and pharmacy	28
Mosque	26
Sewer system	21
Schools	7
Transportation services	7
Other	11

not only in communal terms; they were also at least superficially politicized. This evidence supports Cornelius's observation that "the range of needs viewed by the migrant poor as requiring governmental action is partly a function of the presence or absence of overt governmental attempts to create feelings of dependence among the lower classes."[28] In Kuyi Nuhum-i Aban, the government had already acted by constructing dwelling units for the squatters. It was, therefore, logical for the residents to expect further actions by the government to alleviate other communal problems. The most common channels perceived by the migrants for satisfaction of demands in this particular community were the mayor, the office of the prime minister, and the queen's office. However, not many expected that any concrete benefits would develop as a result of contacting these offices.

The homeowning migrants in two other low-income communities of Tehran, Khazahih-yi Fallah and Mihrabad-i Junubi, also expressed a variety of social- and community-oriented needs. These needs were directed primarily to lack of medical and health facilities, absence of paved streets, inadequate public transportation, and other social services.[29] The residents of Mihrabad-i Junubi were among the most vocal migrants in Tehran. They openly expressed their dissatisfaction with the conditions of the neighborhood and its social environment. No such strong and overt expression of discontent was aired by migrants in other low-income communities of Tehran. Further analysis of the socioeconomic background of this particular sample of migrants revealed a higher rate of educational attainment and income than the average nonsquatting migrant poor in Tehran. However, as with the residents of Kuyi Nuhum-i Aban, there was no clear expectation for amelioration of the community needs by the government.

Some migrant poor neighborhoods of Tehran have occasionally presented petitions to high officials during the past several years. These activities have almost invariably come about either after eradication of a settlement and housing compound or when the residents have perceived such threats to their homes. In the Appendix there is a report of one such petition drive. In another instance, after the municipal employees had destroyed a few houses located on the waqf (pious foundation) lands of Narmak area, a large group of residents gathered to express their collective concern. Three buses were rented for the occasion, and the crowd headed toward the Shah's Niavaran palace.

> Someone in the bus suggested that on the way they shout "Long live the Shah." Others said that if they attracted attention, then the authorities would not allow the buses to reach the Shah's palace. The Shah was expecting an important foreign dignitary when the buses reached the palace. The police officials told the petitioners to gather at the two sides of the street and cheer the Shah and his guest when they arrived. "We will then allow you to see the Shah." The guest arrived and the people cheered,

but the officials did nothing. One of the men whose house had been demolished said, "Twenty people must get killed before this situation is rectified. Without shedding blood the problem will not be resolved."[30]

The next day, after much discussion the group decided to go to the parliament building. Two members of the local neighborhood council tried to dissuade the petitioners from going to the parliament with vague promises. At the entrance to the parliament building, the guards said that this affair did not concern the representatives and that it should be handled by the mayor's office. The petitioners were eventually "persuaded" to go to the local municipality office in Narmak. Nothing came of this petition drive, and the migrants returned empty-handed.

The migrants generally have not had extensive interactions with government-sponsored or privately formed associations and institutions. Many of the migrants have contacted, at one time or another, some of the existing charitable organizations or civic associations. However, because of the unresponsiveness of these institutions, the migrants have not felt encouraged to return. They freely share their stories about how they were mistreated or even abused by institutions that were established ostensibly to help the poor. Perhaps the only broad exception to this pattern is the several clinics, day-care centers, and apprentice shops organized by the College of Social Work in the southern part of Tehran. There has been a small but regular flow of the poor migrants to these centers seeking assistance in regard to occupation, health, and family matters.

The relative absence of overt expression of political demand making, even when the objective needs are felt strongly, has been widespread among all strata of the Iranian migrant poor. Either the needs were not politicized at all or they were not made into demands presented to the government. This was particularly true about individual needs related to employment. The majority of the migrants did not expect to find employment through government channels. The only individual need the migrants hoped would be satisfied by possible government action was in the area of housing. There were vague expectations that someday the government would provide low-income housing for the poor.

The infrequency of political demand making among the migrant poor can be explained partly by the nonresponsiveness of the political system to the migrants' demands. In Mexico City, for example, political demand making by the migrant poor has been reasonably high because, among other reasons, the regime has "ensured a relatively high level of responsiveness to petitioning."[31] No such counterpart can be found in the Iranian case. The Iranian bureaucracy, notorious for its inefficiency and corruption, would be highly unresponsive to such demands, especially when presented by the migrant poor. This explains why almost none of the migrant perceived the

81

regular bureaucratic channels as possible sources for satisfaction of their needs. It was rather the apex of bureaucracy--the queen, the prime minister, and the mayor-- who were viewed as potentially responsive to their demands.[32]

Another explanation for the migrants' relative nonparticipation in political demand making is the limitations of voluntary associations or other forms of organized and collective political activity among the migrant poor. Because of the relative ineffectiveness of these organizations, the migrants are denied access to an important arena for training of leaders. Without organizations and community leaders, aggregation and collective expression of demands have become exceedingly difficult. The situation was further exacerbated by the fact that the regime-controlled political organizations and parties were highly centralized and have in no way served as demand articulators for the lower classes.

Migrant Radicalism

Political participation through demonstrations, protests, collective violence, and other acts of radicalism is not a regular or common feature of the migrant poor's behavior. Although the traditional literature has put much evidence on the anomic, violent, and radical behavior of the migrant poor, the recent empirical research in the Third World cities disputes these long-held views. Studies by Wayne Cornelius, William Mangin, Janice Perlman, Alejandro Portes, and others have reported that slum and squatter radicalism is not a basic feature of the Latin American cities.[33] Myron Weiner's study of voting behavior for extremist parties in the Calcutta elections of 1957 and 1962 has found no evidence "to support the commonly held hypothesis that migrants to urban centers are politically more extremist than city-born residents."[34] In another study of violence in Calcutta over the tram fare in 1953 and 1954, Weiner discovered that the demonstrators came from many social classes but that the most violent demonstrations were those "in which the middle classes form the core."[35]

The Iranian poor migrants present no exception to this general pattern. As a rule, they are not involved in acts of political protest or radicalism in the city. Violent political action in Iranian cities is more in the domain of traditional and city-born residents, such as artisans, tradesmen, people from the bazaar, and more recently the factory workers. Unless mobilized because of extraordinary circumstances, the poor migrants do not engage in collective acts of political protest and radicalism.

Several different explanations may be advanced to account for the migrant poor's noninvolvement in political protests. In the first place, important socioeconomic preconditions for participation in politics, whatever the form, are absent among the migrant poor in Tehran. These include higher literacy, income, and general socioeconomic position than the Iranian poor migrants usually possess. The migrants' sense of political cognition is low, and their sense of political efficacy is practically nonexistent. The government is not normally viewed as a logical source for demand satisfaction. Moreover, the migrants' fundamental concerns are centered on efforts to obtain housing and better employment for themselves and their family members. The strenuous daily struggles in pursuit of such basic goals do not leave much room for political activity. The absence of indigenous leadership and organizational means for political action has further limited the potential for involvement in politics. The net effect of the migrant poor's socialization experience in the city has not been to promote sustained interest in politics or various forms of political action.

Second, the migrants, like most groups who challenge a given political regime, are guided by certain rational calculations of chances for success. As Portes points out, "the political behavior of the poor is governed . . . by rational adaptation to what structural circumstances permit and encourage."[36] It is not unlikely for an unresponsive or repressive regime to crush the migrants' protest movement in a harsh manner. As indicated in a study of urban settlements in Chile and Peru, "actual repression or the threat of it may under such conditions be sufficient to discourage any behavior that might antagonize the establishment."[37] Unless the migrants can count on assistance from external sources, they probably would not challenge the authorities. The migrants' perception of the regime's response and the remote possibility of obtaining the desired goals through collective protest often served as barriers to radical action.

Third, the migrants tend to have limited aspirations, and when these aspirations are thwarted it is rare for the government to be blamed. As Joan Nelson states, the poor do not "perceive the connection between government policies and programs and the general economic conditions which perpetuate their poverty."[38] The migrants' failure to link their destitution to the socioeconomic structure and government policies reduces their potential for revolutionary action.[39]

Fourth, the poor migrants in Tehran do not have the sense of anomie, social isolation, and uprootedness that some scholars have viewed to be an important precondition leading to the migrants' espousal of radical ideologies, causes, and parties. As already seen, the migrants maintain an extensive network of communication with friends and relatives both in the city and the village of origin.

Finally, the frustration-aggression theory of radicalism is not a plausible explanation of the migrant poor's behavior in Tehran. The basic idea here is that aggression is the result of frustration and that frustration comes about when one's goals and expectations are thwarted. The most comprehensive recent analysis of frustration-aggression theory of political violence is presented by Ted Gurr. Gurr links frustration-aggression to the notion of relative deprivation, defined as "perceived discrepancy between men's value expectations and their value capabilities."[40]   The causal sequence in the process leading to political violence is, in Gurr's view, first the development of deprivation-induced discontent, "second the politicization of that discontent, and finally its actualization in violent action against political objects and actors."[41]

Empirical evidence collected among the migrant poor has consistently questioned the validity of frustration-aggression analysis of political violence. Much of this research indicates that the migrants consider themselves better off in the city than they were in the country and that they are not dissatisfied with their lives.[42] Similarly, the poor migrants in Tehran, although deprived in a multitude of ways of many amenities, perceive their lives to be better in the city than they were in the village. In my 1977 survey, 84 percent of the migrants mentioned that they preferred living in Tehran rather than their rural villages. When asked to state their reasons for preferring Tehran, nearly all of them mentioned better work and higher income in the city.[43] Considering the migrant poor's deplorable conditions in the city, this underlines the migrants' perception of an even more deplorable life in the countryside.[44] The poor migrants in Tehran were also happy with their work. Only 16 percent expressed outright displeasure with their occupation. Tehran may have monumental problems affecting all residents, but fully 78.5 percent of the migrants were content with life in the capital.

Another deficiency in the frustration-aggression explanation of the migrant poor's radicalism is the assumption that the frustrated migrants express their anger in political forms. The migrants may be frustrated, deprived, and angry, but as Nelson perceptively observes, they

> can express their frustration in an infinite variety of ways. They may turn their anger inward in withdrawal and defeat; they may beat their wives or quarrel with their neighbors; they may seek oblivion in alcohol or solace in religion. In addition to these individual reactions, there are many associational responses with little or no political relevance. Political action, whether individual or associational, moderate or extremist, legal or illegal, is only one class of reactions to frustration among many others.[45]

The migrants' frustration with their lot is often turned inward. There is a strong tendency among the migrants to blame themselves or fate for their socioeconomic problems and the resultant frustrations. It is rare for the migrants to place blame for their frustrations on structural features of social order such as social injustice or exploitation of the poor.[46] Hence collective violence, along the lines envisaged in the frustration-aggression theory, is not a likely outcome of the migrant poor's behavior.

84

Legal and Institutional Violence

Although the poor migrants are not usually perpetrators of violence, they are frequently its victims. It can be argued that the migrants, like other poor, are often subjected to social injustice or, as Johan Galtung calls it, "structural" violence.[47] In Galtung's view, this form of violence "is built into the structure and shows up as unequal power and consequently as unequal life chances."[48] Although there may be some merit in such a broad conception of violence, it is more appropriate to characterize these situations in terms of social injustice or inequality of opportunity.[49] Perhaps a more useful and restricted notion of violence in this regard would be to identify those areas where specific acts of violence by the agents of social order have been committed. These are acts of violence stemming from the institutions of the state and hence are labeled "legal" violence.[50]

It is not uncommon to find "legal" violence inflicted on the migrant poor by the agents of the state. Forceful removal and eradication of squatter settlements are among the most often committed acts of "legal" violence in many cities of the world. The Iranian squatter settlements have had no better fate. There have been several examples of forceful eradication of squatter settlements in Tehran during recent years. Two such episodes are worth recounting.

The first concerted act of squatter settlement eradication in Tehran took place in November 1958 in an area known popularly as the South City Pits. These pits consisted of enormous hollows dug into the ground in which the squatters had built shacks, hovels, and cavelike dwellings. According to the reports, 1,356 squatters lived in these pits at the time. On a cold night at 8:30 P.M., a large group of government officials and workers surprised the residents and attacked their homes. The official eradication party included 130 soldiers; 100 policemen; 120 officers of the police relief organization; 300 municipal officers, workers, and street sweepers; as well as 30 military trucks, 100 police trucks, 3 fire engines, 2 ambulances, 25 large bright lamps, and a few other pieces of equipment.[51] An eyewitness account described the action in detail.

> As planned, the official activities began behind the police precinct at the "Haji Mo'in Pit," located on the northern section of Ghar Avenue. A group of soldiers hurriedly stepped down from their trucks and surrounded the Pit. A large number of bright lamps immediately set the Pit's huge space ablaze. Loudspeakers filled the air: "Brothers and sisters, in accordance with the Shah's order, we have come to save you from misery. Brothers, don't be frightened. The government will provide you with houses, quilts, space heaters, food, clothes, and work." Dumbstruck, the squatters, many of whom

85

had been asleep, emerged from the pits and shacks.
The sight of so many people--soldiers, policemen,
and street sweepers carrying shovels and picks--
frightened and worried them. . . . The mayor and
other high officials entered the Pit; each, in his
own way, tried to convey the Shah's order and the
Cabinet's decision. The mayor called to one of the
women: "Don't be frightened, sister. Do you always
want to live in this filthy and putrid shack? Now
you face happiness; gather your belongings quickly
and give your children the good tidings that from
now on a better and more comfortable life awaits
them." Another high official spoke baby talk to a
squatter child shivering in his arms. At this time,
groups of officers walked into the Pit carrying
shovels and picks. Another group, holding lamps
and searchlights, entered the shacks and hovels.
. . . A few of the squatters tried to escape, but
were prevented by the soldiers' tight encirclement.
After half an hour, about 25 squatters got into
the waiting trucks. The first pit was now
evacuated. Then the mayor ordered the shacks'
destruction. The remainder of the squatters'
belongings were set on fire, and the work of "Haji
Mo'in Pit" was completed. The officials along with
their entourage climbed back into their cars and
sped off in the direction of the "Farahani Pit."[52]

The eradication efforts were finished by two in the
morning. The squatters were taken to large government storage
rooms for temporary housing. Meager attempts were made to
find employment for a few of the squatters. Some were forced
to return to their villages. Others were set free in a few
days or were placed in an overcrowded institution for
beggars. The net result of the whole effort was futile, as
these squatters or others soon reestablished themselves in
the old habitat. Those sent to their villages were back in
the streets of Tehran in a few days.[53]

The second example of squatter settlement eradication
concerns a series of attempts by the officers of Tehran
Municipality to evict squatters from their homes on the
pretexts of illegal occupation and residence in areas outside
the city limits. These sporadic acts of eviction took place
on a few occasions in late 1977 and in 1978. The basic
pattern of action was based on a decision by the Tehran
Municipality to forcefully terminate all residential units
or business operations that had not conformed to the city's
stated regulations. Several supermarkets, business
enterprises, and housing units owned by the well-to-do were
destroyed by the Municipality's squad of workers. As part
of this decision, a few of the newer squatter settlements,
which were mushrooming on the outskirts of Tehran, were
singled out for destruction. However, in contrast to the
1958 situation, occasionally the squatters put up stiff
resistance and defended the settlements. Many of the
squatters tried to physically prevent destruction of their

86

homes and were consequently either forcibly detained by the officers or injured in the melee. For example, in Sulaymaniyih a few vehicles belonging to the Municipality were set on fire. In Tehran Pars acid was reportedly thrown at the demolition crew. There were rumors of similar acts of resistance by the squatters in various other parts of Tehran.

In a particularly harsh fight with the officers of Tehran Municipality in August 1978, 200 men and women of a settlement known as Shahbaz-i Junubi fought the invaders for five hours. The squatters' efforts were, however, to no avail, as their 50 shacks were leveled by bulldozers. About 13 of the squatters were injured also, some seriously enough to require hospitalization. One of the injured residents expressed his bitterness, shared by others, about the government's action:

> The high cost of tenancy forced us to build a small shack with scraps of metal and oil cans in this location. I then brought my wife and four children here to lead a Stone Age life in a place that has no water or electricity. But the officers of the Municipality, without prior warning and with no regard to their own timetable stated in the eviction notice, destroyed our shacks over our heads. My children's birth certificates and my other documents are all buried under the debris. I don't know how I am going to find them.[54]

Sometimes resistance to eradication took passive forms. The squatters simply remained inside their shacks and refused to move out. At other times, the authorities were showered with insults. There were also frequent expressions of frustration. An extreme case of this was the attempt at self-immolation of a young poor migrant homeowner in Majidiyih. He recounted the episode in the following manner:

> They destroyed my home last spring. I was furious and wanted to attack them but my brother physically restrained me. I went and poured kerosene over my head and lit a match. Everybody gathered and tried to put the fire out. I spent five months in a hospital and have no energy left. . . . Now I sift dirt here and make a living selling it. The Municipality officers bother me. But ever since the self-immolation attempt, they say "don't go near him, he'll burn himself."[55]

The demolition of the poor migrants' homes left a bitter residue. The problem was exacerbated when the government made no attempt to relocate the squatters. In the 1958 removals at least an initial effort was exerted to house the squatters and to find what the authorities considered to be solutions to their problems. In the more recent removals the squatters were left homeless and with nowhere to go. At the minimum, the squatters blamed the government for their loss of homes. As word of the government's increasingly hostile attitude toward the settlements got around, more squatters

mobilized and prepared to defend their homes. Clearly,
through its harsh policy, the regime created much ill feeling
among the squatters and left them with no choice other than
to stand against what they considered to be unbearably
repressive action. Hence, when the antiregime demonstrations
and riots of 1978 began in earnest, the task of mobilizing
the poor against the Shah's regime was made considerably
easier.

The Revolution

Massive political protests, demonstrations, and riots
shook the basic foundations of the Iranian political system
in 1978 and 1979. These acts of political protest were
directed against the Shah's regime and the Pahlavi dynasty.
The protests were expressed by practically all segments of
the social order and united disparate groups and factions
behind the goal of toppling the government. The regime's
harsh measures against the demonstrators intensified the
conflict and brought an increasingly larger number of people
into active opposition to the Shah. The causes and
precipitants of the revolution are multiple, and it is not
my purpose here to analyze either the causes or the events
themselves.[56] My primary interest is rather to discuss the
conditions for the poor migrants' mobilization against the
regime and the extent of their participation in the
revolutionary events. It is clear that elements of the
migrant poor, like other groups of Iranians, rose against
the Shah's regime. It also appears that the nonsquatting
poor migrants were more actively involved in anti-Shah
demonstrations than the poorer squatters, although segments
of both groups had been mobilized against the regime. The
key concern is to underline those factors responsible for
the mobilization of the migrant poor against the government.

Mobilization can be defined in broad terms, in Charles
Tilly's words, as "the process by which a group goes from
being a passive collection of individuals to an active
participant in public life."[57] Political mobilization has
generally involved an attempt to change the norms and
structures of the existing authority.[58] In order for
political mobilization to take place, usually several
conditions for political action need to be present. First,
there must be an awareness of certain needs, issues, and
grievances that can be expressed in political terms. Second,
linkages between these issues and national or higher-level
politics must be established. Third, it is essential that
leadership and organizational means for expression of the
needs and issues exist to provide direction and focus to the
action groups.[59]

These conditions were largely met in the recent crisis
and resulted in mobilizing groups of poor migrants, normally
politically passive, into active opponents of the regime.
The issues that were of particular concern to the migrants

involved perception of new threats to their endeavors to obtain employment, food, and housing. The migrant squatters felt specifically threatened by the government's new policy of eradication of squatter settlements. The manner and form of removal acts left the squatters bitter and homeless. Many of them banded together and decided to resist the eviction attempts. The new sentiment of solidarity was vividly expressed by a Virdabad squatter:

> There is nothing they can do it we are united. As lower classes we must have solidarity. Otherwise, no one will care about our problems. After all, doesn't the Shah's family depend only on the well-to-do?[60]

The nonsquatting poor migrants were severely affected by the rapid increase in the cost of renting rooms or other forms of dilapidated housing. A much larger share of their income now had to be set aside for housing than ever before. For many of these migrants, the exponential rise in the price of even low-income housing destroyed the hope of ever owning a home.

Added to the migrants' problems was the annual inflation rate of about 30 percent, which affected the price of all commodities, including the basic food items. The only staple not touched by the steep rise in prices was bread, the price of which was kept artificially low by the government for fear of strong popular reaction. Finally, the credit squeeze in 1976 that resulted in a slowdown of the construction industry adversely affected the migrants' employment opportunities. Since a substantial number of the migrant poor were employed in construction or related jobs, the slowdown left many migrants with no steady source of income. Longer periods of unemployment or less frequent temporary construction jobs became a more regular feature of the migrant poor's daily lives.

It is apparent that the migrant poor's economic difficulties were aggravated by the mid-1970s. The direct connection between their worsening economic position and government policies, however, was not necessarily clear to all migrants. The linkage was made by the regime's opposition forces, most of whom had suffered not only from economic hardship but also from the government's authoritarian and repressive actions. The opposition had correctly judged that success against the regime and its well-entrenched military and security forces was largely contingent upon the extent of popular participation and street demonstrations. The migrants and other groups of the urban proletariat could provide an important numerical support for the antiregime organizations. Hence, the stage was set for politicizing the poor's needs and grievances and directing them against the Shah's government.

The task of the opposition was made easier by the great inequality of wealth in the country. Available statistical evidence points to a society on a path of increasing maldistribution of wealth (Table 5.5). In 1973-74 in the

89

Table 5.5

Four Measures of Inequality of Consumption Expenditure

	1969-1970	1970-1971	1971-1972	1972-1973
Rural				
Gini Coefficient	0.3559	0.3685	0.3899	0.3659
Share of Top 20%	44.88	45.85	45.67	43.59
Share of Middle 40%	32.08	31.62	30.58	31.73
Share of Bottom 40%	18.03	18.17	17.55	18.40
Urban				
Gini Coefficient	0.4161	0.4227	0.4152	0.4032
Share of Top 20%	49.24	47.83	48.33	47.11
Share of Middle 40%	27.99	28.43	29.64	30.21
Share of Bottom 40%	16.06	15.36	16.25	16.69
Total				
Gini Coefficient	0.4188	0.4545	0.4363	0.4228
Share of Top 20%	49.66	52.48	50.00	48.83
Share of Middle 40%	28.91	28.28	28.28	28.89
Share of Bottom 40%	16.77	14.41	14.98	15.40

SOURCE: M. A. Pesaran, "Income Distribution in Iran," Iran: Past, Present, and Future, ed. Jane Jacqz (New York: Aspen Institute for Humanistic Studies, 1976), p. 280.

urban areas, the highest 10 percent of households accounted for 37.9 percent of total expenditure; the lowest 10 percent accounted for only 1.3 percent (Table 5.6). Inequality of income was most pronounced in Tehran where, in 1974, 60 percent of the city's total income was distributed among the top 20 percent income group.[61] The opposition did not need statistical evidence to prove the growing impoverishment of the many for the benefit of the few. The extreme concentration of wealth in a small group was amply demonstrated by the wealthy's conspicuous consumption and eager display of opulence. It was particularly difficult to justify or rationalize the maldistribution of resources in the wake of the oil boom of the post-1973 years and the expectations that is had raised among the population. Instead of a better and more comfortable life, the poor discovered a relative deterioration of their economic life and faced greater difficulties in making ends meet.

The decisive external support needed for the poor's mobilization was provided by the religious hierarchy and to a lesser degree by the secular National Front. Both groups, particularly the religious establishment, had the organization and leadership required to draw the disenfranchised elements into taking action against the regime. The initially tacit and later explicit tactical alliance between the religious groups and the National Front allowed for a direct attempt to

Table 5.6

Decile Distribution of Household Expenditure:
Urban Areas (Percent)

Deciles (lowest to highest)	1959-1960	1969-1970	1970-1971	1971-1972	1972-1973	1973-1974
1st	1.77	1.59	1.48	1.34	1.37	1.37
2nd	2.96	2.86	2.62	2.39	2.51	2.40
3rd	4.09	3.96	4.07	3.60	3.36	3.42
4th	5.08	4.58	4.54	4.32	4.64	4.77
5th	6.17	5.94	5.60	5.66	5.16	5.08
6th	7.37	7.96	7.68	6.94	6.98	6.85
7th	8.92	8.48	8.23	8.57	9.51	9.36
8th	11.85	11.72	11.48	11.70	11.14	11.19
9th	16.42	16.05	16.18	16.00	18.38	17.57
10th	35.37	36.86	38.12	39.48	36.95	37.99

SOURCE: M. H. Pesaran, "Income Distribution in Iran," Iran: Past, Present, and Future, ed. Jane Jacqz (New York: Aspen Institute for Humanistic Studies, 1976), p. 278.

reach the poor. In a pattern reminiscent of the century-old clerical-liberal alliances, the two organizations put aside their fundamental political differences and united in opposition to the Shah.

The religious hierarchy was logistically in a much better position than the National Front to reach the poor, address their grievances, and give focus and direction to their demands. This was due to at least two factors: (1) the pervasiveness of the Shi'i religious institution and its permeation of most levels of social order, especially the lower classes; and (2) the strong affinity of the poor with traditional beliefs, values, and practices of Shi'i Islam.

Ever since 1501 when Shi'ism was adopted as the state religion of Iran by the Safavid dynasty, Shi'i institutions have had the opportunity to develop and expand in various parts of the country. The Safavids came to power adhering rigidly to the Shi'i platform. As part of their campaign to convert all of Iran into Shi'ism, and thus win more support for their rule, the Safavids helped to build up the Shi'i ulama into an effective organization.[62] The Shi'i ulama in due time acquired administrative control of waqf and religious taxes in the forms of khums and zakat. The waqf were pious foundations or endowments that were established to support public works or religious institutions. Khums and zakat were canonical payments or almsgivings required of all Shi'is and collected by the religious authorities. Khums (one fifth) was the share of the Imam, and zakat was distributed among the needy.

Owing to the peculiar nature of the twelver Shi'i belief system, which gave the ulama the right to guide the community in all matters of life during the absence of the hidden Imam, the relationship between the clergy and the state was not always harmonious. Some members of the ulama occasionally questioned the right to rule and the legitimacy of the secular authority. This issue became more acute after the collapse of the Safavid dynasty, and especially in the late Qajar period.

When the Pahlavi dynasty was established by Reza Shah in 1925, attempts were made to reduce the power of the clergy in the affairs of the state and society. Reza Shah's reforms, particularly in the areas of education and the judiciary, undermined the clergy's authority and control. The ulama's challenge to Reza Shah was diminished as the monarch's authoritarian rule severely curtailed the clergy's role. The ulama's opposition was, therefore, muted and limited in its impact. When Muhammad Reza Shah replaced his father in 1941, the religious leaders attempted to regain some of the lost power. Although initially the ulama made important gains, their activist opposition to the Pahlavis was blunted in due time. The decline of the clergy's power became especially evident after the riots of June 1963, led by Ayatullah Ruhullah Khumayni, were suppressed.

The causes of the 1963 riots and the ensuing events are not directly relevant to my discussion of the migrant poor.

It is, however, important to note that after this date Khumanyi emerges as the chief and dominant spokesman among the ulama against the abuses of the Shah's regime.[63] Although the riots were brutally crushed by the military and Khumanyi was exiled, the oppositional role of the clergy was firmly reestablished. Led by a charismatic figure who made masterful use of Shi'i and popular symbols rejecting unjust rule, the opposition remained alive abroad and as an underground movement within Iran.

After 1963 the Shah's regime made a more vigorous and concerted effort to dominate the institution of the clergy. Elements from within the ulama who supported the government were rewarded handsomely. Those who did not, but remained passively acquiescent, were let alone. Others were made to pay for their opposition through imprisonment and harassment by the SAVAK, the Shah's secret police. In spite of these efforts, the government failed to gain control of or pacify the religious institution. The clergy remained strong even though their control over waqf had been drastically reduced for some time and the land reform program had redistributed charitable land previously administered by them. Through the network of Shi'i mosques and the flow of voluntary religious "tax" payments, the ulama effectively maintained their ties with the people. The presence of several thousand mosques and shrines and many more mullahs in all corners of the country kept the religious institution a vital element of the Iranian social structure.[64] Hence, the religious hierarchy was not forced to abandon the distribution of welfare among the poor even though its conventional sources of funds had been restricted. Many individuals and groups in the bazaar merchant community, who were financially affected by, and disenchanted with, the Shah's economic policies, sustained or increased their contribution to the ulama.

The Shi'i clergy in Iran had always been close to the poor. In addition to welfare distribution, the relationship between the clergy and popular classes is cemented by the deeply ingrained values and practices of Shi'i Islam. This relationship is formalized by the poor's attendance at mosques and holy shrines and their participation in the Shi'i festivals, especially those commemorating Imam Husayn's martyrdom by the Ummayyad Sunni Caliph, Yazid. This episode has had a profound impact on the Shi'i psyche. To the Shi'is, Husayn (the grandson of prophet Muhammad) exemplifies the quest for the noblest heroism and self-sacrifice for the sake of justice, whereas Yazid is considered as the personification of evil. The Manichaean dualism inherent in such explicit juxtaposition of good and evil is celebrated regularly with passion plays, marches, and flagellations.[65] To commemorate these events, the popular classes are mobilized through the extensive network of mosques, shrines, and hay'at missions.[66] The poor participate fully in all phases of these festivals and reaffirm not only their faith but also their contacts with the ulama and the bazaar organizers of the ceremonies.

The symbolism of Husayn's quest for justice and his eventual martyrdom was repeatedly evoked by Khumanyi and other ranking leaders of the ulama during the course of the revolution. Khumanyi linked pauperization of the masses to the wastefulness and corruption of the Shah's monarchy.[67] He exhorted the masses: "Do not remain silent. When they hit you on the head, protest. Do not give in to injustice as it is worse than perpetrating evil. Protest, deny untruths, and shout."[68] The Shah's regime, which had always suffered from a serious problem of legitimacy, was now likened to the traitors and oppressors of the Shi'i cause. The Shah was designated as "the Yazid of the age."[69] The frequency of Khumanyi's exhortion to rise against the Shah increased as the month of Husayn's martyrdom, Muharram, drew near.

> Moharram, the month of courage and sacrifice, has arrived. This is the month during which the blood of martyrs defeated the sword and Truth overcame falsehood, rendering the satanic rule of tyrants futile. Moharram has taught generations of people throughout history how to defeat oppression and it has been remembered as the month in which Truth prevailed over secular super-powers. In this month, our Imam Hossein taught us how to fight against tyranny. He showed us how the clenched fists of freedom fighters can crush the tanks and guns of the oppressors, ultimately giving the victory to Truth. . . . Islam is for the oppressed and the peasants and the poor. . . . Today nobody has any excuse to be passive, and silence or withdrawal is suicidal, aiding the oppressors. . . . I consider martyrdom for truth an everlasting honour.[70]

The Shah-Yazid analogy, which was used by Khumanyi as far back as the 1963 riots,[71] was perceived as relevant by at least some of the poor migrants. In one instance, for example, when a squatter's shack was destroyed by the government, he was reported to have said that "Yazid did not commit the injustice that they are doing."[72] The clear implication was that the Shah's regime was even worse than Yazid's--a theme often used by the clergy to evoke responses from the masses.

The National Front also made attempts to help the poor's mobilization against the Shah. The task was made easier after the leader of the National Front, Karim Sanjabi, met with Khumanyi in Paris and reached broad agreements about the struggle against the Shah. Calling the monarchy illegal, Sanjabi and other National Front leaders held some of their meetings and rallies in the migrant poor areas of South Tehran. Emphasizing economic and political discontent, the National Front leaders urged actions to topple the government in the hope of a better future.

The end result of the joint National Front-clergy alliance was that many migrant poor areas of Tehran witnessed demonstrations and riots aimed at the regime. These demonstrations were noted on several occasions in the large migrant poor area of Javadiyih in South Tehran. Although the mobilization of the poor was helped by both the clergy and

94

the National Front, the response of the migrant poor was overwhelmingly in religious terms. Whether in the form of shouting Allahu Akbar (God Almighty) from rooftops at night or facing the Shah's military forces head-on in the streets of Tehran, the religious dimension remained the dominant mode of expression for the migrant poor.[73]

Although significant segments of the migrant poor were mobilized during the revolution, it is important to note that not all poor migrants participated equally in the revolution. Among the most active participants were the nonsquatting factory workers. Their involvement in factory life and organized occupational activities provided an important basis for collective action. Not only did most factories participate in the general strikes, but the workers became actively involved in street demonstrations.

In many street demonstrations and riots in Tehran, large numbers of very young participants were also observed. Although it would be difficult to state definitively, it is nevertheless likely that many of these youthful demonstrators were second-generation migrants. Their upbringing in the city and their socialization in the Iranian education and school environment probably contributed to their willing and forceful participation in the revolutionary struggle. Clearly, the regime's massive indoctrination efforts through the educational system (which included classes discussing the Shah's reform program based on his book, The White Revolution) did not succeed in gaining support for a monarch whose legitimacy was continuously questioned and challenged.[74]

In contrast to the nonsquatting migrant poor and the second-generation migrants, mobilization of the squatters was not as effective. Groups of squatters banded together to defend their homes and prevent forceful removals, but they were not as actively involved in political protests and demonstrations. Their preoccupation with the immense problems of day-to-day survival was far too great to permit sustained antiregime activities. This point was made clear in some of the interviews conducted by newspaper reporters in the squatter settlements during the crisis. In one instance, a squatter living in an abandoned brick factory told a reporter that he had heard about the demonstrations but stressed that they did not take part in them. To demonstrate, he said, "you have to have a full stomach."[75] Another squatter in a different settlement mentioned that he had no time for demonstrations but knew "that things will get better once the King goes."[76]

It is apparent that mobilization of the squatters was at best incomplete. The squatters' perception of relevance of politics to their lives, even in a revolutionary situation, was limited, and consequently political action by them was less forthcoming. The one issue that directly concerned their basic needs and threatened their survival was eradication of the settlements. The squatters were swift in joining together and making every possible effort to prevent such removals. Some of the squatters participated in antiregime demonstrations, but it is likely that many took no part in these activities.

The nonsquatting poor migrants, however, were largely mobilized against the regime. The relevance of politics to their socioeconomic position, especially in the areas of housing and employment, was driven home by both the religious organization and the National Front. External support by these groups was decisive in prompting the migrants to join forces with millions of other Iranians to overthrow the existing authority structure. The independent contribution of the migrant poor in the revolution, however, was limited. As with other marginal groups in different cities of the world, the migrants' mobilization merely reinforced the already initiated process of structural change.[77] Nevertheless, their participation was important both in providing numerical support to the antiregime forces and as a highly significant symbolic outcry by the poor against the injustices of the Iranian political and social system.

CHAPTER VI

MIGRANT FACTORY WORKERS

Upon arrival in Tehran, most poor migrants hope to find
regular employment in the many factories that surround the
city. Joining the industrial labor force as a steady wage
earner is a wish, however, that is not fulfilled for all
migrants. Although factories and industrial establishments
have multiplied rapidly in Tehran in the past decade, there
are still a large number of migrants who cannot find regular
employment in these establishments. Those who can find jobs
in the factories take a significant step toward consolidating
their economic position and improving their chances of
survival in the city.

Not only does factory work mean regular employment, but
it adds several important dimensions to the poor migrants'
lives that are not usually in evidence in nonindustrial
occupations. These features of factory life are discussed
extensively by Alex Inkeles and David Smith in their
comparative study of conditions of modernity in six developing
nations. Asserting that the factory is "an effective school
in modernity," Inkeles and Smith discuss the various forms
and processes of new learning inherent in factory work that
promote modern attitudes and values.[1] They further maintain
that new learning as part of the factory environment is
especially relevant to those who have left the farm and
agricultural occupations for city life and factory work.
These men, Inkeles and Smith assert, are "much more often
modern than . . . their 'cousins' who continued in agriculture."[2]

To assess to what extent the factory is an important
arena of new learning and socialization, a sample of poor
migrant factory workers in Tehran was selected for study.
The sample consisted of three separate groups of 30 factory
workers each in two different industrial establishments. The
first two groups were made up of male factory workers who had
migrated to Tehran from villages located mostly in the Central
Province. They were employed in a large privately owned
factory that manufactured refrigerators, space heaters, air
conditioners, and other machinery. The third group was
composed of female factory workers in a small fabric-making
establishment organized and operated by the Tehran College
of Social Work. Practically all female workers were second-
generation migrants, either born or reared in Tehran.
Without exception, their parents had been villagers who left
their rural homes in search of better jobs and higher income
in the capital.

The sample was chosen with the specific purpose of
determining whether significant political learning takes

97

place among the migrants subsequent to their regular employment at the factory in a major metropolitan center. Since the two groups of male factory workers had spent a different length of time at the factory and, consequently, in Tehran, it was possible to evaluate the impact of factory life on their political socialization.[3] The sample of female factory workers, although second generation, permitted interesting comparisons and contrasts with the male workers in terms of two dimensions--gender and length of stay in Tehran.

The general line of inquiry emphasized adult political socialization because until recently most studies have largely stressed political learning early in life, particularly during childhood. Although significant political learning does take place during childhood,[4] the critical importance of political socialization later in adult life is now receiving greater recognition.[5] Allan Kornberg and Norman Thomas, for example, point out in their comparative study of Canadian parliamentary leaders and American congressmen that a substantial proportion of their elite sample had no real interest in politics during the preadult years. They conclude that "political sociali- zation is a phenomenon which can occur at various stages of the life cycle rather than primarily in the pre-adult period."[6] Adult political socialization is especially relevant to individuals or groups who for a variety of reasons, experience major changes in their adult lives-- changes that may in turn result in significant modifications in political orientation. The sample of male factory workers in Tehran had in fact experienced major occupational, economic, and social changes as adults. Hence, a study of their political socialization subsequent to employment at the factory seemed appropriate.

In order to gauge the migrants' political learning and participation, a series of structured and open-ended question- naires was administered at the factory. The survey instrument was designed to tap five general dimensions: knowledge of politics, organizational affiliation, mass media partici- pation, social class awareness, and political demand making. In each case, the purpose was to determine whether important differences existed between the following two groups of male factory workers: (1) Group A, consisting of migrants with less than ten months of work at the factory and less than one year of stay in Tehran; and (2) Group B, consisting of migrants with at least two years of factory work and longer residence in Tehran.[7] In addition, the sample of female factory workers, Group C, was used for purposes of comparison and contrast. Although none of these groups constituted a random sample, it is likely that these workers were represen- tative of a much larger population of unskilled and semiskilled migrant factory workers in Tehran.

Analysis and Findings

My principal assumption was that the factory serves as an important arena for political learning and socialization of the rural migrants. Normally, therefore, those who had been at the factory longer in an urban setting should have higher levels of political knowledge, mass media participation, organizational affiliation, and the like. The underlying concern may be rephrased in terms of Harold Lasswell's well-known query about the process of communication: "(a) who (b) learns what (c) from whom (d) under what circumstances (e) with what effect?"[8] The answer is that the new migrants in the factory learn about politics from a variety of sources (such as peer groups, mass media, secondary associations) and become more knowledgeable and conscious politically--a process that may in turn create or increase political demands made upon the regime.

Knowledge of Politics and the Political System

Increased knowledge of politics can take place both directly and indirectly.[9] Direct learning results from political education and experience, indoctrination by the regime and its agents, and membership in organizations with explicit or implicit political purposes. Indirect learning is a function of the development of certain attitudes toward authority in both the factory and the society at large. Both forms of political learning are significant aspects of the migrant factory workers' political socialization.

The migrant factory workers were given a series of questions geared to tap their basic knowledge of politics and the Iranian political system. They were asked to name a few key government leaders and to recount the most critical political events of the past six months. The respondents were also asked to describe the functions of some of the more important political institutions and organizations in Iran. In all cases, I attempted to discern the extent of factory workers' political knowledge and sustained interest in governmental affairs. Since knowledge and interest in politics and the sense of political efficacy are often highly interrelated, it was assumed that acquisition of greater political knowledge would probably eventually result in more active involvement in the political system.

Overall analysis of the responses by the factory workers indicates that the most knowledgeable group was the male workers with the longest stay at the factory. The recent male migrants and the second-generation female factory workers had only a superficial and elementary knowledge of the political system. Furthermore, they showed no sustained interest in following the more conspicuous domestic political events of the time. I was in fact astonished to learn that substantial portions of these two groups (approximately

99

35 percent) were not able to name the current Iranian prime
minister who, at the time, had been at the helm of government
for an unprecedented ten years. Some of these respondents
actually confused the office of the prime minister with that
of the monarch.

Since both groups of male factory workers came from
similar rural socioeconomic backgrounds, it was likely that
the longer the time spent at the factory, the greater the
level of the workers' political knowledge. Another factor
that contributed to a higher level of political awareness
among the workers with lengthier factory stay was the increase
in their literacy levels. None of these factory workers was
illiterate. Many had managed to obtain a sixth-grade
certificate by attending adult literacy classes at the
factory, which were organized and operated by the government.
Clearly, greater educational attainment increased these
workers' political knowledge and awareness.

The recent male migrants were less literate and had less
education. About 20 percent were illiterate; the remainder
had completed no more than four years of elementary school
in their villages of origin. All were attending literacy
classes, however, at the place of work. It is reasonable to
assume that in due time recent migrant factory workers will
also achieve higher levels of both literacy and political
learning. The only discontinuity concerned the female factory
workers who, despite some level of literacy, had limited
knowledge of politics. In their case, educational attainment
had not resulted, in any discernible way, in more political
cognition or interest in governmental affairs.

Political Participation and
Organizational Affiliation

Political participation in the form of voting in
parliamentary or city council elections was a nonexistent
phenomenon for both the recent migrants and the female
workers. The only exception consisted of four male factory
workers who had voted, prior to migration to Tehran, for the
elected members of either the village councils or the rural
Houses of Justice. None had participated in any form of
electoral politics while in Tehran. This contrasted sharply
with individuals in Group B--male workers with longer stay at
the factory--who had invariably voted in parliamentary or city
council elections. All members of this same group also
belonged to the labor unions, and about 50 percent had joined
one of the then existing political parties. Neither the
recent migrant workers nor the female factory workers were
members of trade unions or political parties. It thus
appears that longer stay at the factory, for the male workers
at least, resulted in greater organizational affiliation and
political participation as measured by voting at elections.

Valid questions may be raised about the meaning of
electoral participation or trade union membership in the

Iranian political system. The Shah's regime organized and controlled political parties and unions without much opportunity provided for meaningful grass-roots participation. Nevertheless, the fact that workers were organized, even in government-controlled unions, and regularly attended union meetings had to have some effect on the workers' consciousness of themselves as a group and of their potential role in the Iranian social system. Sensitivity to politics, developed through participation in organizational activities, was bound to make the workers more aware of existing political realities.

Mass Media Participation

The workers' participation in mass media increased with the length of their experience at the factory. In the case of written media, greater participation was partly a function of increased ability to read. All three groups of factory workers listened regularly to radio programs and occasionally watched television when it was available to them. However, in terms of program content on the radio, the recent migrants and female workers hardly paid any attention to news and current events programs. They were primarily interested in radio broadcasts of popular Persian music and stories. Female workers who occasionally read weekly magazines pointed out that their major interest centered on articles about family affairs, well-known local film stars, or short stories. Rarely did they attempt to read anything about politics or public affairs. The male workers with lengthier stay at the factory, however, showed slightly more interest in political news. Although they continued to be primarily preoccupied with nonpolitical matters in their media participation, they at least exhibited a more pronounced concern with public and civic affairs. It is probable that this new concern with political news was prompted by their involvement in organizational activities and electoral participation.

Social Class Awareness

Questions geared to measure social class awareness caused much difficulty; they were often not understood at all by many of the respondents. The problem of identifying class awareness is not restricted to this particular sample in Iran. As Joseph Lopreato and Lawrence Hazelrigg point out, most empirical studies of class awareness "report the existence of a rather sizable minority of people who either do not know 'what classes are' or deny their very existence."[10] While this may be an indication of absence of class awareness, Lopreato and Hazelrigg are careful to note that "it is almost certain that at least some of those classified as 'class-unaware' are merely unable to articulate verbally their class conceptions in the interview situation."[11] Since the interview format for my sample of factory workers allowed for open-ended answers and flexibility in oral communication with the respondents, it was possible to probe deeper and to overcome some of the initial problems in articulation.

Basically, the structured part of the interview asked the workers to name how many social classes there were in Iran and to which one of these social classes they belonged. Whenever the concept of social class was not comprehended, a ladder of four classes with brief descriptions of each was shown to them. To some respondents, even this further clarification did not simplify the matter, and questioning on the subject had to be discontinued. Generally, most individuals in the three groups were aware of economic and status differences but did not exhibit any extensive class consciousness. Although they all had aspirations of bettering their economic position, none expected to achieve any drastic change in life style or economic well-being in the near future. To them economic and status advancement was invariably related to the hope of obtaining more education. The factory workers conceived of social mobility simply as something that would come about after they achieve more literacy.

Within this limited scale, levels of class awareness ranged from a practically nonexistent state for the recent migrants to very pronounced for the female workers. Class awareness of the male migrants who had spent longer time at factory work fell somewhere between the two groups. Although greater class awareness for more experienced workers was expceted, the female workers' more highly developed state was unusual. This may well be due to the fact that the female workers were second-generation migrants and consequently had had more exposure to the widespread class differences that exist in an urban environment such as Tehran.

Political Demand Making

In order to discover the extent and form of demand making among the three groups of factory workers, each respondent was asked a series of questions based on important stages of political demand making. Like other poor migrants, the factory workers identified a few socioeconomic needs such as security of tenure, improvement of living conditions, and better employment opportunities as their primary concerns. Although all three groups felt these objectively defined needs strongly, their perceptions of the necessity for ameliorative action varied. Such perceptions were most strongly apparent among the female workers. The recent male migrants who objectively were most in need of ameliorative action to improve their living conditions seemed to be the least aware of their situation. The second group of male workers, with longer tenure at the factory, who had reasonably adequate dwellings in factory-owned compounds, expressed the need for better housing or the desire to become homeowners.

The recent migrants did not envisage the government as a channel for satisfying their needs. They frequently

102

mentioned literacy, hard work, and fate as possible ways of overcoming their deficiencies. The more experienced male factory workers viewed the government only partially as a means of fulfilling their objective needs. Indeed, they generally expressed a hope for government action rather than an expectation of its occurrence. The female workers, however, clearly expected and wanted the government to act to improve their lot. They perceived the government as the primary channel for need satisfaction. When asked how they would go about influencing the government to take action on their behalf, the female workers mentioned the possibility of contacting certain influential public figures and political organizations. The recent male migrants had no clear notion of channels that could be used to precipitate governmental action. The more experienced male workers did talk about bringing their needs to the attention of a few important officials, but they made no mention of government organizations.

It is, therefore, apparent that political demand making was most highly developed among the female workers. Although the more experienced male workers had greater awareness of political demand making than the recent migrants, they had not yet reached the level of the female workers. It is again possible that the female factory workers' greater demand making was conditioned by their socialization in Tehran and their second-generation status. However, the higher level of demand making was rarely expressed in terms of mutual and collective action to affect government policy outcome. The expression of demand making for both the female and the more experienced male factory workers was in terms of individual rather than of collective or organizational pressures on the political system.

Political Socialization of Factory Workers

The overall conclusion based on the five dimensions of the survey indicates that the male factory workers underwent a fairly rapid process of political socialization in their adult lives. Both groups of male factory workers came from very similar socioeconomic backgrounds, yet they exhibited different degrees of knowledge and involvement with the political system. These variations in political knowledge and experience can be explained on two levels. First, these migrant factory workers experienced several important and basic changes in their adult lives.[12] Second, the Shah's regime had made a concerted effort to socialize migrants through the factory institution into patterns of political behavior acceptable to its goals and purposes. Hence, longer stay at the factory exposed the workers to greater pressures for political socialization from agents of the regime.

Moreover, other important structural changes affecting the factory workers also contributed to adjustment in their political outlook and behavior. The factory life in itself is a critical environment for new learning. As Inkeles and Smith point out, "by bringing together a much wider variety of men than one commonly finds in the village, the factory offers the worker an encounter not only with new ways of doing mechanical things, but with new people whose thinking and customs may be quite different from his own."[13] The factory workers in the present study were exposed systematically to new social experiences, reference groups, and socializing agents. These encounters pressured the workers to acquire new or different social and political values and norms.

The factory workers also experienced important patterns of geographic and social mobility. Having left the self-contained and inward-looking village world of sharecropping and farming, they had taken employment on the assembly line at a large modern factory in an ever expanding metropolis. They perceived this step as a significant movement upward on the economic and social ladder. This was apparent not only in changes in their residence, occupation, or income but also in novel experiences as members of trade unions and as participants in parliamentary and city council elections.

The regime's more direct actions in this process of politicization can be seen in the efforts to control trade unionism and the factory workers' other organized activities. The regime's agents overtly limited the range and form of acceptable political activity and influenced the contents of political information communicated to the migrants. Although political learning increased with length of stay at the factory, it did not necessarily result in a higher degree of identification with the political regime. Greater interaction and involvement with the political system was, therefore, not equivalent to increased support for the Shah's government. It is also significant that neither of the two groups of male factory workers exhibited any sustained level of political demand making. Although longer stay at the factory resulted in more pronounced identification of objective needs and hopes for ameliorative action, the male workers had not yet converted these needs into fully articulated demands placed upon the political system. Clearly, there are other factors that mitigate, or partly limit, the crucial importance of longer stay at the factory--at least insofar as political demand making is concerned.

The case of the female factory workers was generally different. Unlike their male counterparts, the women expressed a very low level of political cognition, yet they articulated concise political demands and expected response from the regime. Several possible explanations may be advanced for the female workers' seemingly unusual behavior pattern. First, these are women workers and, given the cultural and social milieu of modern Iran, their socialization experience was different from that of men. Second, they generally had higher degrees of literacy than the male workers--an education that was obtained not in adult literacy classes but in regular educational programs and in a school environment. Most important, the female workers were second-generation migrants who were either born or reared in the capital. Their long process of socialization had taken place almost exclusively in an urban setting. For them, advancement and increased well-being did not necessitate comparisons with past life in backward rural villages. They were consequently more aware of economic and class differences in the city than their migrant brethren and more conscious of the material possessions they lacked. Thus, although uninformed and lacking sustained knowledge of politics, the female factory workers were highly political on matters with a direct bearing on their well-being. Given the circumstances and the need, it would not be difficult for the female workers to acquire the necessary knowledge of politics. If such knowledge is acquired as part of these workers' involvement in organizations, then more direct political action and collective demand making are likely to emerge.

The Industrial Working Class and Political Activity

With the increased pace of industrialization in Iran, a larger proportion of poor migrants will be able to join the industrial working class as regular wage earners. Membership in this class is bound to involve the migrants more intensely with both political authority and opposition movements. Attempts by various forces to gain the allegiance of this expanded urban industrial working class will clearly be a major theme of Iranian politics in the coming years. Traditionally the industrial working class has not been a highly influential force in politics. Although the workers have at times played important roles in certain sociopolitical movements, they have rarely been a critical weight in Iranian politics. This has been due mostly to their relatively small size and fragmentation as well as the regime's control of workers' organizations.

Origin and Development

The development of a modern industrial working class in Iran is closely associated with Reza Shah Pahlavi's industrialization policy. As a result of Reza Shah's modernization program, a number of factories, manufacturing establishments, and other industrial organizations were created in the interwar period. Furthermore, the expansion of the mining and oil industries increased the size of the country's industrial labor force. In the past two decades, additional large-scale growth of industry took place. By 1976 employment in industry surpassed the 2.5 million mark-- a substantial increase over the 1956 figure of slightly over 800,000. There was also a parallel growth in the number of large industrial establishments employing ten or more workers. These establishments increased from 1,581 in 1960 to 6,626 by 1972. Important concentration of workers can be found in

the new steel mill complex in Isfahan, the automobile and
bus assembly plants, and in several electronics and machine-
tool factories. The oil industry, with about 40,000 workers,
however, has retained its position as the largest and single
most important place of worker concentration.

A serious problem confronting Iran's industrial labor
force derives from its limited productivity and shortage of
skilled manpower.[14] Many factories attempt in-service
training of unskilled workers for semiskilled positions "to
prepare them in a rudimentary way for machine operation
within a relatively short period of time."[15] The consequence
of such inadequate on-the-job training is that workers are
rarely able to reach the appropriate level of productivity
and skill required for efficient operation of these
establishments.[16] The fact that many unskilled workers are
hired haphazardly from among those appearing at the factory
gates adds additional strain to effective recruitment and
management of industry.[17] A substantial portion of these
workers are rural migrants with limited education, no skill,
and practically no prior experience in an industrial
establishment. Since there is always a surplus of unskilled
migrants looking for employment in factories, sizable groups
of them are inevitably unsuccessful in locating regular wage
earning industrial occupations. It is clear, then, that
although more migrants have been hired by the factories than
ever before, Iran's industrialization program has not so far
absorbed anywhere near a majority of those seeking industrial
employment.

Trade Unions and Labor Radicalism

The course of trade union activities and labor radicalism
in Third World countries has generally been somewhat different
from the Western European and American experience. Samuel
Huntington suggests that in the initial stages of development,
labor was more radical in Europe and America because
industrialization preceded unionization. "In these countries,
the mobilization of labor easily outran the organization of
labor, and consequently radical and extremist movements often
gained support among the alienated working class before unions
became strong."[18] In the Third World countries industrial-
izing later, unions were organized concomitantly with the
development of the industrial labor force and, in some cases,
preceded its formation.[19] Thus, as Huntington maintains,
"not only is labor less radical because unions are formed
early, but the unions themselves also tend to be less radical
because they are often outgrowths of the establishment rather
than protests against the establishment."[20]

Huntington's analysis is not completely applicable to
the Iranian labor movement. It is at best a partial
explanation of a complex phenomenon. The Iranian trade
unions have assumed important radical postures, expressed
intermittently in political action during the various phases
of their organization and development. With the formation

of the printers' union in 1906, the first modern labor union
emerged on the Iranian industrial scene.[21] Other unions were
established a year later, and the nucleus of a trade union
movement began in earnest. In the succeeding years, three
separate phases of union and labor radicalism are discernible:
first, in the two decades before Reza Shah's consolidation of
power in the 1920s; second, the period toward the end of
World War II to the downfall of Prime Minister Muhammad
Musaddiq in 1953; third, in the years following the oil boom
of 1973 and especially in the latter phases of the destruction
of the Iranian monarchy.[22]

In the first stage of union activity, labor radicalism
was not extensive largely because the working class was small.
Labor, however, was able to stage several major strikes in
different Iranian cities and thereby obtain better working
conditions. On the political level, a few of the labor
unions were influenced by communist elements, and in 1921,
some of Tehran's unions affiliated with Pofintern, the Trades
Union International, based in Moscow.[23] Labor radicalism
diminished with Reza Shah's consolidation of power. From
this time on, strikes were mostly unsuccessful and came to an
abrupt end in 1936 when a law banning labor unions was
passed.[24]

With the onset of World War II and Reza Shah's
abdication, trade unions were once again able to organize and
press for economic and political rights. This new phase of
union activity was largely due to the efforts of the Tudeh
(Communist) party in organizing trade unions and engaging
them in active political struggles. By 1944, the Tudeh had
succeeded in unifying four independent unions and in forming
the Central Council of United Trade Unions, which claimed a
membership of 400,000.[25] The strength of these unions was
concentrated in the major cities of Tehran, Isfahan, Tabriz,
and in the southern oil fields, especially the Abadan
refinery.[26] The Tudeh party was the force behind a number
of labor strikes, some of which resulted in violent confrontation with the authorities. In the oil industry strike of
1946 in Abadan and Ahvaz organized by the Tudeh party, 196
workers were reported killed.[27] The Tudeh was also
instrumental in other key strikes, particularly in Isfahan's
textile factories and Tehran's brick kilns.[28]

The main rival to the party's labor activities was the
government-sponsored organization of workers' syndicates
(ESKI), which was established in 1946 and eventually
affiliated with the International Conference of Free Trade
Unions. In the same year, the Ministry of Labor was created
to control, in Leonard Binder's words, "labor organization,
to draw workers away from the Tudeh, and to deal with
interested international parties."[29] The government soon
initiated a labor law that regulated the workers' relations
with employers and provided for a 48-hour week. Labor,
however, was basically neglected and the Ministry of Labor
remained "the least important of the ministries"[30] for some
time. The Tudeh party, accused of the attempted assassination
of Muhammad Reza Shah, was banned in 1949 and its trade union

activities outlawed. The party, however, continued to exercise influence among segments of the industrial labor force until the coup d'état of 1953 and the Shah's return to power.[31]

The Shah's return signaled the beginning of a serious effort to control all forms of dissent and potential opposition to the regime. The labor unions' freedom of action was, therefore, severely curtailed. Many new labor organizations, established and run by the regime, replaced the traditional unions. In 1971, about 397 such unions were in operation (Table 6.1). The number of these organizations is reported to have surpassed 1,000 by 1978.[32]

The Labor Law of 1959 and its supplementary regulations of 1969 and 1970 provided the principal framework for the operation of workers' syndicates and the settlement of disputes and grievances.[33] But as Fred Halliday points out, in the basic 1959 Labor Law "no mention is made of the right of strike."[34] Opportunities for strike were also hampered by the excessive fragmentation of the workers' unions and the uniquitous presence of the Shah's secret police, the SAVAK. All attempted strikes were dealt with severely and terminated through violent interference of police and security agents. Fearful of labor unrest, the Shah's government made an effort to win the workers' support by various forms of enticement, propaganda, and indoctrination. The most noted of these gestures for labor support was point four of the Shah's White Revolution program, which called for "the industrial workers to share in the net profits of the factories in which they work."[35]

In spite of these efforts, the Shah failed to win the allegiance of the industrial working class. Even the dreaded SAVAK was not able to keep the lid on the workers' unrest for long. Sporadic industrial strikes occurred in many places, especially during the 1959-61 period. The frequency and intensity of strikes increased after the 1973 oil boom. It is reported that the number of these strikes grew from a handful in 1971-73 to "as many as 20 or 30 per year in 1975."[36]

Although most of these strikes concerned ostensibly economic issues, they often had certain underlying political overtones--if only for the fact that they were challenges to the Shah's absolutist authority. This political dimension sometimes surfaced because of the government's harsh measures in putting down the strikes or its decision to view demands for better wages and working conditions as political threats and insubordination. During the revolutionary period of 1978 the workers continued to present serious problems for the Shah's government. With extensive support from other groups in the society forthcoming, the industrial labor force inflicted a severe blow to the Shah's chance of survival. When the oil workers in the southern fields struck, it was clear that the strikes had assumed a predominantly political posture and that the regime's downfall was only a matter of time.

Table 6.1

State-Run Trade Unions, 1971

Kind of Activity	Number of Organizations	
	Workers	Employers
Automobile	7	–
Metal Working	13	5
Textile	43	7
Transport	42	64
Water and Power	18	3
Leather and Intestine	9	2
Oil	26	–
Chemistry	5	1
Printing	4	3
Services	56	30
Food	68	22
Abattoirs	20	–
Construction	24	10
Art, Cinema, and Theatre	6	–
Clothing	13	3
Communication	2	–
Glass and Crystal	2	1
Banks	7	–
Paper Manufacturing	2	–
Health Services	4	9
Carpet Weaving	10	2
Miscellaneous	16	6
TOTAL	397	168

SOURCE: United Nations, ILO Mission, Labour Legislation, Practice and Policy, Working Paper IX, 1973. Reported in Fred Halliday, Iran: Dictatorship and Development (New York: Penguin, 1979), p. 204.

The Tudeh party has always been strong in the southern oil fields, and its presence was evident in the oil workers' latest strike. The workers in other large industrial establishments have also showed their radicalism in the period since the Shah's downfall. Many of these workers, now fully and effectively mobilized politically, have expressed their desires to operate and manage the factories through their own workers' organizations. To what extent they will succeed in achieving this goal is an open question. However, it is apparent that no longer can any regime in Iran impose its will on the industrial workers without incurring an extremely high cost. Although workers in smaller industrial establishments have not so far expressed similar demands, it is possible that they will eventually be affected by these developments and desires for autonomous class action.

The Migrant Poor and the Working Class

When the Iranian revolution is finally consolidated, it is likely that a larger number of migrant poor will be able to find employment in industrial organizations. The strong populist dimension of the revolution is bound to pressure the Iranian government to absorb as many of the poor migrants as possible in regular wage-earning jobs in the economy. A logical first step is to hire the migrants in industrial establishments. If such a step occurs, it is likely that the poor migrants will be organized in grass-roots trade unions and thus have ample opportunities for political learning and activity. Under these circumstances, the poor migrants, like other workers, will develop class awareness and consciousness. There is some evidence that indicates the development of class awareness among industrial workers as early as a decade before the revolution in some urban centers. A survey of workers in an industrial settlement in Tehran, conducted by Ahmad Ashraf in 1969, points to the rising class awareness of the workers. In this settlement, a member of

> the industrial working class identifies himself as
> a worker, and makes a sharp distinction between his
> class and the traditional working class [artisans]
> and lumpenproletariat. To make this distinction
> clear, instead of the three-class terminology used
> by the upper classes, they usually use a four-class
> terminology, and thus identify themselves with the
> members of the third class, while identifying the
> lumpenproletariat with the fourth class.[37]

The intriguing question about the poor migrants as members of the industrial working class is to know when their incipient class awareness will be transformed into the full-fledged class consciousness necessary for political action. Karl Marx's differentiation between a "class-in-itself" (Klasse an sich) and a "class-for-itself" (Klasse fur sich)[38] is a highly relevant theoretical problem for the migrant industrial workers. Although as members of the industrial

110

working class they are a class against capital, it does not
mean that they have developed sufficient unity and consciousness to act as a class for the preservation of their
interests. Given the Iranian working class' history of
involvement in politics and its mobilization during the
recent crisis, it will probably not be long before they
develop such consciousness and act as a "class-for-itself."

CONCLUSION: THE FUTURE

In the recent past, the Iranian political system has been forced to confront several basic problems stemming from critical structural imbalances in the spheres of economy, politics, and social affairs. In each sector, the policies and actions of the regime intensified and exacerbated existing imbalances and only increased the discontent of the aggrieved population. Indeed, it seemed as if every step taken by the Shah's regime resulted in expanding the opposition's demands for a fundamental transformation of the authority structure. The scenario finally unfolded with full mobilization of the Iranian masses against the Shah and the collapse of the Pahlavi dynasty.

During the Shah's rule many of the problems specifically affecting the migrant poor derived from certain economic and political developments. In the economic realm, the imbalances created in the post-1973 oil boom period and the infusion of massive capital into Iran accentuated the difficulties in the plan for economic development and deleteriously affected the poor migrants' well-being. The basic strategy was to use Iranian and Western management skills to develop the country's resources for purposes of economic growth and expansion. The management and entrepreneurial skills lacking in Iran were to come from the Western countries, particularly from the United States. The petroleum sector was viewed as the primary source of capital needed to finance this economic development.

Before 1973 when capital was not as plentiful, the development plans were financed through careful manipulation of oil revenues and foreign and domestic loans.[1] Important overall growth rates were attained during the 1962-72 period with relative price stability and limited inflationary pressures.[2] With the dramatic rise in the price of oil after 1973, however, an enormous amount of capital entered the economy and disrupted the basic development strategy. The dominance of the petroleum sector was now firmly established. The government also faced major problems due to uncontrolled expenditure, shortages of skilled manpower, congestion of ports, and shortages of essential items, as well as other similar bottlenecks.[3] This situation resulted in high levels of inflation, which were especially intolerable to the city dwellers, who were most directly affected by the steep rise in prices.

These conditions were further aggravated when the effects of the failure in the agricultural sector and in the land reform program became apparent. Masses of poor peasants were forced to flee the countryside for the cities in search of better jobs and higher income. Uncontrolled settlements and shanty towns mushroomed on the outskirts of major urban centers, especially Tehran. The intolerable living conditions, occupational difficulties, and income instability of the poor migrants dramatized the extent of urban poverty

112

in Iran and emphasized the marginality of large segments of
the population. The poor migrants' situation worsened with
the slowdown in construction in 1976. Many migrants were made
jobless and, because of their lack of skills, could not find
employment in other sectors. The migrants' widespread
unemployment and insecurity made their poverty and inability
to make ends meet even more pronounced. Indeed, their plight
represented the ultimate situation of marginality--the
underclass once again was systematically excluded from
partaking of the benefits of power, wealth, and status brought
about by the new oil wealth that was enjoyed by the superordinate groups.

To prevent the influx of poor migrants to the urban
centers and to control the expansion of squatter settlements,
the Shah's regime attempted a number of haphazard actions.
Fearful of the potential political impact of the poor migrants
in Iranian cities, the government discouraged cityward
migration. Minor incentives such as limited cash grants were
provided to those former peasants who were willing to return
to their villages of origin. In early 1975, a makeshift
headquarters was set up in a major Tehran park to take the
names of those who wanted to return. On several occasions I
witnessed long lines of poor migrants who had gathered hoping
to receive some of the grants. Although a few migrants were
beneficiaries in this deal, the program was too limited in
scope to have any real impact on the rate of cityward
migration. Even those who returned to their villages were
probably back in the streets of Tehran within a short time.

Clearly, the regime's action amounted to no more than
futile window dressing. The fundamental issue of failure in
the agricultural sector and land reform, which was the primary
cause of cityward migration, was not addressed in an effective
manner. Three other factors also have some bearing on the
difficulties faced by the government in stemming the tide of
cityward migration. First, it is virtually impossible to
prevent rural to urban migration when it is caused by basic
socioeconomic factors. Hardly any regime has succeeded in
eliminating mass migration in the past. Not even the fascist
regime of Italy under Mussolini was able to accomplish this
feat successfully.[4] Second, cityward migration may be viewed
as a significant step to reduce excess population in the
countryside and to deflect rural discontent.[5] As William
Mangin points out, "migration to cities has been the most
successful adaptation for peasants under pressure."[6] It is,
therefore, possible for the political regime to regard
cityward migration as a reasonable move, at least for the
time being, toward displacement of peasant discontent. Since
there had been some alienation and discontent among the
Iranian poor peasants, particularly those who did not receive
land during the land reform program, the government may not
have been too displeased with their departure from the rural
areas. Finally, the vast majority of poor migrants have no
desire to return to their villages of origin. They usually
consider themselves better off in the city than in the
village and have no overwhelming incentive to reestablish

113

their previous rural life. The Iranian government's extremely limited program was an inadequate response to the needs of the poor migrants and did not result in any significant back-to-village patterns.

Faced with the steady rise of the poor migrant population, the regime undertook a few other direct and indirect steps to adjust to the situation. One measure was to respond to the squatters' deplorable living arrangements by constructing a few low-income settlements and moving portions of the squatters to these areas. The settlement known as Kuyi Nuhum-i Aban in the southern part of Tehran was the most notable of these endeavors. Although this settlement provided reasonable and efficient housing to some of the former squatters, it was too limited in scope and size to alleviate the migrant poor's living problems. Only a small segment of the squatters could be housed in this settlement; the vast majority were left to find alternative housing arrangements. Many of the squatters were forced to find shelter in dilapidated shacks, hovels, and brick kilns in various parts of South Tehran. The nonsquatting poor migrants established residence in small rented or owned dwelling units in slums or low-income communities of the capital.

The rapid increase in the rate of cityward migration by the poor peasants further underscored the inadequacy of the government's low-income housing program. The existing limited program could not accommodate even a small portion of the new migrants. Rather than expanding low-income housing, the government chose instead to devote its resources to constructing large upper-income complexes for the well-to-do. These complexes were irrelevant to the needs of the poor migrants but were vivid manifestations of the government's lack of concern with the plight of the urban poor.

In the area of employment, the migrants benefited for a while because of the great boom in the construction industry during the early 1970s. Many of the poor migrants were able to secure jobs as unskilled construction laborers. Their employment was disrupted, however, by the general slack in the construction industry beginning in 1976, which caused many migrants to lose their jobs. Given the fact that the poor migrants have limited opportunities for social and occupational mobility, this new phase of unemployment made their daily struggle for subsistence all the more difficult.

Under the Shah, the Iranian government's overall policy toward the migrant poor can perhaps be described, at its best, as one of benign neglect. Not much systematic attention was paid to the poor migrants, and they were left to themselves to eke out a subsistent life. It seemed as if the government felt that by ignoring the migrants' plight, the problems would disappear. The situation, however, changed dramatically as important segments of the politically passive poor migrants mobilized against the Shah's regime. Although many factors were responsible for this mobilization, it was the opposition groups' attempts to gain the support of the underclass that ultimately led to the migrants' active participation in the revolutionary struggles.

114

The success of the Iranian revolution in toppling the Shah has not brought about any immediate and drastic changes in the conditions of the poor migrants. Consolidation of the revolution has created innumerable problems on many fronts. Once the sanctions imposed by the Shah's authoritarian regime were finally removed, many groups and factions made vigorous demands for shares in the decision-making centers of the new and chaotic political system. An important part of this development has been the attempt by various groups to solicit the support of the urban masses. The extent to which the poor migrants are responding to these overtures is conditioned by at least two factors. First, the migrant poor's economic aspirations were raised as the result of the massive infusion of capital in the wake of the oil boom of 1973. But these aspirations remained essentially unfulfilled. Second, the revolution with its strong religious and populist under-currents raised the masses' political expectations as well as their level of politicization. Thus, any group or organization hoping to gain the support of the migrant poor will have to satisfy, first and foremost, their economic needs and, to a lesser degree, their political aspirations.

The problem of satisfying the migrants' economic and political aspirations has been acute in the factories and larger industrial establishments. Many factory workers have pressed demands to have some control over the management of factory affairs. These demands have been supported by the two leftist urban guerrilla groups, Chirikha-yi Fada'i-yi Khalq-i Iran (Sacrifice Guerrillas of the People of Iran) and Mijahidin-i Khalq-i Iran (Warriors of the People of Iran). The extent to which the migrants are involved in these activities is not completely clear. There is, however, some evidence that points to the participation of migrant factory workers.[7] Aggravating the situation is the fact that not all factories have reopened and that the operation of some has suffered from lack of adequate supplies, from managerial difficulties, and from other related problems.

An important factor that may result in greater political activity by the migrant industrial workers is the "work-no-work" phenomenon--that is, losing one's job after having been employed as a regular wage earner for some time. Under these circumstances, chances for labor unrest usually increase. Employment of large numbers of migrants in industrial establishments would thus also necessitate efforts to prevent mass layoffs. Otherwise, demonstrations and riots on the part of the laid-off workers are distinct possibilities. The migrant factory workers, because of their low skill level, would be prime targets in such layoffs. Since they have always been the most politicized segment of the migrant poor, it is logical to expect collective responses and assertiveness on their part. One possible way to prevent labor unrest among the migrant poor in the future is for the current Iranian government to embark on a labor-intensive economic program that increases employment opportunities for the poor.

The employment condition of other poor migrants, especially the squatters, remains a major problem. In some respects, their situation worsened in the months immediately following the revolution. The construction industry came almost to a complete standstill, and there were not many other realistic employment prospects for the poor migrants. As a result, some migrants decided to return to their villages of origin and begin a new life. This return migration was partly prompted by the new government's public announcements emphasizing rehabilitation of agriculture and assistance to rural residents. Although the extent of this back-to-village migration is not yet clear, it is apparent that substantial numbers of poor migrants continue to reside in Tehran.

The great majority of poor migrants who have opted to remain in Tehran face several immediate problems. Aside from the recurrent difficulties in securing wage-earning jobs, the migrants have to grapple with inflation and unresolved housing problems. Inflation remains unabated, affecting the basic staples of life as before. Although the squatter settlements are no longer being eradicated, most poor migrants are unsatisfied with their present housing situation. A revealing report in the newspaper Kar highlights the squatters' discontents about housing and employment in the postrevolutionary era. In response to the investigator's question, "What is your most important problem?" one squatter of the South City Pits replied bitterly:

> Our total life is a problem. From the moment we
> recognized ourselves, we had nothing but problems.
> Look at the present situation. Now they say that
> the old regime is gone and the hands of exploiters
> and oppressors are cut off. But my problem, and
> that of thousands of other squatter families, is
> lack of jobs and living quarters. I have had no
> income for the past year. I have eaten whatever I
> had. There is no food for tomorrow. Believe me,
> I don't know how I am going to live tomorrow.[8]

The response of the Khumanyi regime to the plight of the urban masses has focused on two related areas. First, the regime has made strong ideological appeals emphasizing the poor's needs. Second, a few concrete steps have been taken toward alleviating the poor's most pressing problems. The ideological dimension has stressed populist themes and the urgency of economic redistribution to benefit the poor. This theme is repeated regularly in pronouncements and speeches of Khumanyi and his entourage.[9] Furthermore, the newly adopted constitution both in the preamble and several articles makes specific references to the economic needs of the poor. The preamble states that the revolution was "a move towards complete victory of the poor over the powerful."[10] Article 43 requires the government to provide for the basic needs of all, including "housing, food, clothing, health and medical care, education, and establishment of the necessary conditions for the setting up of a family."[11] The poor have also been given the official designation of mustaz'ifin (the weakened and disinherited). The reference to the poor as the disinherited underscores both their special status and the government's avowed determination to remove those conditions that led to their plight in the first place.

The regime's few concrete but haphazard steps to help the urban poor's pressing problems have been aimed at providing food and housing. One of the government's most important decisions has been to direct the Alavi Foundation (the former Pahlavi Foundation) to distribute welfare among the poor. Some of the poor migrants have benefited from this policy. A few of the squatters have also received free food delivered regularly by government trucks to selected settlements. On other occasions, unclaimed merchandise in the possession of government agencies has been given to the needy. In a recent case, the governing Revolutionary Council ruled that if the owners of thousands of tons of food and clothing, currently stored in various Iranian ports and customs centers, did not claim their goods by a set date, they would be doled out to the poor.[12]

Some action has also been taken to provide housing for the poor. An organization for this purpose is being created under the direction of Ayatullah Hadi Khusrushahi. A sizable number of dwelling units belonging to those accused of collaborating with the Shah's regime, and other vacant properties, have been confiscated by the government and redistributed. The migrant poor, however, have not been the principal beneficiaries of this policy.[13] A substantial majority of them still have to cope with inadequate or squatter housing as in the past. This situation has prompted a few of the squatters to occasionally invade a vacant building and claim it for themselves. In a recent episode, 100 squatter families invaded and occupied a vacant twelve-story building and refused to move out. One of those involved in the invasion plan told a reporter that the building's owner was "an important agent of the old regime who disappeared after the revolution's victory." A supporter of the squatters' action standing outside the building said: "When thousands of our brothers and sisters live in damp and cold shacks of the squatter settlements, such fully equipped buildings, constructed from the people's blood, should not remain empty."[14] There have also been reports of a few Robin Hood-style robberies where gunmen forcibly expropriate the wealthy's funds and distribute the cash in the squatters settlements.[15]

On the political front, the future direction of the poor migrants' activities is ambiguous. For the migrant factory workers, the future points to increased political activity and greater expressed class consciousness. They are likely to become politically integrated in left-of-center organizations operating within the industrial establishments. The second-generation migrants are also particularly susceptible to political involvement and increased organizational participation. For the rest of the migrant poor the situation is much less clear. This stems in part from the fact that it is generally more difficult to translate the poor's limited demands into sustained political activity.[16]

There are several groups and organizations that have made efforts to solicit the migrant poor's support. In the late spring of 1979, the new regime helped establish the Committee to Settle Tehran Squatters. The squatters were urged to vote for their representatives in the committee. Many squatters participated in the election hoping that the committee would be able to promote their well-being. These forms of political activity, organized by the government, will most likely continue in the future. They can serve potentially as important channels for expressing demands to the government and maintaining the ties that were affirmed during the revolution.

Another possible alliance could be forned between the poor migrants and individual religious leaders who are personally attractive to the poor. This would be a situation resembling a patron-client relationship where the mullah acts essentially like the Latin American cacique. A prime candidate for such a role is Shaykh Sadiq Khalkhali and his organization, the Fada'iyan-i Islam (Devotees of Islam). Known as "Judge Blood" for his role in condemning many of the Shah's collaborators and postrevolutionary dissidents to the gallows, Khalkhali enjoys some support among the poor migrants. Khalkhali's organization and its theocratic extremism have always had a strong base among the uneducated and semieducated masses on the fringes of urban society. If secular elements in Iran regain their lost position in the future, then Khalkhali's organization may be able to give focus and direction to the migrant poor's demands on the government. By invoking religious slogans such as the Qur'anic concept of "Command the Good and Forbid the Evil," now enshrined in the Iranian constitution, Khalkhali or someone like him can mobilize the poor against their perceived oppressors.

The two guerrilla organizations, the People's Sacrifice Guerrillas and the Warriors of the People of Iran, have also made extensive and concerted efforts to reach the poor migrants, and especially the squatters. Internal divisions within the respective organizations and their leftist orientations have prevented a more effective recruitment of the migrant poor. However, both groups are keenly aware of the migrant poor's concrete needs and vigorously publicize their support of the squatters. It is less likely that the National Front or its offshoot, the National Democratic Front, will be able to recruit effectively from among the poor migrants. The secular ideological posture of these two organizations is closely tied to the professional classes and the intelligentsia and hence is less attractive to the poor migrants. Moreover, the National Front's activities have been curtailed by the current leadership of the religious establishment. Consequently, the National Front groups have been forced into a situation where they neither possess adequate institutional means nor have the opportunity to recruit among the disenfranchised urban poor.

Whether it is the religious establishment or some other urban group, attempts will undoubtedly be made to recruit the poor migrants into Iranian politics. Alienation of this class from the existing political system would be too costly-- an event that no Iranian regime can afford to ignore any longer. But the recruitment efforts will have to recognize the migrants' needs and economic aspirations. The urban poor of Iran have come to realize their potential political power and have learned the slogans and ways of the revolution. They can use these slogans against those who would thwart their goals. Yet it remains to be seen whether recognition of the migrant poor's legitimate needs succeeds in eliminating their marginality.

THE LIFE HISTORY OF A SQUATTER FAMILY

In 1974 a team of researchers affiliated with the
Institute for Social Research (Tehran University) conducted
a series of interviews at a number of squatter settlements in
Tehran. The interviews were geared to provide complete life
histories of some of the squatter households. Unfortunately,
the results of this research were not published or made
available to the scholarly community. A member of the
research team, Professor Ali Banuazizi of Boston College, has
kindly given me one of the most complete life histories of a
squatter family prepared by him in 1974. Although unlike
most poor migrants, members of this particular family do not
come from a rural area of Iran, nevertheless the story of
their lives reflects many of the problems and frustrations
encountered by the migrant poor in Tehran. What follows is
a translation from the Persian of an unpublished report on
the Nava'i family.

The Nava'i Family

Family Members

    Hamid Nava'i, 50 years old
    Uzra Nava'i, 41 years old
    Ni'mat Nava'i, 21 years old
    Muhammad Qasim Nava'i, 19 years old
    Shukat Nava'i, 15 years old
    Baqir Nava'i, 13 years old

Living Conditions at the Settlement

    The Nava'i family lives in a shack in a squatter
settlement known as the "Professor Brown Squatter Settlement."
The settlement is located at the entrance to Professor Brown
Avenue adjacent to the central building of Tehran University.
In an area of 2,400 square meters, surrounded by walls and
buildings, stand about 100 shacks of different sizes. These
shacks are connected to one another by small winding alleys
that lead to the main entrance of the settlement. The main
entrance is a wooden door that opens into Professor Brown
Avenue. The shacks usually consist of a 2 by 2.5 meter room
constructed with primitive and minimum material. The open
winding space in front of the shacks is used as the residents'
yards. In the northern section of the settlement, at the two
sides of Professor Brown Avenue, about fifteen makeshift
stores, carts, and boxes have been set up for the sale of

120

fruit. Most of these belong to the squatters who apparently have reasonable sales during the summer months.

The land of the settlement was used as a British military camp during World War II. Later the property passed to different individual owners. About two years ago, the owner of the land threatened the residents, with an eviction order in hand, that they must leave the settlement. He even offered cash to some of the residents who had lived at the settlement for fifteen to twenty years to entice them to leave. However, because of this group's refusal and the strong resistance of other residents, the owner failed to remove the squatters.

The number of shacks in the settlement increases regularly. In the past ten years, the shacks have doubled. Apparently, until five years ago all the residents had migrated from villages in Arak. But in the more recent years, migrants from areas around Nishapur, Sabzavar, and Hamadan have also settled in the area. The newcomers usually had to purchase their shacks from the previous "owners." Presently a shack is valued from 20,000 to 40,000 rials. The residents maintain that they will not leave their homes unless the government constructs housing for them. Practically all squatters point to the Kuyi Nuhum-i Aban settlement as an example of desirable public housing. They assert that they have no monetary claims from the land's owner.

Initial Contact with the Family

With the appropriate information about the living conditions of the Professor Brown Squatter Settlement on hand, we set out one morning to visit Javad Rabi'i, a young resident of the settlement. Javad was not at home, but his mother and two aged neighbors mentioned that he would be back in an hour or two. They promised to "keep him" there until we came back. We returned in two hours. Javad and another young man were in the process of constructing one of the shack's walls. His mother said that they had purchased a dresser but the height of the dresser was greater than the ceiling of the shack. After consulting with his parents and wife, Javad decided to raise the shack's ceiling and enlarge the living area by moving one of the walls farther back. In addition to Javad and his friend, two boys and a sixteen-year-old girl were helping in the construction. A group of children were also gathered around the shack watching and occasionally teasing Javad and his coworkers.

Javad came down from the roof when he saw us. He apologized for not being able to stop his masonry. He said that if the work was not completed by the afternoon, a city official might show up the next day and object to his illegal construction. He was afraid the official might destroy whatever he had already built. It was suggested that we come back at night for a longer and more leisurely conversation with his family.

121

At this time, a few women and children who had gathered around us, asked: "Mister, doesn't the government want to destroy the shacks?" Another responded: "I pray to God that the government destroys these shacks and gives us homes like those of the Kuyi Nuhum-i Aban so that we will be eternally thankful. We are frightened to death worrying when they are going to destroy these dilapidated shacks." An older woman who was washing clothes in front of her shack angrily called out (without raising her head): "What are you frightened of? Let them destroy these shacks. What will be worse? We have neither summer nor winter, neither day nor night. We are sick from lack of water and electricity, heat and cold, and filth. Let them destroy and see what God wants." We assured them that our visit had nothing to do with either eradicating the settlement or constructing houses for them; we are here only to do research about their living conditions for Tehran University.

One of the ten to fifteen children around us insisted that we take an individual picture of him, even though he had seen no cameras in our hands. We tried to take advantage of the situation and asked the children about their education and the distance to the school. A thirteen-year-old girl volunteered that she had reached the seventh grade when her parents arranged an engagement with a distant relative who is a fruit peddler. As a result, she had to quit school. She was upset because before the marriage, it had been agreed that she would be allowed to continue school for another two to three years. Apparently after the wedding, her husband refused to give her permission to continue her education.

Another youth with a large yellowish face and fairly long hair, who had been standing near us and obviously wanted to talk, came toward us. After pulling up the pants of his black pajamas, he began to describe his life and the family's situation. He said that there were six of them in one shack and he was therefore not able to concentrate and study. "Just as I am about to resolve a mathematical problem, all of a sudden my mother screams at my brother to stop playing with the radio or writing poetry and start studying. My brother gets angry and screams back at her. I lose my concentration and have to start all over. This situation caused five low grades in my subjects this year alone. Sometimes I wait to study until they all go to sleep, but then they insist that I turn off the light to keep the mosquitoes out. In the winter, the cold weather doesn't allow studying outside; in the summer, the neighbors either sleep outside or talk until the wee hours of the morning." This youth introduced himself as Muhammad Qasim Nava'i and asked us to go to his shack and meet the family, which we did.

The Family's Living Conditions

The Nava'i shack consists of a small but relatively solid room, said to have been left behind from the days of the British camp. The floor is covered with small beat-up old rugs and cloths. The walls are adorned with pictures of the royal family, religious figures, members of the national soccer team, and singers such as Gugush, Arif, and Vigin. Below a small window that opens onto Professor Brown Avenue, a bed covers a variety of household items such as old shoes, papers and envelopes, boxes, and pots. Two small shelves are constructed at the eastern and western sides of the room. A few books, notebooks, pencils, glasses, socks, and a transistor radio are placed on the shelves. Near the entrance, an old dresser and a dilapidated closet meet the eye. To the left side of the room, a rack is attached to the wall from which hang two old pants and a cloth.

After our initial introduction to the Nava'i family, we sat outside to talk and observe the scene. We had just settled down when a neighbor asked Muhammad Qasim to lend her the iron. Muhammad Qasim immediately took out an electrical iron from the closet and handed it over to the neighbor. We were surprised to see an electrical iron at a place that has no electricity. Muhammad Qasim explained that they heat the iron over a cooking stove and then use it for ironing clothes.

We visited the Nava'i family five more times at various hours of the day and night. Each time we were warmly greeted, brought tea, and sometimes fruit. Hamid Nava'i, the father and head of the household (who although fifty years old looked as if he were sixty-five), his wife Uzra, who frequently monopolized the conversation, and the four offspring participated in our discussions. They responded to our questions either individually or as a group. Twice we visited the family when the parents were not at home. What follows is based on these visits and discussions.

The Cause and Pattern of Migration to Tehran

Many years ago, Hamid Nava'i had been selling sugar in Nishapur and had apparently been relatively well-off. However, because of a sharp decline in the price of sugar and the fact that he had hoarded sugar in hopes of large profits, he suddenly went bankrupt. With the money collected from the sale of his property, Hamid opened a confectionary and then a grocery store.

At the same time, his daughter Shukat developed extensive pains in her eyes and had to terminate her education. They operated on Shukat's eyes but the problem did not disappear. The expenses of the operation and medicine severely taxed Hamid's financial resources, and he was forced to close down his grocery store. Fortunately, Hamid's brother, who owned an electrical shop in Nishapur, came to Hamid's aid. Hamid was hired as an assistant at the store for a daily wage of 50 rials. (While Hamid was describing this situation to us, his son Ni'mat interrupted his father and in a grateful tone said: "Father, my uncle never said that you were his assistant. He told everyone that you were his partner so that you would not lose face in the community.")

123

After a while, Hamid's brother migrated to Tehran, opened an electrical shop in Majidiyih and prospered. Hamid's situation grew worse after his brother's departure. His pride did not allow him to become another person's store assistant or to work as a construction laborer. Hoping to find work, Hamid migrated to Tehran. Just before departing for Tehran, one of his twin daughters died as a result of both illness and the family's inability to provide proper medical care for her. The other twin dies on the way to Tehran from an illness probably contracted in a truck that transported them along with some animals.

At first Hamid and the family stayed with his brother in Majidiyih. After a few months, the shortage of space forced them to leave the brother's house. They rented a room in the Kuyi Nuhum-i Aban settlement. They all liked living in their new home. The availability of water and electricity, a shared yard, paved streets, the closeness to clinics and social workers were unexpected advantages for the family. However, after a period of unemployment, their inability to pay rent as well as the rising cost of living made the family decide to buy a shack in the Professor Brown Squatter Settlement. With money borrowed from his brother and a few others, Hamid was able to buy his shack for 34,000 rials on installment.

Problems at the Professor Brown Squatter Settlement

After their move to the new home, Hamid started selling fruit from a box in front of the settlement. In a few days, the local police officer asked Hamid for regular extortion payments. Since Hamid could not pay the fee, he was taken to the police station and charged with obstructing traffic. Hamid protested at the station that selling fruit was not illegal and that others in the same location made a similar living. The police captain retorted that "the filth and irregular" life of Hamid and others like him in the settlement and other parts of the city has caused the foreigners to think that Iran was a backward country. Hamid responded: "Then, your highness, why doesn't the government build houses and find work for us so that foreigners would not have such thoughts about us?"

Hamid's daily struggles with the police officer continued and he was eventually told to terminate his business. As a result, Hamid was unemployed for two years. During this time, the family's only source of income was the money brought in by Uzra and Shukat, who did various chores in people's homes outside the settlement. The income was not enough for food, clothing, medicine, and the educational expenses of the three boys. The two older sons, who were in high school, were pressured to find employment. Ni'mat, the eldest son, who was in the eleventh grade, found work in a company for 150 rials' daily wage. Muhammad Qasim was allowed to continue his education. During his employment, Ni'mat learned radio and television repair work and the family income improved.

124

But after two years, Ni'mat was fired from the company. He claims that due to curiosity, he took notes about the chemical solutions at work. This made the supervisor suspicious and resulted in the termination of his employment. Without his income, the family was once again faced with poverty and its related features.

A few months later, Ni'mat was able to find part-time work in a lawyer's firm as an office boy. Hamid, the father, also began work as a car washer at the Tehran-Tajrish taxi stop. Uzra and Shukat kept intermittent jobs cleaning and washing in various homes in the vicinity of the settlement.

Living in a squatter settlement continues to create many difficulties and problems for this family. Water has to be transported in buckets from a faucet in Professor Brown Avenue. Since they have no storage facilities, water must be brought in several times a day. The number of outhouses (constructed in the most primitive manner) is very limited. There is approximately one outhouse for every five to ten families. The absence of regular piped water, the shallowness of the outhouse sewage wells, and the accumulation of garbage in various locations of the settlement attract flies, bugs, mosquitoes, and mice. This is one of the most difficult daily living problems of the inhabitants. For bathing, water is heated in summer, while in the winter, once a month the family members go to a public bathhouse in Amirabad Avenue.

None of the members of the Nava'i family, and as far as they knew none of their neighbors, have health insurance. On a few occasions because of severe illness they had to go to Pahlavi Hospital for treatment. They mentioned that even though they paid 30 to 50 rials and waited for several hours, the attending physician spent only a few minutes with them. In one case, they were not able to purchase the prescribed medicine because of its high cost. In spite of this, it seemed that health problems were not central to this particular family (perhaps because their children were grown). If we had not questioned them about medical problems, they probably would not have mentioned them.

According to the Nava'i family, their daily food intake is very similar to that of other households in the settlement. It consists of bread and tea for breakfast, bread and fruit for lunch in the summer, and bread and cheese or halva in the winter. For supper, they often have soup. Uzra and Shukat frequently eat their lunches at the homes where they work. Sometimes they bring food for the rest of the family from these homes.

Relationships among the Settlement's Inhabitants

When we asked Hamid Nava'i about the squatters' relations with one another, he responded in a proud tone: "At least here there are no bosses or servants, wealthy or beggar. We all consider one another human beings and have respect for everyone, especially for old men and women."

Generally migrants from the same area mix more frequently with each other. Migrants from some towns have more organized group activities. For example, the Arakis have organized a hay'at or group so that during the months of Muharram and Safar and other religious holidays they can mourn together. Those from the Nishapur area go to Kuyi Nuhum-i Aban and participate in the roving hay'ats of the Nishapuris of that settlement. These gatherings take place once a week at a different member's home. Ni'mat had this to say about the hay'ats: "Nothing brings us together more than the love for Imam Husayn. My personal view is that these hay'ats have a positive aspect in uniting us and keeping us informed about each other's affairs. But gatherings alone are not enough. I told our own hay'at: 'What is the point of killing Imam Husayn every year and then mourning his death. We also have Muhammad and Ali whose words are worth billions.' I gave examples from our religious books, Nahaj al-Balaqih and Nahaj al-Fasahih, and pointed out that they should follow their orders. But where are the listening ears?" Ni'mat had proposed to the Nishapuris' hay'at that rather than spending their time and effort setting up mourning sessions and engaging in self-flagellation, they should build a mosque. "Then people would come to the mosque for prayers and meditation. They could also add a lending library to the mosque." On another occasion, Ni'mat suggested that his hay'at organize a cooperative society to provide low-priced groceries for the members and work for some of the unemployed. Neither of the two proposals ever materialized.

In contrast to the unity of migrants from the same geographical region, relations among migrants from different regions are not so smooth. Some of these squatters have quarreled, fought physically, and in a few instances injured one another. The police had to be called in to mediate some of these fights. Most of the quarrels start among children who get into fights because of the limited space. (There are 102 households in a 2,400-square-meter area.) Children's quarrels increase especially in the summer months when hot weather, the absence of recreation facilities, and the difficulty of getting away from the settlement's monotonous environment add to the tensions. In the past year or two, the squatters' relations have improved. As Hamid said: "The people have realized that these quarrels and fights benefit no one and make life more difficult for all." During our visits with the Nav'ai family at least three times nearby neighbors quarreled. In each case, however, the two sides quickly reconciled their differences. The cause of the arguments in all three cases involved the neighbors' children.

In regard to only one issue are all the inhabitants of the Professor Brown Squatter Settlement completely united: opposition to those who claim the settlement's land and their resistance to eviction. About a year ago, the present owner of the settlement's land obtained an eviction order and told the inhabitants that he would soon demolish their shacks. This event created much commotion among the inhabitants, who decided to resist the owner. At first they collected several

126

Iranian flags and wrote slogans on white cloths such as,
"Now that the landlord-peasant system is overturned, do not
allow the wealthy property owners to rule the poor." Then
about eighty squatters gathered in the Twenty-fourth of Isfand
Square and chartered a bus to take them to the Shah's Sa'dabad
Palace in order to present their case. At the palace gates,
the police stopped them. They were told to wait until their
case was reported to the Shah's office. The squatters waited
for about two hours until two police officers appeared and
assured them that the government officials were concerned
about their living conditions. They pointed out that unless
sanctioned by the government, no one would be allowed to
destroy their shacks. This news pleased everyone and the
group returned to the settlement with a sense of success.
They were not disturbed after that date.

The Head of the Family's Opinions and Views

Although Hamid Nava'i attributed his problems in life
to fate and God's will, his only hope for improving his
family's living conditions was the government. He believed
that only the government could save him, and others like him,
from poverty by finding regular and respectable employment
for them. He thought the government could prevent discrimination against the poor in the bureaucracy; it could construct
low-cost housing similar to the Kuyi Nuhum-i Aban settlement
for the squatters; it could provide opportunities for his
children to continue their disrupted education. "If the
government does not want to do them, there is nothing that
I am able to do." Hamid did not envisage any ways of
attracting the government's attention to these matters or
pressuring the officials to respond to these needs. Hamid's
views are in some ways reflected in one of our interviews
with him.

Question: What is needed to solve your family's living
problems and do you have hopes that your situation will
improve in the future?

Hamid: By God, this all depends on what the government wants.
There is nothing we can do.

Question: What do you mean by the government?

Hamid: Government means the prime minister, ministers, and
the Majlis.

Question: Do you know who is the prime minister?

Hamid: I have heard that Mr. Huvayda is the prime minister
and I have seen his picture in the newspapers a few times.

Question: What do you know about the Majlis?

Hamid: Do you mean what I personally know about the Majlis?

Question: Yes.

Hamid: I basically have never gotten involved in politics.
There are no records and dossiers on me even though I am
fifty years old.

127

Question: Have you ever voted in elections?

Hamid: In Nishapur we, the small merchants, voted for someone we knew. After coming to Tehran, one of our acquaintances told us that these matters are not our concern. I listened to his advice.

Question: How many social classes do you think there are in the country or any city and what types of people are part of each class?

Hamid: Well, this is obvious. Every village, town, or country has masters and serfs. But overall, I think, first comes the top class headed by the Shahinshah and then the prime minister, ministers, and important officials of the government and the armed forces; that is, those whose income is more than two to three thousand tumans a month. The second class is made up of major businessmen and merchants who have a good income but do not have the status of the government officials. Members of the third class are the workers, laborers, and peasants who don't have much income and live from day to day. Then there are those who don't fit into a social class. These are connected neither to the earth nor to the sky. They have no regular income and no home. They are left out in the middle to fend for themselves.

Question: To which of these social classes do you belong?

Hamid: Around here they say we belong to the third class. Thank God, if this is true.

It may not be immaterial to point out that Hamid and his wife were familiar with the names and poetry of Khayyam, Attar, Sa'di, and Hafiz. The only time they expressed real joy and felt comfortable and even equal to us was when we asked them to speak about "The Notables of Nishapur" and recite a few lines of poetry with the Nishapuri accent. They told us that the family had visited Khayyam's tomb many times. Hamid was also proud to relate that he had seen Kamal al-Mulk. To prove his point, Hamid referred to Kamal al-Mulk's blindness in one eye.

Problems of Poverty and Social Conditions as Seen by the Elder Sons

Ni'mat was twenty-one years old and had quit his studies in the eleventh grade to find work and help the family's financial situation. His brother, Muhammad Qasim, was nineteen and hoped to pass the tenth grade. (We found out a few weeks later that Muhammad Qasim had failed his tests. Apparently he handed in blank exam papers for two of his subjects.) Both brothers seemed much better informed on social matters and general knowledge than other inhabitants of the settlement. For this reason we tried to get to know them better and asked their views about poverty and living conditions in the settlement. Fortunately, both enjoyed conversation with us and were pleased to find an audience. The two brothers, and particularly Ni'mat, were very

128

articulate. (For example, this is how Ni'mat greeted us the very first time we saw him: "Yes, my brother has informed me that you wish to speak with us about the problems encountered by the squatter youth. I am very pleased about your concern with our affairs. However, as you are aware, there are unfortunately no accurate methods for research on youth such as us." After further conversation, Ni'mat modified his official and partially artificial language.) What follows is a summary of many hours of conversation with the two brothers.

Both brothers were aware of the wide gap that separated their squatter lives from the middle and upper classes, especially those who lived not far from their settlement. The discrimination, deprivation, and other social and psychological pressures felt by them caused occasional anger, depression, or a sense of defeat in the two boys. For Muhammad Qasim, who was still at school, the problem was manifested in various encounters with classmates and teachers. He claimed that he was not accepted by his classmates because of his poverty-stricken appearance. They had often pointed to his squatter life and teased him about it. When he was no longer able to put up with their jokes, he struck fellow students. In one case, he was taken to the local police station and imprisoned for twenty-three hours. Muhammad Qasim explained the fight in this manner: "Believe me, the two of us were equally responsible. But when the school officials complained, they arrested only me. The reason was the fact that my poor father has no influence but the other boy's father was an important person."

Muhammad Qasim thought that some of the teachers discriminated against him and at times ridiculed him publicly. He explained that once he let his hair grow a bit longer since that was the popular style. One of the teachers told him in the classroom: "Do you too have to grow your hair? Your face looks more and more like a butcher's." The teachers have accused and bothered him many times. For example, he felt he was frequently criticized in the classroom by the teachers. Last year when his father, after much effort, borrowed 158 tumans to pay his tuition, the school principal told him: "I don't know why some of the southern residents of Tehran insist on placing their children in northern schools. Next year please put your son in a school in your neighborhood more suited for him."

Studying and reading in the settlement is a major problem for the two brothers. It is impossible to concentrate in the settlement. Outside, the noise and traffic in summer and the cold weather in winter make reading difficult. A few times they went to the Farah Park for quiet reading. At first the sight of girls freely strolling in the park or with other boys made them eager to return. However, they gradually realized that concentration in the park was impossible for them. As Ni'mat said: "We reached puberty at the age of twelve and have feelings and desires like other youths. It makes no sense for us to go to these places when we rarely have the opportunity to even talk to a girl. Going to the park only gives us new complexes."

A while back the two brothers decided to register in a public lending library. They went to the Farah Library and asked for the registration forms. Since this library was for younger children, they were rejected because of their ages. Then they went to the Park-i Shahr Library to get their cards. When the person in charge asked them for their address and telephone number, they responded: "Professor Brown Avenue, Nurullah Khan Enclosure, and we are awaiting our turn for a telephone." The official thought the brothers were joking with him. He told them angrily and emphatically: "Whenever you get a correct address come back and I will give you the library cards."

When we discussed recreation possibilities, they mentioned that their primary problem was lack of money. For example, it costs 25 rials to see a film; it was rare for them to have 50 extra rials. Both enjoyed reading books and had purchased a few inexpensive volumes. They showed their books to us and briefly discussed their contents and the authors. The following list encompasses most of their collection:

Iraj Dihqan, The Broken Bridges
Kurush Salahshur, The Small Dragon
Shapur Qarib, The Fall Evening
Azinfar, Principles of Radio and Its Repair
Honoré de Balzac, Father Goriot

Muhammad Qasim added that in addition to these books, he has also read Les Misérables, The World That I Know, The Story of Beehives, and Papillon. His most cherished book was Victor Hugo's Les Misérables.

Ni'mat, who spoke clearly, occasionally used beautiful and poetic words in his conversation. When he came to trust us more, we were shown a notebook of personal poems and memoirs. He explained that he had been writing about life and the difficulties he and other youths had to face because of social and economic deprivation. He hoped to be able to read these writings to other youth on the radio. Since he was not inclined to show us the few pages that he had written, we did not insist. However, he calmly and quietly read aloud his introduction. The introduction was addressed to "Fellow Countrymen, Dear Brothers and Sisters." The contents discussed his future talks about the deprivation suffered by some youth who were engulfed in poverty. He mentioned two or three times in the introduction that these problems did not concern the present situation in Iran and that most of these issues had been resolved due to the country's recent progress.

In addition, Ni'mat had written two or three short stories and composed a few lines of poetry. Most of his poems dealt with failure in love and expressed his despair.

I am among those lovers in the world
Who mourn unrequited love,
They say drink to forget
But if I drink I am no longer a person.

* * *

Relatives scorn me if I drink,
Before others they demean and debase me,
Wine drinking, it is said, is a sin,
But relatives leave me when I am in sorrow and pain.

* * *

Because of you, my life grew dark,
All my heart's desires destroyed,
My vision of your lovely face
Brought me the moon and the poets' inspiration.

Ni'mat explained that in the fourth line of the last poem he was referring to the poets' dreams about the moon as the source of beauty and inspiration. He lamented that the image of the moon had been destroyed ever since human beings landed on the moon and came back with pictures of its surface showing the craters.

Once when we were speaking with the two brothers, Muhammad Qasim indirectly implied that his brother had another problem. Ni'mat with some hesitation said: "That situation is not so important now. I will explain the problem for them in full some other time." We later discovered that the problem was Ni'mat's marriage. Over four years ago because of his mother's insistence, even though he had no desire or readiness for marriage, Ni'mat agreed to marry his cousin. Apparently Uzra had decided that her son should get married. Without any prior consultation with Ni'mat, Uzra arranged the marriage for her son, who was then only eighteen years old and still in high school. On the engagement day, she took Ni'mat to the cousin's house carrying a large mound of lump sugar. In approximately three weeks the wedding took place. Soon Ni'mat and his wife realized their incompatibility and the marriage was terminated.

Uzra did not learn from this example and, a few months after Ni'mat's divorce, again insisted that he should start his own family. About this time, Ni'mat's uncle had decided to marry his daughter to a low-ranking military officer who was over forty and had three children from his first marriage. Uzra encouraged Ni'mat to perform his family duty and "save" his cousin. Since Ni'mat also liked this cousin, he agreed to the marriage, which took place two years ago.

Ni'mat and his wife had hoped to rent a room close to his parents' home. But even though both worked (his wife washed clothing in different homes), they were not able to rent their own room because a good portion of their income went to help their respective parents' households. Ni'mat also feared possible obligatory military service. In that

131

case, his wife could not have lived alone in one room.
Consequently, his only contact with his wife was a once-a-week
visit to her father's house.

* * *

The last time we saw the brothers we asked them what
they wanted in the coming year and how they saw their future.
Muhammad Qasim, the younger brother, answered: "I wish to get
my twelfth-grade diploma. I like engineering most, but they
say engineering is not for third-class members like us. . . .
Basically, what difference does it make what we want?"

Ni'mat said: "We don't even have control over our daily
lives, much less our future. I am always afraid of military
conscription. If I could manage financially, I would pull
myself out of this squalor and rent a room to take my wife
there. Now the relatives are saying that a person who can't
take his wife away after two whole years should not have
gotten married in the first place. God willing, one day I
want to write the story of our lives. We Nishapuris love
literature and poetry. Our present living conditions have
taught us a lot and have created feelings that the upper-class
youth have perhaps never experienced. Isn't it true that most
writers have come from the lower classes?"

REFERENCES

CHAPTER I

1. See Ervand Abrahamian, "The Crowd in Iranian Politics, 1905-53," Past and Present, 41 (December, 1968), pp. 184-210, and Richard Cottam, Nationalism in Iran (Pittsburgh: University of Pittsburgh Press, 1964).

2. Abrahamian, "The Crowd in Iranian Politics," pp. 189-90.

3. For a discussion of the extent of urban violence in the 1946-68 period see Farhad Kazemi, "Social Mobilization and Domestic Violence in Iran: 1946-1968" (Ph.D. dissertation, University of Michigan, 1973), pp. 114-85.

4. Farhad Kazemi and Ervand Abrahamian, "The Nonrevolutionary Peasantry of Modern Iran," State and Society in Iran, special issue of Iranian Studies, Vol. 11, ed. Amin Banani (Boston: Society for Iranian Studies, 1978), pp. 259-304.

5. Cottam, Nationalism in Iran, p. 37.

6. Ibid.

7. Robert Park, Race and Culture (Glencoe, Ill.: The Free Press, 1950), p. 373.

8. Everett Stonequist, The Marginal Man: A Study in Personality and Culture Conflict (New York: Charles Scribner's Sons, 1937), p. 215.

9. Ibid., p. 2.

10. Ibid., p. 140.

11. Ibid., p. 6.

12. Park, Race and Culture, p. 356.

13. Stonequist, Marginal Man, p. 221.

14. See for example Aaron Antonovsky, "Toward a Refinement of the 'Marginal Man' Concept," Social Forces, 35 (October, 1956), pp. 57-62; Milton Goldberg, "A Qualification of the Marginal Man Theory," American Sociological Review, 6 (February, 1941), pp. 52-58; David Golovonsky, "The Marginal Man Concept: An Analysis and Critique," Social Forces, 30 (March, 1952), pp. 333-39; Alan Kerckhoff and Thomas McCormick, "Marginal Status and the Marginal Personality," Social Forces, 34 (October, 1955), pp. 40-55; J. S. Slotkin, "The Status of the Marginal Man," Sociology and Social Research, 28 (September-October, 1943), pp. 47-54.

15. Golovensky, "Marginal Man Concept," p. 335.

16. H. F. Dickie-Clark, The Marginal Situation: A
Sociological Study of a Colored Group (London: Routledge &
Kegan Paul, 1966).

17. Ibid., p. 10.

18. Ibid., p. 47.

19. Ibid., p. 22.

20. See Dickie-Clark's discussion, ibid., p. 21.

21. Ibid., p. 185.

22. Ibid., pp. 29-30.

23. Ibid., p. 31. Dickie-Clark further breaks down
the barriers into "efficacy" and "criterion of membership."
See pp. 31-32.

24. Gino Germani, "Consideraciones metodológicas y
teóricas sobre la marginalidad urbana en América Latina,"
Revista de la Sociedad Interamericana de Planificación, 6
(December, 1972), p. 5, quoted in Lisa Peattie, "The Concept
of 'Marginality' as Applied to Squatter Settlements," Latin
American Urban Research, ed. Wayne Cornelius and Felicity
Trueblood, Vol. 4 (Beverly Hills: Sage Publications, 1974),
p. 102. See also Germani's recent book in which marginality
is discussed more systematically: Gino Germani, Marginality
(New Brunswick, N.J.: Transaction, 1980), especially pp. 3-48.

25. Janice Perlman, The Myth of Marginality: Urban
Poverty in Rio de Janeiro (Berkeley: University of California
Press, 1976), p. 118.

26. Roger Vekemans and Jorge Giusti, "Marginality and
Ideology in Latin American Development," Studies in
Comparative International Development, 5 (1969-1970), p. 229.
See also Perlman, Myth of Marginality, pp. 118-23; and John
Robin and Frederick Terzo, Urbanization in Peru (New York:
Ford Foundation, 1972), pp. 13-15.

27. Vekemans and Giusti, "Marginality and Ideology,"
p. 229.

28. Perlman, Myth of Marginality, pp. 93-97.

29. Wayne Cornelius, Politics and the Migrant Poor in
Mexico City (Stanford: Stanford University Press, 1975);
William Mangin, "Latin American Squatter Settlements: A
Problem and a Solution," Latin American Research Review, 2
(Summer, 1967), pp. 65-98; Peattie, "The Concept of
Marginality"; Alejandro Portes, "Rationality in the Slum:
An Essay on Interpretive Sociology," Comparative Studies in
Society and History, 14 (June, 1972), pp. 268-86.

30. Perlman, Myth of Marginality, p. 243.

31. Ibid., p. 161.

32. Ibid.

33. On how the poor are marginalized, see Joan Nelson,
Access to Power: Politics and the Urban Poor in Developing
Nations (Princeton: Princeton University Press, 1979), p. 130.

34. See relevant articles in Robert Rhodes, ed., _Imperialism and Underdevelopment: A Reader_ (New York: Monthly Review, 1970); Janet Abu-Lughod and Richard Hay, Jr., eds., _Third World Urbanization_ (Chicago: Maaroufa, 1977).

35. James Petras, _Critical Perspectives on Imperialism and Social Class in the Third World_ (New York: Monthly Review, 1978), pp. 47-54.

36.. See Johan Galtung, "A Structural Theory of Imperialism," _Journal of Peace Research_, 8 (1971), pp. 81-117.

37. See Samir Amin, _Unequal Development_ (New York: Monthly Review, 1976), and _Imperialism and Unequal Development_ (New York: Monthly Review, 1977); Karl Deutsch, "Imperialism and Neocolonialism," _Papers of the Peace Science Society (International)_, 23 (1974), p. 16; Larrisa Lomnitz, _Networks and Marginality: Life in a Mexican Shantytown_ (New York: Academic Press, 1977), pp. 4-5; Germani, _Marginality_, pp. 5-6.

38. Diego Robles Rivas, "Development Alternatives for the Peruvian Barriada," in Abu-Lughod and Hay, _Third World Urbanization_, pp. 322-23; Peter Lloyd, _Slums of Hope? Shanty Towns of the Third World_ (Middlesex, England: Penguin, 1979), p. 61.

39. Petras, _Critical Perspectives on Imperialism_, p. 51.

CHAPTER II

1. Ira Lapidus, "Traditional Muslim Cities: Structure and Change," _From Madina to Metropolis: Heritage and Change in the Near Eastern City_, ed. L. Carl Brown (Princeton, N.J.: Darwin Press, 1973), p. 59. See also Ira Lapidus, "The Evolution of Muslim Urban Society," _Comparative Studies in Society and History_, 15 (January, 1973), pp. 21-50.

2. Gustav Von Grunebaum, "The Structure of Muslim Towns," "Islam: Essay on the Nature and Growth of a Cultural Tradition," Memoir 81, _American Anthropological Association_, 57 (April, 1955), p. 152.

3. Lapidus, "Traditional Muslim Cities," p. 60.

4. Albert Hourani, "Introduction: The Islamic City in the Light of Recent Research," _The Islamic City_, ed. Albert Hourani and S. M. Stern (Philadelphia: University of Pennsylvania Press, 1970), p. 16.

5. _Ibid._, p. 17.

6. _Ibid._, pp. 21-23.

7. L. Carl Brown, "Introduction," _From Madina to Metropolis_, p. 34.

8. Max Weber, _The City_, trans. by D. Martindale and G. Neuwirth (Glencoe, Ill.: The Free Press, 1958), p. 81.

9.   Hourani, "Introduction: The Islamic City," p. 13.

10.   Ibid.

11.   V. F. Costello, Urbanization in the Middle East
(Cambridge, England: Cambridge University Press, 1977), p. 9.
It has now been determined by S. M. Stern and others that
Louis Massignon's claim that Islamic cities possessed
corporate institutions is unfounded. See S. M. Stern, "The
Constitution of the Islamic City," in Hourani and Stern, The
Islamic City; Claude Cahen, "Y a-t-il eu des Corporations
Professionelles dans le Monde Musulman Classique?" in ibid.;
Ira Lapidus, "Muslim Cities and Islamic Societies," Middle
Eastern Cities, ed. Ira Lapidus (Berkeley: University of
California Press, 1969); Dale Eickelman, "Is There an Islamic
City? The Making of a Quarter in a Moroccan Town,"
International Journal of Middle Eastern Studies, 5 (June,
1974), pp. 274-94; Michael Bonine, "From Uruk to Casablanca:
Perspectives on the Urban Experience of the Middle East,"
Journal of Urban History, 3 (February, 1977), pp. 148-57.

12.   Ahmad Ashraf, "Vizhgiha-yi Tarikhi-yi Shahrnishini
dar Iran: Dowrih-yi Islami," Ulum-i Ijtima'i, 1 (Tir, 1353/
1974), pp. 24-41. See also Michael Bonine, "The Morphogenesis
of Iranian Cities," Annals of the Association of American
Geographers, 69 (June, 1979), pp. 208-24.

13.   Ashraf, "Vizhgiha-yi Tarikhi," pp. 41-48. Paul
English's analysis of Kirman in the 1960s suggests that the
city-village linkage is still in existence in the Kirman
basin. Based on this research, English maintains that "the
villager of Iran, whether sharecropper, weaver, or herder, is
inextricably involved in an urban-dominated, regional economic
organization and probably was so in the past." See Paul
English, City and Village in Iran: Settlement and Economy in
the Kirman Basin (Madison: University of Wisconsin Press,
1966), p. 88.

14.   Charles Issawi, ed., The Economic History of Iran:
1800-1914 (Chicago: University of Chicago Press, 1971), pp.
26-27.

15.   Charles Issawi, "Economic Change and Urbanization
in the Middle East," in Lapidus, Middle Eastern Cities, p.
108.

16.   University of Tehran, Institute for Social Research,
"Takvin-i Shahr-i Abadan," Ulum-i Ijtima'i, 1 (Tir, 1353/
1974), pp. 50-56; Costello, Urbanization in the Middle East,
pp. 25-26.

17.   The discussion of these four factors and the
corresponding figures is based on Iran, Plan and Budget
Organization, Iranian Statistical Center, "Darrisi-yi
Ijmali-yi Muhajirat bih Manatiq-i Shahri" (mimeographed), pp.
1-2. There is a discrepancy of 81,662 for total urban
population given in this report and the census data reported
in Table 2.1. The urban population of Iran in 1966 was
9,794,246.

18. See ibid.

19. Mark Jefferson, "The Law of the Primate City," Geographical Review, 29 (April, 1939), pp. 226-32.

20. Philip Hauser, "The Social, Economic, and Technological Problems of Rapid Urbanization," Industrialization and Society, ed. Bert Hoselitz and Wilbert Moore (Paris: Mouton, 1966), p. 201.

21. Philip Hauser, "Some Cultural and Personal Characteristics of the Less Developed Areas," Political Development and Social Change, ed. Jason Finkle and Richard Gable (New York: John Wiley, 1968), p. 56.

22. Hauser, "Problems of Rapid Urbanization," pp. 203-205. See also Alan Peshkin and Ronald Cohen, "The Values of Modernization," Journal of Developing Areas, 2 (October, 1967), p. 18; Arnold Linsky, "Some Generalizations Concerning Primate Cities," The City in Newly Developing Countries: Readings on Urbanism and Urbanization, ed. Gerald Breese (Englewood Cliffs, N.J.: Prentice-Hall, 1969), pp. 285-94.

23. Janet Abu-Lughod, "Urbanization in Egypt: Present State and Future Prospects," Economic Development and Cultural Change, 13 (April, 1965), pp. 315-17.

24. David Kamerschen, "Further Analysis of Overurbanization," Economic Development and Cultural Change, 17 (January, 1969), p. 246.

25. Surrinder Mehta, "Some Demographic and Economic Correlates of Primate Cities: A Case for Revaluation," in Breese, The City in Newly Developing Countries, p. 299. See also N. V. Sovani, "The Analysis of 'Over-Urbanization,'" Economic Development and Cultural Change, 12 (January, 1964), pp. 120-33; Brian Berry, "City-Size Distributions and Economic Development," Economic Development and Cultural Change, 9 (July, 1961), p. 584. See also the seminal article by Kingsley Davis and Hilda Hertz Golden that was partly responsible for this controversy, "Urbanization and the Development of Pre-Industrial Areas," Economic Development and Cultural Change, 3 (October, 1954), pp. 6-26.

26. Bert Hoselitz, Sociological Aspects of Economic Growth (Glencoe, Ill.: The Free Press, 1960), p. 187. See also Gerald Breese's discussion of overurbanization in his Urbanization in Newly Developing Countries (Englewood Cliffs, N.J.: Prentice-Hall, 1966), pp. 133-36.

27. Abdul'aziz Javahir-Kalam, Tarikh-i Tehran, Part 1 (Tehran, 1325/1946), pp. 1-7.

28. See Laurence Lockhart's discussion of both Ray and Tehran in his Persian Cities (London: Luzac, 1960), pp. 1-9.

29. Javahir-Kalam, Tarikh-i Tehran, p. 71.

30. Lockhart, Persian Cities, p. 5. See also George Curzon, Persia and the Persian Question, Vol. 1 (London: Frank Cass, 1966), p. 302.

31. Lockhart, Persian Cities, p. 5.

32. _Ibid._ See also Javahir-Kalam, _Tarikh-i Tehran_, p. 83.

33. Abbott, "Report on Trade for 1841," FO 60/92, reprinted in Issawi, _Economic History of Iran_, p. 118.

34. Thomson, "Report on Persia," A and P 1867-68, 19, reprinted in Issawi, _Economic History of Iran_, p. 28.

35. Mihdi Amani, "Avvalin Sarshumari-yi Jam'iyyat-i Tehran," _Ulum-i Ijtima'i_, 1 (Bahman, 1348/1970), p. 89. The discussion of Tehran's first census is based primarily on Amani's report of the census.

36. Various estimates are given for Tehran's population at this time. See Mihdi Amani, _Shahgara'i va Shahrnishini dar Iran_ (Tehran: University of Tehran, 1350/1971), pp. 62-63; Paul Vieille, _Marché des Terrains et Société Urbaine_ (Paris: Editions Anthropos, 1970), pp. 224-25; Fredy Bemont, _Les Villes de l'Iran: Des Cités d'Autrefois à l'Urbanisme Contemporain_ (Paris: l'Auteur, 1969), pp. 117-18; Gad Gilbar, "Demographic Developments in Late Qajar Persia, 1870-1906," _Asian and African Studies_, 2 (1976), pp. 147-51.

37. Mohammad Hemmasi, "Tehran in Transition: A Study in Comparative Factorial Ecology," _The Population of Iran: A Selection of Readings_, ed. Jamshid Momeni (Honolulu: East-West Center, 1977), p. 362.

38. For discussion of Tehran's transformation under Reza Shah see Amin Banani, _The Modernization of Iran: 1921-1941_ (Stanford: Stanford University Press, 1961), pp. 144-45. On Tehran's geographic organization and structure see Vieille, _Marché des Terrains_, pp. 85-86, and Bemont, _Les Villes de l'Iran_, pp. 109-17.

39. See the chapters by Mehta and Linsky in Breese, _The City in Newly Developing Countries_.

40. Costello, _Urbanization in the Middle East_, p. 35. Costello also finds regular rank-size distributions for both Turkey and Jordan even when the top five cities are included in the analysis.

41. Issawi, "Economic Change and Urbanization," p. 116.

42. Berry, "City-Size Distributions," p. 582. Berry also mentions that primate cities tend to develop in small countries that previously possessed extensive empires (e.g., Spain, Portugal), or in areas where economies of scale are such that intermediate-sized cities are not necessary.

43. _Ibid._, p. 585.

44. Marvin Zonis, _The Political Elite of Iran_ (Princeton: Princeton University Press, 1971), pp. 139-40.

45. Echo of Iran, _Iran Almanac and Book of Facts, 1971_; for 1971/72 academic year.

46. Ferydoon Firoozi, "Tehran--A Demographic and Economic Analysis," _Middle Eastern Studies_, 10 (January, 1974), p. 67; for 1968/69.

47. Ibid.

48. Iran, Plan and Budget Organization, Shakhisha-yi Ijtima'i-yi Iran, 1978; for 1975.

49. Robert Looney, The Economic Development of Iran: A Recent Survey with Projections to 1981 (New York: Praeger Publishers, 1973), p. 129; for 1967.

50. Ibid.

51. Ibid.

52. Iran, Plan and Budget Organization, Iranian Statistical Center, Amar-i Muntakhab, 1973; for 1972.

53. Iran, Bank-i Markazi, Annual Report and Balance Sheet, 1968; for 1968.

54. Iran, Plan and Budget Organization, Iranian Statistical Center, Salnamih-yi Amari-yi Kishvar, 1976; for 1975.

55. Iran, Plan and Budget Organization, Iranian Statistical Center, Amar-i Muntakhab, 1976; for 1975.

56. Ibid.

57. Iran, Plan and Budget Organization, Iranian Statistical Center, Salnamih-yi Amari-yi Kishvar, 1976; for 1975.

58. Ibid.

59. Ibid.

60. For a discussion of "heterogenetic" and "orthogenetic" cultural roles of cities see Robert Redfield and Milton Singer, "The Cultural Role of Cities," Economic Development and Cultural Change, 3 (October, 1954), pp. 53-73.

61. E. G. Ravenstein, "The Laws of Migration," Journal of the Royal Statistical Society, 48, Part 2 (June, 1885), pp. 167-227, and "The Laws of Migration," Journal of the Royal Statistical Society, 52 (June, 1889), pp. 241-301.

62. Everett Lee, "A Theory of Migration," Demography, 3 (1966), p. 47.

63. Ibid., p. 49.

64. Ibid., p. 50.

65. Ibid., p. 51.

66. Michael Todaro, Internal Migration in Developing Countries: A Review of Theory, Evidence, Methodology and Research Priorities (Geneva: International Labour Office, 1976), p. 20.

67. Ibid., p. 31. For a critique of Todaro's work see T. G. McGee, "Rural-Urban Mobility in South and Southeast Asia, Different Formulations . . . Different Answers?" in Abu-Lughod and Hay, Third World Urbanization, p. 198. See also the "ecological model of migration" in Lomnitz, Networks and Marginality, pp. 38-40. For other models and studies of

migration see Alan Brown and Egon Neuberger, eds., _Internal Migration: A Comparative Perspective_ (New York: Academic Press, 1977); Brian du Toit and Helen Safa, eds., _Migration and Urbanization: Models and Adaptive Strategies_ (The Hague: Mouton, 1975).

68. Todaro, _Internal Migration_, p. 66.

69. _Ibid._, p. 7.

70. Julian Bharier, "The Growth of Towns and Villages in Iran, 1900-66," _Middle Eastern Studies_, 8 (January, 1972), p. 56.

71. _Ibid._

72. Julian Bharier, _Economic Development in Iran: 1900-1970_ (New York: Oxford University Press, 1971), p. 30.

73. Iran, Plan and Budget Organization, Iranian Statistical Center, "Barrisi-yi Ijmali," pp. 1-2.

74. Habibullah Zanjani _et al._, _Jam'iyyat Shinasi-yi Tatbiqi-yi Jahan_ (Tehran: University of Tehran, 1350/1971), p. 172.

75. Amani, "Avvalin Sarshumari," p. 90.

76. Bharier, "Growth of Towns and Villages," p. 57.

77. Bharier, _Economic Development in Iran_, p. 30. Todaro includes Tehran as one of the twelve fastest-growing cities of the world, a fact that is due mostly to migration. See Todaro, _Internal Migration_, p. 8.

78. See Todaro, _Internal Migration_, p. 27.

79. This percentage is based on the total number of city-dwelling migrants, excluding those who migrated for reasons of marriage and other secondary migrants who were dependents of principal migrants.

CHAPTER III

1. The above figures are based on Bharier, _Economic Development of Iran_; M. A. Katouzian, "Oil Versus Agriculture: A Case of Dual Resource Depletion in Iran," _Journal of Peasant Studies_, 5 (August, 1978), pp. 347-69; annual reports of Iran's Central Bank.

2. For more elaboration of these terms see Hamza Alavi, "Peasants and Revolution," _The Socialist Register_, ed. Ralph Miliband and John Saville (New York: Monthly Review Press, 1965), p. 244.

3. Ann K. S. Lambton, _The Persian Land Reform: 1962-1966_ (London: Clarendon Press of Oxford University Press, 1969), p. 20.

4. See Kazemi and Abrahamian, "The Nonrevolutionary Peasantry of Modern Iran." See also Ann K. S. Lambton,

Landlord and Peasant in Persia: A Study of Land Tenure and Land Revenue Administration (London: Oxford University Press, 1953), pp. 275-82.

5. Lambton, Landlord and Peasant in Persia, p. 295.

6. Javad Safinizhad, Bunih (Tehran: Tus, 1353/1974).

7. Khusrow Khusravi, Pazhuhishi dar Jami'ih-yi Rusta'i-yi Iran (Tehran: Payam, 2535/1976), pp. 67-83.

8. Eric Hooglund, "The Khwushnishin Population of Iran," Iranian Studies, 6 (Autumn, 1973), pp. 229-45.

9. Ibid., p. 256.

10. James Bill, The Politics of Iran, Groups, Classes and Modernization (Columbus, Ohio: Charles E. Merrill, 1972), p. 137.

11. Cottam, Nationalism in Iran, p. 271; Lambton, Persian Land Reform, p. 37.

12. Lambton, Persian Land Reform, pp. 41-43.

13. Ibid., p. 56.

14. Ibid., p. 294.

15. Ibid., pp. 293-94.

16. Jane Carey and Andrew Carey, "Iranian Agriculture and Its Development: 1952-1973," International Journal of Middle East Studies, 7 (July, 1976), p. 364; R. Doroudian, "Modernization of Rural Economy in Iran," Iran: Past, Present, and Future, ed. Jane Jacqz (New York: Aspen Institute for Humanistic Studies, 1976), pp. 159-60. A variant of farm corporations known as production cooperatives were also established. In production cooperatives the farmers retained their land titles; in farm corporations land titles were exchanged for shares in the corporation. See Doroudian, "Modernization of Rural Economy," p. 161.

17. Marvin Weinbaum, "Agricultural Policy and Development Politics in Iran," Middle East Journal, 31 (Autumn, 1977), p. 439; Katouzian, "Oil Versus Agriculture," p. 360. Khuzistan Province was selected as the primary area for these operations.

18. Bill, Politics of Iran, p. 146.

19. K. S. McLachlan, "Land Reform in Iran," The Cambridge History of Iran, Vol. 1: The Land of Iran, ed. W. B. Fisher (Cambridge, England: Cambridge University Press, 1968), p. 710.

20. Ibid., p. 711.

21. Lambton, Persian Land Reform, p. 100.

22. Ibid.

23. Ibid., p. 103.

24. Zonis, Political Elite of Iran, p. 59.

25. Bill, Politics of Iran, p. 142, n. 17.

26. See Zonis's interesting discussion of Arsanjani's "resignation" in Political Elite of Iran, pp. 53-61.

27. Hossein Mahdavy, "The Coming Crisis in Iran," Foreign Affairs, 44 (October, 1965), p. 142.

28. Lambton, Persian Land Reform, p. 360.

29. Doroudian, "Modernization of Rural Economy," p. 158.

30. Weinbaum, "Agricultural Policy and Development," p. 438.

31. Ahmad Ashraf and Marsha Safai, The Role of the Rural Organizations in Rural Development: The Case of Iran (Tehran, 1977), p. 37.

32. Ibid.

33. Ibid., pp. 55-58.

34. Ibid., pp. 64-65.

35. Inayatullah, Cooperatives and Development in Asia: A Study of Cooperatives in Fourteen Rural Communities of Iran, Pakistan and Ceylon (Geneva: United Nations Research Institute for Social Development, 1972), p. 117; Ashraf and Safai, p. 58; Daniel Craig, "The Impact of Land Reform on an Iranian Village," Middle East Journal, 32 (Spring, 1978), pp. 147-49.

36. Inayatullah, Cooperatives and Development, p. 125.

37. Katouzian, "Oil Versus Agriculture," p. 358.

38. Weinbaum, "Agricultural Policy and Development," p. 438.

39. Ibid.

40. Katouzian, "Oil Versus Agriculture," p. 359.

41. Oddvar Aresvik, The Agricultural Development of Iran (New York: Praeger Publishers, 1976), p. 111.

42. Ashraf and Safai, Role of Rural Organizations, p. 23.

43. Aresvik, Agricultural Development of Iran, p. 112.

44. Katouzian, "Oil Versus Agriculture," p. 361.

45. Ibid.

46. Ibid. For another critique of the Iranian agricultural projects see Thierry Brun and Rene Dumont, "Iran: Imperial Pretensions and Agricultural Dependence," Merip Reports, 8 (October, 1978), pp. 15-20. See also Paul Vieille and Abol-Hassan Banisadr, Pétrole et Violence (Paris: Editions Anthropos, 1974), pp. 19-22.

47. Weinbaum, "Agricultural Policy and Development," p. 440.

48. Katouzian, "Oil Versus Agriculture," p. 361. For a devastating critique of agribusiness operations see Helmut Richards, "Land Reform and Agribusiness in Iran," Merip Reports, 43 (December, 1975), pp. 3-18, 24.

49. Farhad Daftary, "Development Planning in Iran: A Historical Survey," Iranian Studies, 6 (Autumn, 1973), p. 209.

50. Ibid., p. 212.

51. Aresvik, Agricultural Development of Iran, p. 33; Weinbaum, "Agricultural Policy and Development," p. 435.

52. Katouzian, "Oil Versus Agriculture," p. 365.

53. Aresvik, Agricultural Development of Iran, p. 129. The situation was not much better for meat production. In 1975-76, for example, 75 percent more red meat was imported than the previous year. See Weinbaum, "Agricultural Policy and Development," p. 446.

54. Katouzian, "Oil Versus Agriculture," p. 347.

55. Nikki Keddie, "The Iranian Village Before and After Land Reform," Journal of Contemporary History, 3 (July, 1968), p. 86. See also Nikki Keddie, "Stratification, Social Control, and Capitalism in Iranian Villages: Before and After Land Reform," Rural Politics and Social Change in the Middle East, ed. Richard Antoun and Iliya Harik (Bloomington: Indiana University Press, 1972), p. 387; Farhad Khamsi, "Land Reform in Iran," Monthly Review, 21 (June, 1969), p. 28.

56. William Bartsch, Problems of Employment Creation in Iran (Geneva: International Labour Office, 1970), p. 14, n. 3.

57. Bartsch, Problems of Employment, p. 67.

58. United Nations, International Labour Office, Employment and Income Policies for Iran (Geneva: International Labour Office, 1973), p. 25.

59. Isma'il Ajami, "Khulqiyyat, Mu'taqidat, va Arizuha-yi Shughli-yi Rusta'iyyan," Ulum-i Ijtima'i, 1 (Bahman, 1348/1970), pp. 36-39.

60. Employment and Income Policies for Iran, p. 32; Bartsch, Problems of Employment, pp. 9-17.

61. Employment and Income Policies for Iran, p. 32. The Plan Organization's study of migration to Tehran reports 20.7 percent unemployment rate immediately before migration to Tehran. Iran, Plan and Budget Organization, Pazhuhishi Amari Baray-i Ira'i-yi Sima-yi Muhajiran dar Tehran va Tabriz (Tehran: Plan and Budget Organization, 1977), p. 3.

62. Shakhisha-yi Ijtima'i-yi Iran, p. 322.

63. Ismail Ajami, "Agricultural and Rural Development in Iran: Agrarian Reform, Modernization of Peasants and Agricultural Development in Iran," in Jacqz, Iran, p. 153.

64. Employment and Income Policies for Iran, pp. 12, 25.

65. Salnamih-yi Amari-yi Kishvar, 1976, p. 252/11.

66. As the evidence from the developing countries indicates, urban unemployment has greater ill effects than rural underemployment. See Paul Bairoch, Urban Unemployment in Developing Countries: The Nature of the Problem and

Proposal for Its Solution (Geneva: International Labour Office, 1973), p. 76.

67. Employment and Income Policies for Iran, p. 25.

68. Marc Howard Ross, The Political Integration of Urban Squatters (Evanston, Ill.: Northwestern University Press, 1973), p. 40.

69. Bairoch, Urban Unemployment, p. 33.

70. Employment and Income Policies for Iran, p. 69.

71. Kazim Izadi, "Savadamuzi va Rabitih-yi on ba Taharruk-i Shugli va Jughrafiya'i-yi Savadamuzan," Ulum-i Ijtima'i, 1 (Tir, 1353/1974), pp. 77-89.

72. In a report on migrants in a low-income community of southwest Tehran known as Yakhchiabad, 74.6 percent of the sample's respondents stated that the principal reason for their migration was job-related problems and low income. See Mihdi Salamat et al., Ilal-i Muhajirat va Barrisi-yi Awza'-i Farhangi, Iqtisadi, va Ijtima'i-yi Muhajirin-i Mantaqih-yi Yakhchiabad (Tehran: College of Social Work, 1350-1351/1971-1972).

73. Similarly, a study of nonmigrant residents of two villages in Azerbaijan indicated an illiteracy rate of 83 percent among 1,203 heads of households and their spouses. See the report on Suhrab and Tazihkand in Pazhuhishi Amari, p. 651.

74. Mohammad Hemmasi, Migration in Iran: A Quantitative Approach (Shiraz: Pahlavi University, 1974), p. 46.

75. Although certain provinces (e.g., Central, Azerbaijan, Khurasan) usually send a larger number of migrants to Tehran, distance is not a satisfactory measure of migration flows. This is further documented in the Plan Organization's study, Pazhuhishi Amari, and in the report on Tehran squatters, Tehran University, Institute for Social Research, Barrisi-yi Hashiyih Nishinan-i Tehran: Shinasa'i-yi Vahidha (Jami'ah-yi Amari) (Tehran: Institute for Social Research, 1350/1972).

76. Kemal Karpat, The Gecekondu: Rural Migration and Urbanization (Cambridge, England: Cambridge University Press, 1976), p. 84; Perlman, Myth of Marginality, p. 40.

77. Wayne Cornelius, "Urbanization as an Agent in Latin American Political Instability: The Case of Mexico," American Political Science Review, 63 (September, 1969), pp. 843, 855; Perlman, Myth of Marginality, pp. 70-71.

78. In a survey of migrants to Shiraz, Ali Paydarfar similarly reports that about one half of the migrants had relatives in the city with whom they had been in contact before the decision to leave the countryside was taken. See Ali Paydarfar, Social Change in a Southern Province of Iran (Chapel Hill: Institute for Research in Social Science, University of North Carolina, 1974), p. 97.

1. John F. C. Turner, "Uncontrolled Urban Settlement: Problems and Policies," in Breese, The City in Newly Developing Countries, p. 508n.

2. United Nations, Conference on Human Settlements, Urban Slums and Squatter Settlements in the Third World (A/CONF. 70/RPC/9, 1975), p. 3n. See also Elizabeth Colton, "Community Programs for Low-Income Populations in Urban Settlements of Developing Countries," report prepared for the United Nations (mimeographed), p. 2.

3. Urban Slums and Squatter Settlements, p. 3n.

4. Ibid.

5. Charles Abrams, Man's Struggle for Shelter in an Urbanizing World (Cambridge: M.I.T. Press, 1964), p. 12.

6. Turner, "Uncontrolled Urban Settlement," p. 526. See also Charles Stokes's interesting distinctions between slums of "hope" and slums of "despair," in "A Theory of Slums," Land Economics, 38 (August, 1962), pp. 187-97.

7. Barrisi-yi Hashiyih Nishinan.

8. See Abrams's discussion of squatter tenancy and other forms of squatting in Man's Struggle for Shelter, pp. 21-22.

9. Reported in Iran Times, July 8, 1978, p. 8. Another report in the same newspaper discusses the discovery of the "cheapest house in the country" in the Karaj area. This "house" has a four-square-meter area, four walls, but no roof. Inside the compound a tent is set up in which a seven-member household resides. The owner wants to sell his property for about $1,430 which includes a profit of $571. He argues the worth of his house in the following manner: "It is true that my house has no rooms but a husband and wife without children can sleep in the tent and free themselves from having to depend on rentals. Living here is difficult for us because of our four children and the fact that my newly married son has brought his wife to live here. If I sell my house for the asking price, then with the addition of a loan I would be able to find a larger place for us to live in." Iran Times, August 4, 1978, p. 6.

10. Abrams, Man's Struggle for Shelter, p. 21.

11. There is one report of organized mass invasion by squatters in the Tehran Pars wastelands. The invaders were dispersed after aerial shootings by the gendarmerie officers. See Chirikha-yi Fada'i-yi Khalq-i Iran, Guzarishati az Mubarizat-i Daliranih-yi Mardum-i Kharij az Mahdudih (Tehran: 1357/1978), p. 23.

12. Abrams, Man's Struggle for Shelter, p. 12.

13. See the discussion by Portes refuting the validity of such views in "Rationality in the Slum," pp. 277-79.

14. Husayn Yazdani, "Alunaknishini dar Hashiyih-yi Shahrha," Khwandaniha (June 5, 1976), p. 39. This article was originally published in the government-sponsored magazine, Talash. The view of this author is probably representative of attitudes of many high government officials.

15. Perlman, Myth of Marginality, pp. 196-97; Portes, "Rationality in the Slum," pp. 278-79.

16. See Turner's distinctions of the two terms in "Uncontrolled Urban Settlement," p. 526.

17. Portes, "Rationality in the Slum," p. 281.

18. College of Social Work, Tasviri as Awza'-i Ijtima'i-yi Kuyi Nuhum-i Aban (Tehran: College of Social Work, 1345/1966).

19. Ibid., p. 77. According to official reports, in 1973 in the city of Bandar Abbas in South Iran only 5 percent of the squatters were fully employed. See Yazdani, "Alunaknishini," p. 16.

20. Ahmad Ashraf, "Iran: Imperialism, Class and Modernization from Above" (Ph.D. dissertation, New School for Social Research, 1971), p. 226.

21. Karl Marx, The Communist Manifesto (New York: Appleton-Century-Crofts, 1955), p. 20. Also cited in Bertell Ollman, "Marx's Use of 'Class,'" American Journal of Sociology, 73 (March, 1968), p. 575.

22. This is a free translation of an introductory passage in Sattarih Farmanfarmayan, Piramun-i Ruspigari dar Shahr-i Tehran (Tehran: College of Social Work, 1349/1971), pp. 23-24. Some observers of migrant neighborhoods have stressed the incidence of crime in these areas. Although crime, drug addiction, and prostitution can be found in some of the poor migrant neighborhoods, it is dangerous to attribute these factors to poverty or overemphasize their occurrence in the absence of systematic statistical evidence. While visiting some of the poor migrant areas of Tehran, I was occasionally told stories about drug addiction and prostitution. One account related a story about the intermittent gatherings of hard-core and poverty-stricken opium addicts who use the common name "Abbas Aqa" to refer to each other. In addition to opium smoking, these gatherings (or so I was told) are also used to exchange information and sometimes even map "strategies" to ensure availability of drugs to the group.

23. Karl Marx, The Class Struggles in France: 1848-1850 (New York: International Publishers, 1972), p. 50. Perhaps there is no better description of the lumpenproletariat's life than Samad Behrangi's short story, "24 Restless Hours." Behrangi's powerful story captures the plight of the lumpenproletariat through the life of a poverty-stricken migrant boy in the streets of Tehran. See Samad Behrangi, The Little Black Fish and Other Modern Persian Stories, trans. Eric and Mary Hooglund (Washington, D.C.: Three Continents Press, 1976).

24. College of Social Work, "Barrisi-yi Awza'-i Iqtisadi, Ijtima'i, va Bihdashti va Barrisi-yi Niyazmandiha-yi Sakinan-i Mantaqih-yi Khazanih-yi Fallah" (mimeographed).

25. Mangin, "Latin American Squatter Settlements," pp. 76-78.

26. This discussion is based on Nelson, Access to Power, pp. 24-43, and Lloyd, Slums of Hope, pp. 140-47.

27. Lloyd, Slums of Hope, p. 143.

28. Nelson, Access to Power, p. 31.

29. Michael Todaro in his model of labor migration in the urban areas of the Third World posits a two-stage sequence. First the migrant spends some time in the "urban transitional sector" before finding more permanent employment in the modern sector. Michael Todaro, "A Model of Labor Migration and Urban Employment in Less Development Countries," American Economic Review, 59 (March, 1969), p. 139.

30. Hauser, "Problems of Rapid Urbanization," p. 211. See Nelson's comprehensive review of these issues in her Access to Power, pp. 91-109.

31. Hoselitz, Sociological Aspects of Economic Growth, p. 180.

32. Lucian Pye, "The Political Implications of Urbanization and the Development Process," p. 401.

33. Oscar Lewis, "Further Observations on the Folk-Urban Continuum and Urbanization with Special Reference to Mexico City," The Study of Urbanization, ed. Philip Hauser and Leo Schnore (New York: John Wiley, 1965), p. 494. See also Cornelius, "Urbanization as an Agent," p. 845.

34. Douglas Butterworth, "A Study of the Urbanization Process among Mixtec Migrants from Tilatongo in Mexico City," Peasants in Cities: Readings in the Anthropology of Urbanization, ed. William Mangin (Boston: Houghton Mifflin, 1970), p. 105.

35. Janet Abu-Lughod, "Migrant Adjustment to City Life: The Egyptian Case," in Breese, The City in Newly Developing Countries, p. 386. See also Janet Abu-Lughod, "Varieties of Urban Experience: Contrast, Coexistence and Coalescence in Cairo," in Lapidus, Middle Eastern Cities.

36. Karen Peterson, "Villagers in Cairo: Hypotheses versus Data," American Journal of Sociology, 77 (November, 1971), p. 571. Peterson also points out that the data from Cairo "support the proposition that migrants are not likely to come into contact with those from markedly different backgrounds on their job." See ibid., p. 569.

37. Paul Doughty, "Behind the Back of the City: 'Provincial' Life in Lima, Peru," in Mangin, Peasants in Cities, p. 43. See also Lloyd, Slums of Hope, p. 109.

38. Karpat, Gecekondu, pp. 139-40.

39. Ned Levine, "Old Culture-New Culture: A Study of Migrants in Ankara, Turkey," Social Forces, 51 (March, 1973), p. 360.

40. A squatter settlement in North Tehran, known as Kashnak, is one of the few examples of an isolated and homogeneous migrant settlement.

41. Lomnitz, Networks and Marginality, p. 132.

42. Ibid., pp. 132, 209.

43. Nelson, Access to Power, p. 253.

44. See the Appendix.

45. Butterworth, "A Study of Urbanization Process," p. 103.

46. Karpat, Gecekondu, p. 169.

47. Ibid., p. 166.

48. Pazhuhishi Amari. The discussion of Tabriz migrants is based exclusively on data reported in this survey.

CHAPTER V

1. Daniel Lerner, The Passing of Traditional Society: Modernizing the Middle East (New York: The Free Press, 1964), p. 61.

2. Ibid., p. 58.

3. Ibid.

4. Donald McCrone and Charles Cnudde, "Toward a Communications Theory of Democratic Political Development: A Causal Model," American Political Science Review, 61 (March, 1967), pp. 72-79.

5. Gilbert Winham, "Political Development and Lerner's Theory: Further Test of a Causal Model," American Political Science Review, 64 (September, 1970), pp. 810-18.

6. Karl Deutsch, Nationalism and Social Communication: An Inquiry into the Foundations of Nationality (Cambridge: M.I.T. Press, 1966), p. 153. See also David Cameron, J. Stephen Hendricks, and Richard Hofferbert, "Urbanization, Social Structure, Mass Politics: A Comparison Within Five Nations," Comparative Political Studies, 5 (October, 1972), p. 261.

7. Karl Deutsch, "Social Mobilization and Political Development," American Political Science Review, 50 (September, 1961), p. 494.

8. Ibid., p. 498.

9. Ibid., p. 499.

10. Gabriel Almond and G. Bingham Powell, Comparative Politics: A Developmental Approach (Boston: Little, Brown, 1966), p. 53.

11. Cornelius, "Urbanization as an Agent," p. 846.

12. Clifford Kaufman, "Urbanization, Material Satisfaction, and Mass Political Involvement: The Poor in Mexico City," Comparative Political Studies, 4 (October, 1971), p. 299. See also John Peeler, "Urbanization and Politics," Sage Professional Papers in Comparative Politics, 6 (1977), pp. 5-17.

13. Cameron, Hendricks, and Hofferbert, "Urbanization, Social Structure, Mass Politics," p. 273.

14. Norman Nie, G. Bingham Powell, and Kenneth Prewitt, "Social Structure and Political Participation: Developmental Relationships," American Political Science Review, 63 (June, 1969), p. 365.

15. Ervand Abrahamian, "Social Bases of Iranian Politics: The Tudeh Party, 1941-53" (Ph.D. dissertation, Columbia University, 1969), p. 45.

16. It is, therefore, not surprising to note that 37 percent of my sample of the migrant poor had voted at least once in parliamentary elections while living in the village.

17. Deutsch, "Social Mobilization," p. 499.

18. Norman Nie, G. Bingham Powell, and Kenneth Prewitt, "Social Structure and Political Participation: Developmental Relationships," Part II, American Political Science Review, 63 (September, 1969), p. 826. The obvious case in point is the Islamic clergy's use of the Shi'i networks to mobilize the poor against the Shah during the course of the revolution.

19. Pearson's R coefficient between political awareness index and political party affiliation was not significant. The same was true for the index of socioeconomic status and political party affiliation.

20. Samuel Huntington, Political Order in Changing Societies (New Haven: Yale University Press, 1968), p. 281.

21. Ibid., p. 283.

22. I also studied a third group of second-generation migrants composed of female factory workers. The findings are reported in Chapter VI.

23. Cornelius, Politics and the Migrant Poor, p. 167. For additional studies of political demand making, see Wayne Cornelius and Henry Dietz, "Urbanization, Demand-Making, and Political System 'Overload': Political Participation Among the Migrant Poor in Latin American Cities," paper presented at the annual meeting of the American Political Science Association, New Orleans, September, 1973; Henry Dietz, "Bureaucrat-Client Interactions as Politics: Perceptions and Evaluations by the Urban Poor in Lima, Peru," paper presented

at the annual meeting of the American Political Science
Association, New York, September, 1978.

24. Cornelius, _Politics and the Migrant Poor_, p. 170.

25. _Ibid._, p. 167.

26. "Barrisi-yi Khazanih-yi Fallah." Fred Halliday
underscores the sharp rise in Tehran's rents: "Rents in
Tehran rose by 15 times between 1960 and 1975; they rose by
200 percent in 1974-5 and by another 100 percent in 1975-6."
See Fred Halliday, _Iran: Dictatorship and Development_ (New
York: Penguin, 1979), p. 190.

27. Presentation of the residents' needs is based on
Tasviri as Kuyi Nuhum-i Aban, pp. 86-88.

28. Cornelius, _Politics and the Migrant Poor_, p. 176.

29. The assessment of needs in Mihrabad-i Junubi is
based on my interviews with the residents in 1974-75. For
needs expressed by residents in Khazanih-yi Fallah see
"Barrisi-yi Khazanih-yi Fallah."

30. _Guzarishati az Mubarizat_, pp. 67-71.

31. Cornelius, _Politics and the Migrant Poor_, p. 177.

32. _Guzarishati az Mubarizat_, p. 46.

33. See various studies by Cornelius, Mangin, Perlman,
and Portes, all cited above.

34. Myron Weiner, "Urbanization and Political Protest,"
Civilisations, 17 (1967), p. 48.

35. Myron Weiner, "Violence and Politics in Calcutta,"
Journal of Asian Studies, 20 (May, 1961), p. 277; emphasis
added.

36. Alejandro Portes and John Walton, _Urban Latin
America: The Political Condition from Above and Below_ (Austin:
University of Texas Press, 1976), p. 108.

37. Daniel Goldrich, Raymond Pratt, and C. R. Schuller,
"The Political Integration of Lower-Class Urban Settlements
in Chile and Peru," _Masses in Latin America_, ed. Irving Louis
Horowitz (New York: Oxford University Press, 1970), p. 191.

38. Joan Nelson, _Migrants, Urban Poverty, and
Instability in Developing Nations_ (Center for International
Affairs, Harvard University, 1969), p. 63, and "The Urban
Poor: Disruption or Political Integration in Third World
Cities?" _World Politics_, 22 (April, 1970), p. 404. See also
James White, "Political Implications of Cityward Migration:
Japan as an Exploratory Test Case," _Sage Professional Papers
in Comparative Politics_, 4 (1973), pp. 12-19.

39. Portes, "Rationality in the Slum," p. 284.

40. Ted Gurr, _Why Men Rebel_ (Princeton: Princeton
University Press, 1970), p. 13.

41. _Ibid._, p. 12. Another version of frustration-
aggression theory is the concept of "systemic frustration"

CHAPTER VI

1. Alex Inkeles and David Smith, Becoming Modern: Individual Change in Six Developing Countries (Cambridge: Harvard University Press, 1974), p. 164. Inkeles and Smith point out that the socialization process leading to learning of modern values and attitudes involves four dimensions: modeling, generalization, exemplification, and reward and punishment. These four dimensions of modernity are applied to factory work in Argentina, Chile, East Pakistan, India, Israel, and Nigeria. See pp. 154-91.

2. Ibid., p. 174.

3. Political socialization is defined in the words of vid Easton and Jack Dennis as "those developmental processes ough which persons acquire political orientations and terns of behavior." See David Easton and Jack Dennis, ldren in the Political System: Origins of Political timacy (New York: McGraw-Hill, 1969), p. 7.

4. Robert Hess, "The Socialization of Attitudes Toward ical Authority: Some Crossnational Comparisons," national Social Science Journal, 15 (1963), p. 543.

5. See for example Arnold Rose, "Incomplete ization," Sociology and Social Relations, 44 (1960), -50; Roberta Sigel, "Assumptions about the Learning tical Values," Annals, 361 (1965), pp. 1-9.

Allan Kornberg and Norman Thomas, "The Political ation of National Legislative Elites in the United d Canada," Journal of Politics, 27 (November, 1965),

The average length of work at the factory was six Group A and four years for Group B.

uoted in Fred Greenstein, "Political Socialization on," International Encyclopedia of the Social l. 14, p. 552. See also James Bill and Robert omparative Politics: The Quest for Theory io: Charles E. Merrill, 1973), p. 99.

ert Dawson, Kenneth Prewitt, and Karen Dawson, alization, 2d ed. (Boston: Little, Brown, 1977),

h Lopreato and Lawrence Hazelrigg, Class, obility: Theories and Studies of Class rancisco: Chandler, 1972), p. 131.

Prewitt, and Dawson, Political 81-92.

and Smith, Becoming Modern, p. 159.

ooney, A Developmental Strategy for Iran New York: Praeger, 1977), pp. 42-45. See , "The Iranian Economy 1925-1975: Fifty

used by a number of authors. Although similar to the basic version, "systemic frustration" emphasizes "frustration that is experienced simultaneously and collectively within societies." See Ivo Feierabend, Rosalind Feierabend, and Betty Nesvold, "Social Change and Political Violence: Cross-National Patterns," Violence in America: Historical and Comparative Perspectives, ed. Hugh Graham and Ted Gurr (New York: Bantam, 1969), p. 635. This is a problematic concept and fails, among other things, to demonstrate how psychological traumas in the aggregate add up to mass psychological outburts. For other studies of "systemic frustration" see James Kirkham, Sheldon Levy, and William Crotty, Assassination and Political Violence (Washington, D.C.: U.S. Government Printing Office, 1969); Douglas Bwy, "Political Instability in Latin America: The Cross-Cultural Test of a Causal Model," Latin American Research Review, 3 (1968), pp. 17-66.

42. Perlman, Myth of Marginality, p. 182; Nelson, Migrants, Urban Poverty, p. 15.

43. The statistical evidence partly supports the migrants' view that longer stay in Tehran results in somewhat higher income (Pearson's R coefficient of 0.24, significant at 0.005 level for $n = 210$).

44. Note a similar observation by Nelson, Migrants, Urban Poverty, p. 15.

45. Ibid., p. 20.

46. See Portes's discussion of this issue for the Latin American migrant poor. Portes and Walton, Urban Latin America, pp. 91-92.

47. Johan Galtung, "Violence, Peace, and Peace Research," Journal of Peace Research, 6 (1969), p. 171.

48. Ibid.

49. See Terry Nardin's comments on Galtung's concept of structural violence. Terry Nardin, "Conflicting Conceptions of Political Violence," Political Science Annual: An International Review, ed. Cornelius Potter (Indianapolis: Bobbs-Merrill, 1973), pp. 106-10.

50. See Terry Nardin, "Violence and the State: A Critique of Empirical Political Theory," Sage Professional Papers in Comparative Politics, 2 (1971), pp. 5-72; Barrington Moore, Social Origins of Dictatorship and Democracy: Lord and Peasant in the Making of the Modern World (Boston: Beacon Press, 1967), p. 20, on enclosures in England.

51. Ittila'at, November 13, 1958, p. 1.

52. This is a free translation of an eyewitness account in Ittila'at, November 13, 1958, pp. 1, 17. Additional stories on the eradication effort are reported in later issues of November 15 and 16 of Ittila'at.

53. The only concrete result of the eradication effort was the eventual construction of Kuyi Nuhum-i Aban residential unit in this area.

54. *Iran Times*, August 11, 1978, p. 16. See also Paul Vieille, "Transformation des Rapport Sociaux et Révolution en Iran," *Peuples Méditerranéens*, 8 (Juillet-Septembre, 1979), p. 28.

55. *Guzarishati az Mubarizat*, pp. 54-55.

56. For recent analyses of the 1978-79 revolution see James Bill, "Iran and the Crisis of '78," *Foreign Affairs*, 57 (Winter, 1978/79), pp. 323-42; Robert Graham, *Iran: The Illusion of Power* (London: Croom Helm, 1978); Halliday, *Iran*; L. P. Elwell-Sutton, "The Iranian Revolution," *International Journal*, 34 (Summer, 1979), pp. 391-407; "The Iranian Revolution," special issue of *Race and Class*, 21 (Summer, 1979); Sepehr Zabih, *Iran's Revolutionary Upheaval: An Interpretive Essay* (San Francisco: Alchemy, 1979); Shahram Chubin, "Repercussions of the Crisis in Iran," *Survival*, 21 (May-June, 1979), pp. 98-106; Leonard Binder, "Revolution in Iran: Red, White, Blue or Black," *Bulletin of the Atomic Scientists*, 35 (January, 1979), pp. 48-54; George Lenczowski, "Iran: The Awful Truth Behind the Shah's Fall and the Mullah's Rise," *American Spectator*, 12 (December, 1979), pp. 12-15; "Iran in Revolution," special issue of *Merip Reports*, 9 (March-April, 1979).

57. Charles Tilly, *From Mobilization to Revolution* (Reading, Mass.: Addison-Wesley, 1978), p. 69.

58. J. P. Nettl, *Political Mobilization: A Sociological Analysis of Methods and Concepts* (London: Faber and Faber, 1967), p. 136.

59. See Owen Lynch's discussion of these conditions in his "Political Mobilisation and Ethnicity among Adi-Dravidas in a Bombay Slum," *Economic and Political Weekly*, 9 (September 28, 1974), pp. 1658, 1665. See also Tilly, *From Mobilization to Revolution*, pp. 54-55.

60. *Guzarishati az Mubarizat*, p. 119.

61. *Shakhisha-yi Ijtima'i*, p. 390.

62. Leonard Binder, "The Proofs of Islam: Religion and Politics in Iran," *Arabic and Islamic Studies in Honor of Hamilton A. R. Gibb*, ed. George Makdisi (Cambridge: Harvard University Press, 1965), p. 126.

63. See Hamid Algar, "The Oppositional Role of the Ulama in Twentieth Century Iran," *Scholars, Saints, and Sufis: Muslim Religious Institutions in the Middle East since 1500*, ed. Nikki Keddie (Berkeley: University of California Press, 1978); Nikki Keddie, "The Roots of the Ulama's Power in Modern Iran," in *ibid.*; Shahrough Akhavi, *Religion and Politics in Contemporary Iran: Clergy-State Relations in the Pahlavi Period* (Albany: State University of New York Press, 1980); Michael Fischer, *Iran: From Religious Dispute to Revolution* (Cambridge: Harvard University Press, 1980).

64. The number of mosques and holy shrines in Iran are estimated to be 80,000 and the mullahs about 180,000. See Zabih, *Iran's Revolutionary Upheaval*, p. 20. A final precipitant of the clergy's disenchantment with the Shah was the decision by the government of Prime Minister Jamshid Amuzegar in 1977 to stop the annual cash payment of several million dollars by the government to the clergy. This arrangement had been in oprtation for several years as part of the Shah's effort to appease the clergy after land refor eliminated the ulama's control over *waqf* lands.

65. See Peter Chelkowski, ed., *Ta'ziyeh Ritual and Drama in Iran* (New York: New York University Press, 197'

66. Elwell-Sutton, "The Iranian Revolution," p.

67. Vieille, "Transformation des Rapport Socia p. 34.

68. Ruhullah Khumanyi, *Vilayat-i Faqih* (Tehr p. 158.

69. Algar, "The Oppositional Role of the U

70. Ruhullah Khumanyi, "The Message of A Khomaini to the Brave People of Iran on the Oc Moharram," *Iran Erupts*, ed. Ali-Reza Nobari Iran-America Documentation Group, 1978), pp.

71. Ann K. S. Lambton, "A Reconsider Position of the *Marja' Al-Taqlid* and the F Institution," *Studia Islamica*, 20 (1964),

72. *Guzarishati az Mubarizat*, p.

73. In an interesting recent art revolution, Sharif Arani (pseudonym) remarks about this group's religious uprooted people knew no sophisticat they knew something about their re debating whether Khomeini was the his precursor. Many would chant breakers--Abraham, Mohammed, and Sharif Arani, "Iran: From the S Khomeini's Demogogic Theocracy pp. 12-13.

74. It is interesting indoctrination through the to adult literacy classes. for beginners in adult li Education, the reader is King is kind"; "The Peo country." See Iran, M *Binivisim: Baray-i Am* p. 29.

75. *Washingto*

76. *New York*

77. See ob and Walton, *Urba*

Years of Economic Development," Iran Under the Pahlavis, ed. George Lenczowski (Stanford, Cal.: Hoover Institution Press, 1978), p. 139.

15. William Bartsch, "The Industrial Labor Force of Iran: Problems of Recruitment, Training and Productivity," in Momeni, The Population of Iran: A Selection of Readings, p. 319.

16. Ibid.

17. Ibid., p. 317.

18. Huntington, Political Order in Changing Societies, p. 284.

19. Ibid.

20. Ibid., p. 285.

21. Ashraf, "Iran: Imperialism, Class and Modernization," p. 338.

22. Halliday, Iran, p. 198.

23. Ibid., p. 199.

24. Bharier, Economic Development in Iran, p. 36.

25. Abrahamian, "The Crowd in Iranian Politics," p. 202.

26. For a good discussion of the Tudeh party's activities in the trade unions see Sepehr Zabih, The Communist Movement in Iran (Berkeley: University of California Press, 1966), pp. 149-61.

27. Abrahamian, "The Crowd in Iranian Politics," p. 203.

28. Leonard Binder, Iran: Political Development in a Changing Society (Berkeley: University of California Press, 1962), p. 192.

29. Ibid., p. 188.

30. Ibid.

31. Ashraf, "Iran: Imperialism, Class and Modernization," p. 340.

32. Halliday, Iran, p. 203.

33. Jahangir Amuzegar, Iran: An Economic Profile (Washington, D.C.: Middle East Institute, 1977), pp. 234-36.

34. Halliday, Iran., p. 203.

35. For the six-point program see E. A. Bayne, Persian Kingship in Transition (New York: American Universities Field Staff, 1968), Appendix II, p. 255.

36. Halliday, Iran., p. 207.

37. Ashraf, "Iran: Imperialism, Class and Modernization," p. 345.

38. Karl Marx, The Poverty of Philosophy (New York: International Publishers, 1963), p. 173. See also Lopreato and Hazelrigg, Class, Conflict, and Mobility, pp. 23-24.

1. Firouz Vakil, "Iran's Basic Macro-Economic Problems: A 20-Year Horizon," in Jacqz, Iran, p. 83.

2. Ibid.

3. Looney, A Developmental Strategy for Iran, pp. 4-7.

4. See A. F. K. Organski, The Stages of Political Development (New York: Alfred A. Knopf, 1965), pp. 122-39. This should put another damper on Huntington's recommendations on forced slowdown of social mobilization to prevent political instability. See Samuel Huntington, "Political Development and Political Decay," World Politics, 17 (April, 1965), pp. 419-21.

5. Karpat, Gecekondu, p. 232.

6. William Mangin, "Introduction," in Mangin, Peasants in Cities, p. xxvi.

7. See the interesting report by Ladan Boroumand, "Les Ouvriers, l'Ingenieur et les Militantes Khomeinistes Entretien dans une Usine au Lendemain de la Révolution," Peuples Méditerranéens, 8 (Juillet-Septembre, 1979), pp. 59-76.

8. Kar, 3 Khurdad 1358/1979, p. 5.

9. See for example Abol-Hassan Banisadr, Iqtisad-i Tuwhidi (Tehran: Fadak, n.d.), pp. 335-36, 351.

10. Iran, Preamble to the Constitution, section entitled "The Way of Government in Islam" (1979).

11. Iran, Constitution, art. 43, sec. 1 (1979). I am indebted to Professor Changiz Vafai for bringing these matters in the Iranian constitution to my attention.

12. Iran Express, February 2, 1980, p. 9.

13. As news and rumors about the government's housing policy spread, a steady flow of migrants in serach of free housing to Tehran was noted. This occurred even though the poor migrants had not been a major beneficiary of the policy. Alarmed by this development, the mayor of Tehran had to make several public announcements discouraging the migrants' new influx to the capital.

14. See the full story in Iran Express, February 2, 1980, p. 6.

15. For a report on one such incident see Iran Times, February 8, 1980, p. 12.

16. See Lloyd, Slums of Hope, p. 202.

Abrahamian, Ervand. "The Crowd in Iranian Politics, 1905-53." Past and Present, 41 (December, 1968), 184-210.

————. "The Crowd in the Persian Revolution." Iranian Studies, 2 (Autumn, 1969), 128-50.

————. "Social Bases of Iranian Politics: The Tudeh Party, 1941-53." Ph.D. dissertation, Columbia University, 1969.

Abrams, Charles. Man's Struggle for Shelter in an Urbanizing World. Cambridge: M.I.T. Press, 1964.

Abu-Lughod, Janet. Cairo: 1001 Years of the City Victorious. Princeton: Princeton University Press, 1971.

————. "Migrant Adjustment to City Life: The Egyptian Case." American Journal of Sociology, 67 (July, 1961), 22-32.

————. "Rural Migration and Politics in Egypt." Rural Politics and Social Change in the Middle East. Edited by Richard Antoun and Iliya Harik. Bloomington: Indiana University Press, 1972.

————. "Urban-Rural Differences as a Function of the Demographic Transition: Egyptian Data and an Analytical Model." American Journal of Sociology, 69 (March, 1964), 476-90.

————. "Urbanization in Egypt: Present State and Future Prospects." Economic Development and Culture Change, 13 (April, 1965), 313-43.

————. "Varieties of Urban Experience: Contrast, Coexistence, and Coalescence in Cairo." Middle Eastern Cities. Edited by Ira Lapidus. Berkeley: University of California Press, 1969.

————, and Hay, Richard, Jr., eds. Third World Urbanization. Chicago: Maarufa, 1977.

Ajami, Ismail. "Agrarian Reform, Modernization of Peasants and Agricultural Development in Iran." Iran: Past, Present, and Future. Edited by Jane Jacqz. New York: Aspen Institute for Humanistic Studies, 1976.

————. "Khulqiyyat, Mu'taqidat, va Aruzuha-yi Shughli-yi Rusta'iyyan." Ulum-i Ijtima'i, 1 (Bahman, 1348/1970), 26-47.

Akhavi, Sharough. Religion and Politics in Iran: Clergy-State Relations in the Pahlavi Period. Albany: State University of New York Press, 1980.

Alavi, Hamza. "Peasants and Revolution." The Socialist Register. Edited by Ralph Miliband and John Saville. New York: Monthly Review Press, 1965.

Algar, Hamid. "The Oppositional Role of the Ulama in Twentieth Century Iran." Scholars, Saints, and Sufis: Muslim Religious Institutions in the Middle East since 1500. Edited by Nikki Keddie. Berkeley: University of California Press, 1978.

Almond, Gabriel, and Powell, G. Bingham, Jr. Comparative Politics: A Developmental Approach. Boston: Little, Brown, 1966.

Amani, Mihdi. "Avvalin Sarshumari-yi Jam'iyyat-i Tehran." Ulum-i Ijtima'i, 1 (Bahman, 1348/1970), 87-94.

—————. Shahrgara-i va Shahrnishini dar Iran. Tehran: University of Tehran, 1350/1971.

Amin, Samir. Imperialism and Unequal Development. New York: Monthly Review, 1977.

—————. Unequal Development. New York: Monthly Review, 1976.

Amuzegar, Jahangir. Iran: An Economic Profile. Washington, D.C.: Middle East Institute, 1977.

Antonovsky, Aaron. "Toward a Refinement of the 'Marginal Man' Concept." Social Forces, 35 (October, 1956), 57-62.

Antoun, Richard, and Harik, Iliya, eds. Rural Politics and Social Change in the Middle East. Bloomington: Indiana University Press, 1972.

Arani, Sharif. "Iran: From the Shah's Dictatorship to Khomeini's Demagogic Theocracy." Dissent, 27 (Winter, 1980), 9-26.

Arberry, Arthur. Shiraz: Persian City of Saints and Poets. Norman: University of Oklahoma Press, 1960.

Aresvik, Oddvar. The Agricultural Development of Iran. New York: Praeger Publishers, 1976.

Ashraf, Ahmad. "Iran: Imperialism, Class and Modernization from Above." Ph.D. dissertation, New School for Social Research, 1971.

—————. "Vizhgiha-yi Tarihki-yi Shahrnishini dar Iran: Dowrih-yi Islami." Ulum-i Ijtima'i, 1 (Tir, 1353/1974), 24-41.

—————, and Safai, Marsha. The Role of the Rural Organizations in Rural Development: The Case of Iran. Tehran, 1977.

Baer, Gabriel. "The City." Readings in Arab Middle Eastern Societies and Culture. Edited by Abdulla Lutfiyya and Charles Churchill. The Hague: Mouton, 1970.

—————. Population and Society in the Arab East. Translated by Hanna Szoke. New York: Frederick A. Praeger, 1964.

Bairoch, Paul. Urban Unemployment in Developing Countries: The Nature of the Problem and Proposal for Its Solution. Geneva: International Labour Office, 1973.

Bakhtari, H. *Az Shahr-i Tehran Chih Midanim*. Tehran: Sa'ib, 1345/1966.

Banani, Amin. *The Modernization of Iran: 1921-1941*. Stanford: Stanford University Press, 1961.

Banisadr, Abol-Hassan. *Iqtisad-i Tuwhidi*. Tehran: Fadak, n.d.

Banuazizi, Ali. "Migration and Urban Poverty: Case Studies of Squatters in Tehran." Paper presented at the 8th annual meeting of the Middle East Studies Association. Boston, Mass. November, 1974.

Bartsch, William. *Problems of Employment Creation in Iran*. Geneva: International Labour Office, 1970.

――――――. "The Industrial Labor Force of Iran: Problems of Recruitment, Training and Productivity." *The Population of Iran: A Selection of Readings*. Edited by Jamshid Momeni. Honolulu: East-West Center, 1977.

Bayne, E. A. *Persian Kingship in Transition*. New York: American Universities Field Staff, 1968.

Behrangi, Samad. *The Little Black Fish and Other Modern Persian Stories*. Translated by Eric and Mary Hooglund. Washington, D.C.: Three Continents Press, 1976.

Bemont, Fredy. *Les Villes de l'Iran: Des Cités d'Autrefois à l'Urbanisme Contemporain*. Paris: l'Auteur, 1969.

Benard, Cheryl, and Khalilzad, Zalmay. "Secularization, Industrialization, and Khomeini's Islamic Republic." *Political Science Quarterly*, 94 (Summer, 1979), 229-41.

Benet, Francisco. "The Ideology of Islamic Urbanization." *International Journal of Comparative Sociology*, 4 (1963), 211-26.

Berger, Morroe, ed. *The New Metropolis in the Arab World*. New Delhi: Allied Publishers, 1963.

Berry, Brian. "City Size Distribution and Economic Development." *Economic Development and Cultural Change*, 9 (July, 1961), 573-87.

Bharier, Julian. *Economic Development in Iran: 1900-1972*. New York: Oxford University Press, 1971.

――――――. "The Growth of Towns and Villages in Iran, 1900-66." *Middle Eastern Studies*, 8 (January, 1972), 51-61.

――――――. "A Note on the Population of Iran, 1900-1966." *Population Studies*, 22 (July, 1968), 273-79.

Bill, James. "Iran and the Crisis of '78." *Foreign Affairs*, 57 (Winter, 1978/79), 323-42.

――――――. *The Politics of Iran: Groups, Classes and Modernization*. Columbus, Ohio: Charles E. Merrill, 1972.

――――――, and Hardgrave, Robert. *Comparative Politics: The Quest for Theory*. Columbus, Ohio: Charles E. Merrill, 1973.

Binder, Leonard. _Iran: Political Development in a Changing Society_. Berkeley: University of California Press, 1962.

——————. "The Proofs of Islam: Religion and Politics in Iran." _Arabic and Islamic Studies in Honor of Hamilton A. R. Gibb_. Edited by George Makdisi. Cambridge: Harvard University Press, 1965.

——————. "Revolution in Iran: Red, White, Blue, or Black." _Bulletin of the Atomic Scientists_, 35 (January, 1979), 48-54.

Bonilla, Frank. "Rio's Favelas: The Rural Slum Within the City." _Peasants in Cities: Readings in the Anthropology of Urbanization_. Edited by William Mangin. Boston: Hougton Mifflin, 1970.

Bonine, Michael. "From Uruk to Casablanca: Perspectives on the Urban Experience of the Middle East." _Journal of Urban History_, 3 (February, 1977), 141-80.

——————. "The Morphogenesis of Iranian Cities." _Annals of the Association of American Geographers_, 69 (June, 1979), 208-24.

——————. "Urban Studies in the Middle East." _Middle East Studies Association Bulletin_, 10 (October, 1976), 1-37.

Boroumand, Ladan. "Les Ouvriers, l'Ingenieur et les Militantes Entretien dans une Usine au Lendemain de la Révolution." _Peuples Méditerranéens_, 8 (Juillet-Septembre, 1979), 59-76.

Bourgey, A., and Phares, J. "Les Bidonvilles de l'Agglomeration de Beyrouth." _Revue de Géographie de Lyon_, 48 (1973), 107-39.

Breese, Gerald. _Urbanization in Newly Developing Countries_. Englewood Cliffs, N.J.: Prentice-Hall, 1966.

——————, ed. _The City in Newly Developing Countries: Readings on Urbanism and Urbanization_. Englewood Cliffs, N.J.: Prentice-Hall, 1969.

Brown, Alan, and Neuberger, Egon, eds. _Internal Migration: A Comparative Perspective_. New York: Academic Press, 1977.

Brown, L. Carl. "Introduction." _From Madina to Metropolis: Heritage and Change in the Near Eastern City_. Edited by L. Carl Brown. Princeton, N.J.: Darwin Press, 1973.

——————, ed. _From Madina to Metropolis: Heritage and Change in the Near Eastern City_. Princeton, N.J.: Darwin Press, 1973.

Brun, Thierry, and Dumont, Rene. "Iran: Imperial Pretensions and Agricultural Dependence." _Merip Reports_, 8 (October, 1978), 15-20.

Butterworth, Douglas. "A Study of the Urbanization Process among Mixtec Migrants from Tilantongo in Mexico City." _Peasants in Cities: Readings in the Anthropology of_

Urbanization. Edited by William Mangin. Boston: Houghton Mifflin, 1970.

Bwy, Douglas. "Political Instability in Latin America: The Cross Cultural Test of a Causal Model." Latin American Research Review, 3 (1968), 17-66.

Cahen, Claude. "Y a-t-il eu des Corporations Professionelles dans le Monde Musulman Classique?" The Islamic City. Edited by Albert Hourani and S. M. Stern. Philadelphia: University of Pennsylvania Press, 1970.

Cameron, David, Hendricks, J. Stephen, and Hofferbert, Richard. "Urbanization, Social Structure, Mass Politics: A Comparison Within Five Nations." Comparative Political Studies, 5 (October, 1972), 259-90.

Carey, Jane, and Carey, Andrew. "Iranian Agriculture and Its Development: 1952-1973." International Journal of Middle East Studies, 7 (July, 1976), 359-82.

Chandler, Tertius, and Fox, Gerald. 3000 Years of Urban Growth. New York: Academic Press, 1974.

Chelkowski, Peter, ed. Ta'ziyeh Ritual and Drama in Iran. New York: New York University Press, 1979.

Chirikha-yi Fada'i-yi Khalq-i Iran. Guzarishati az Mubarizat-i Daliranih-yi Mardum-i Kharij az Mahdudih. Tehran, 1357/1978.

Chubin, Shahram. "Repercussions of the Crisis in Iran." Survival, 21 (May-June, 1979), 98-106.

Clarke, John. The Iranian City of Shiraz. Durham, England: University of Durham, Department of Geography, 1963.

—————, and Clark, Brian D. Kermanshah: An Iranian Provincial City. Durham, England: University of Durham, Department of Geography, 1969.

—————, and Fisher, W. B., eds. Populations of the Middle East and North Africa: A Geographical Approach. London: University of London Press, 1972.

College of Social Work. "Barrisi-yi Awza'-i Iqtisadi, Ijtima'i, va Bihdashti va Barrisi-yi Niyazmandiha-yi Sakinan-i Mantaqih-yi Khazanih-yi Fallah. Tehran, n.d. (mimeographed).

—————. Tasviri as Awza'-i Ijtima'i-yi Kuyi Nuhum-i Aban. Tehran, 1345/1966.

Collier, David. Squatters and Oligarchs: Authoritarian Rule and Policy Change in Peru. Baltimore: Johns Hopkins University Press, 1976.

Colton, Elizabeth. "Community Programmes for Low-Income Populations in Urban Settlements of Developing Countries." Report prepared for the United Nations, n.d. (mimeographed).

Cornelius, Wayne, Jr. Politics and the Migrant Poor in Mexico City. Stanford: Stanford University Press, 1975.

————. "Urbanization as an Agent in Latin American Political Instability: The Case of Mexico." American Political Science Review, 63 (September, 1969), 833-57.

————, and Dietz, Henry. "Urbanization, Demand-Making, and Political System 'Overload': Political Participation Among the Migrant Poor in Latin American Cities." Paper presented at the 69th Annual Meeting of the American Political Science Association. New Orleans, La. September, 1973.

————, and Trueblood, Felicity, eds. Latin American Urban Research, Vol. 4. Beverly Hills: Sage Publications, 1974.

Costello, V. F. Kashan: A City and Region of Iran. London: Bowker, 1976.

————. Urbanization in the Middle East. Cambridge: Cambridge University Press, 1977.

Cottam, Richard. Nationalism in Iran. Pittsburgh: University of Pittsburgh Press, 1964.

————. "Revolutionary Iran." Current History, 78 (January, 1980), 12-16, 34-35.

Craig, Daniel. "The Impact of Land Reform on an Iranian Village." Middle East Journal, 32 (Spring, 1978), 141-54.

Curzon, George. Persia and the Persian Question. Vol. 1. London: Frank Cass, 1966.

Daftary, Farhad. "Development Planning in Iran: A Historical Survey." Iranian Studies, 6 (Autumn, 1973), 176-228.

Davis, Kingsley. World Urbanization 1950-1970. 2 Vols. University of California, Berkeley, Institute of International Studies, 1969.

————, and Golden, Hilda Hertz. "Urbanization and the Development of Pre-Industrial Areas." Economic Development and Cultural Change, 3 (October, 1954), 6-26.

Dawson, Robert, Prewitt, Kenneth, and Dawson, Karen. Political Socialization. 2d ed. Boston: Little, Brown, 1977.

Deutsch, Karl. "Imperialism and Neocolonialism." Papers of the Peace Science Society (International), 23 (1974), 1-25.

————. Nationalism and Social Communication: An Inquiry into the Foundations of Nationality. Cambridge: M.I.T. Press, 1966.

————. "Social Mobilization and Political Development." American Political Science Review, 55 (September, 1961), 493-514.

Dickie-Clark, H. F. The Marginal Situation: A Sociological Study of a Colored Group. London: Routledge & Kegan Paul, 1966.

162

Dietz, Henry. "Bureaucrat-Client Interactions as Politics: Perceptions and Evaluations by the Urban Poor in Lima, Peru." Paper presented at 74th annual meeting of the American Political Science Association. New York, N.Y. August 31-September 3, 1978.

Doroudian, Reza. "Modernization of Rural Economy in Iran." Iran: Past, Present, and Future. Edited by Jane Jacqz. New York: Aspen Institute for Humanistic Studies, 1976.

Doughty, Paul. "Behind the Back of the City: 'Provincial' Life in Lima, Peru." Peasants in Cities: Readings in the Anthropology of Urbanization. Edited by William Mangin. Boston: Houghton Mifflin, 1970.

Du Toit, Brian, and Safa, Helen, eds. Migration and Urbanization: Models and Adaptive Strategies. The Hague: Mouton, 1975.

Dwyer, D. J. People and Housing in Third World Cities: Perspectives on the Problem of Spontaneous Settlements. London: Longman, 1975.

Easton, David, and Dennis, Jack. Children in the Political System: Origins of Political Legitimacy. New York: McGraw-Hill, 1969.

Eickelman, Dale. "Is There an Islamic City? The Making of a Quarter in a Moroccan Town." International Journal of Middle East Studies, 5 (June, 1974), 274-94.

Elkabir, Y. "The Assimilation of Rural Migrants in Tripoli." Ph.D. dissertation, Case Western Reserve University, 1972.

El-Shakhs, Salah. "Development, Primacy, and Systems in Cities." Journal of Developing Areas, 7 (October, 1972), 11-35.

Elwell-Sutton, L. P. "The Iranian Revolution." International Journal, 34 (Summer, 1979), 391-407.

English, Paul. City and Village in Iran: Settlement and Economy in the Kirman Basin. Madison: University of Wisconsin Press, 1966.

————. "Culture Change and the Structure of a Persian City." The Conflict of Traditionalism and Modernism in the Muslim Middle East. Edited by Carl Leiden. Austin: University of Texas, Humanities Research Center, 1966.

————. "The Traditional City of Herat, Afghanistan." From Madina to Metropolis: Heritage and Change in the Near Eastern City. Edited by L. Carl Brown. Princeton, N.J.: Darwin Press, 1973.

Farmanfarmayan, Sattarih. Piramun-i Ruspigari dar Shahr-i Tehran. Tehran: College of Social Work, 1349/1971.

Feierabend, Ivo, Feierabend, Rosalind, and Nesvold, Betty. "Social Change and Political Violence: Cross-National Patterns." Violence in America: Historical and

    Comparative Perspectives. Edited by Hugh Graham and Ted
    Gurr. New York: Bantam, 1969.

Firoozi, Ferydoon. "Iranian Censuses 1956 and 1966: A
    Comparative Analysis." _Middle East Journal_, 24 (Spring,
    1970), 220-28.

——————. "Tehran--A Demographic and Economic Analysis."
    Middle Eastern Studies, 10 (January, 1974), 60-76.

Fischer, Michael. _Iran: From Religious Dispute to Revolution_.
    Cambridge: Harvard University Press, 1980.

Freivals, John. "Farm Corporations in Iran: An Alternative
    to Traditional Agriculture." _Middle East Journal_, 26
    (Spring, 1972), 185-93.

Galtung, Johan. "A Structural Theory of Imperialism."
    Journal of Peace Research, 8 (1971), 81-117.

——————. "Violence, Peace, and Peace Research." _Journal of
    Peace Research_, 6 (1969), 167-92.

Gaube, Heinz. _Iranian Cities_. New York: New York University
    Press, 1979.

Germani, Gino. _Marginality_. New Brunswick, N.J.:
    Transaction, 1980.

Gilbar, Gad. "Demographic Developments in Late Qajar Persia,
    1870-1906." _Asian and African Studies_, 2 (1976), 125-56.

Goldberg, Milton. "A Qualification of the Marginal Man
    Theory." _American Sociological Review_, 6 (February,
    1941), 52-58.

Goldrich, Daniel, Pratt, Raymond, and Schuller, C. R. "The
    Political Integration of Lower-Class Urban Settlements
    in Chile and Peru." _Masses in Latin America_. Edited by
    Irving Louis Horowitz. New York: Oxford University
    Press, 1970.

Golovonsky, David. "The Marginal Man Concept: An Analysis and
    Critique." _Social Forces_, 30 (March, 1952), 333-39.

Graham, Robert. _Iran: The Illusion of Power_. London: Croom
    Helm, 1978.

Greenstein, Fred. "Political Socialization." _International
    Encyclopedia of the Social Sciences_. Vol. 14, 552.

Gulick, John. "Baghdad: Portrait of a City in Physical and
    Cultural Change." _Journal of the American Institute of
    Planners_, 3 (1967), 246-55.

——————. _Tripoli: A Modern Arab City_. Cambridge: Harvard
    University Press, 1967.

——————. "Village and City: Cultural Discontinuities in
    Twentieth Century Middle Eastern Cultures." _Middle
    Eastern Cities_. Edited by Ira Lapidus. Berkeley:
    University of California Press, 1969.

Gurr, Ted. _Why Men Rebel_. Princeton: Princeton University
    Press, 1970.

Halliday, Fred. Iran: Dictatorship and Development. New York: Penguin, 1979.

Harrison, Robert. "Migrants in the City of Tripoli, Libya." Geographical Review, 57 (July, 1967), 397-423.

Hauser, Philip. "The Social, Economic, and Technological Problems of Rapid Urbanization." Industrialization and Society. Edited by Bert Hoselitz and Wilbert Moore. Paris: Mouton, 1966.

——————. "Some Cultural and Personal Characteristics of the Less Developed Areas." Political Development and Social Change. Edited by Jason Finkle and Richard Gable. New York: John Wiley, 1968.

Hemmasi, Mohammad. Migration in Iran: A Quantitative Approach. Shiraz: Pahlavi University, 1974.

——————. "Tehran in Transition: A Study in Comparative Factorial Ecology." The Population of Iran: A Selection of Readings. Edited by Jamshid Momeni. Honolulu: East-West Center, 1977.

Hess, Robert. "The Socialization of Attitudes Toward Political Authority: Some Crossnational Comparisons." International Social Science Journal, 15 (1963), 542-59.

Hirschfeld, Yair. "Decline and Fall of the Pahlavis." Jerusalem Quarterly, 12 (Summer, 1979), 20-33.

Hobbs, John. "Land Reform in Iran: A 'Revolution from Above.'" ORBIS, 7 (Fall, 1963), 617-30.

Hooglund, Eric. "The Khwushnishin Population of Iran." Iranian Studies, 6 (Autumn, 1973), 229-45.

Hoselitz, Bert. "The Role of Cities in the Economic Growth of Underdeveloped Countries." The City in Newly Developing Countries: Readings on Urbanism and Urbanization. Edited by Gerald Breese. Englewood Cliffs, N.J.: Prentice-Hall, 1969.

——————. Sociological Aspects of Economic Growth. Glencoe, Ill.: The Free Press, 1960.

Hourani, Albert. "Introduction: The Islamic City in the Light of Recent Research." The Islamic City. Edited by Albert Hourani and S. M. Stern. Philadelphia: University of Pennsylvania Press, 1970.

——————, and Stern, S. M., eds. The Islamic City. Philadelphia: University of Pennsylvania Press, 1970.

Huntington, Samuel. "Political Development and Political Decay." World Politics, 17 (April, 1965), 386-430.

——————. "The Political Modernization of Traditional Monarchies." Daedelus, 95 (Summer, 1966), 763-88.

——————. Political Order in Changing Societies. New Haven: Yale University Press, 1968.

Ibrahim, Saad. "Over-Urbanization and Under-Urbanization: The Case of the Arab World." International Journal of Middle East Studies, 6 (January, 1975), 29-45.

Inayatullah. Cooperatives and Development in Asia: A Study of Cooperatives in Fourteen Rural Communities of Iran, Pakistan and Ceylon. Geneva: United Nations Research Institute for Social Development, 1972.

Inkeles, Alex, and Smith, David. Becoming Modern: Individual Change in Six Developing Countries. Cambridge: Harvard University Press, 1974.

Iran Almanac and Book of Facts. Tehran: Echo of Iran, 1961-1971.

Iran. Bank Markazi. Annual Report and Balance Sheet. 1968.

——————. Ministry of Interior. Guzarish-i Khulasah-yi Sarshumari-yi Umumi-yi Kishvar. 2 vols. 1956.

——————. Ministry of Interior. Kitab-i Jughrafiya va Asami-yi Dihat-i Kishvar. 3 vols. 1329-1331/1951-1953.

——————. Ministry of Labor and Social Affairs. General Department of Statistics. A Study of Manpower of Iran. 1968.

——————. Plan Organization. Fourth National Development Plan: 1968-1972.

——————. Plan Organization. Iranian Statistical Center. National Census of Population and Housing. 168. 1968.

——————. Plan and Budget Organization. Iranian Statistical Center. Amar-i Muntakhab. 1973-1976.

——————. Plan and Budget Organization. Iranian Statistical Center. "Barrisi-yi Ijmali-yi Mujajirat bih Manatiq-i Shahri" (mimeographed).

——————. Plan and Budget Organization. Iranian Statistical Center. Guzarish-i Natyij-i Magadamati-yi Sarshumari-yi Umumi-yi Nufus va Maskan. 1976.

——————. Plan and Budget Organization. Iranian Statistical Center. Salnamih-yi Amari-yi Kishvar. 1972-1976.

——————. Plan and Budget Organization. Pazhuhish Amari Baray-i Ira'i-yi Sima-yi Muhajiran dar Tehran va Tabriz. 1977.

——————. Plan and Budget Organization. Shakhisha-yi Ijtima'i-yi Iran. 1978.

Issawi, Charles. "Economic Change and Urbanization in the Middle East." Middle Eastern Cities. Edited by Ira Lapidus. Berkeley: University of California Press, 1969.

——————. "The Iranian Economy 1925-1975: Fifty Years of Economic Development." Iran Under the Pahlavis. Edited by George Lenczowski. Stanford, Cal.: Hoover Institution Press, 1978.

—————, ed. The Economic History of Iran: 1800-1914.
    Chicago: University of Chicago Press, 1971.

Izadi, Kazim. "Savadamuzi va Rabitih-yi on ba Taharruk-i
    Shugli va Jughrafiya'i-yi Savadamuzan." Ulum-i Ijtima'i,
    1 (Tir, 1353/1974), 77-89.

Jacqz, Jane, ed. Iran: Past, Present, and Future. New York:
    Aspen Institute for Humanistic Studies, 1976.

Javahir-Kalam, Abdul'aziz. Tarikh-i Tehran. Part 1. Tehran,
    1325/1946.

Jefferson, Mark. "The Law of the Primate City." Geographical
    Review, 29 (April, 1939), 226-32.

Kamerschen, David. "Further Analysis of Overurbanization."
    Economic Development and Cultural Change, 2 (January,
    1969), 235-53.

Karpat, Kemal. The Gecekondu: Rural Migration and Urbaniza-
    tion. Cambridge, England: Cambridge University Press,
    1976.

—————. "The Politics of Transition: Political Attitudes
    and Party Affiliation in the Turkish Gecekondu."
    Political Participation in Turkey: Historical Background
    and Present Problems. Edited by Engin Akarli with
    Gabriel Ben-Dor. Istanbul: Bogazici University
    Publications, 1975.

Katouzian, M. A. "Oil Versus Agriculture: A Case of Dual
    Resource Depletion in Iran." Journal of Peasant Studies,
    5 (August, 1978), 347-69.

Kaufman, Clifford. "Urbanization, Material Satisfaction, and
    Mass Political Involvement: The Poor in Mexico City."
    Comparative Political Studies, 4 (October, 1971), 295-
    319.

Kayhan Publishers. Kitab-i Sal, Bazar-i Sal. Tehran:
    Kayhan, 1341/1962.

Kazemi, Farhad. "The Migrant Population of Tehran: Political
    Attitudes and Behavior." Paper presented at the 9th
    annual meeting of the Middle East Studies Association.
    Louisville, Ky. November, 1975.

—————. "Rural-to-Urban Migration and Political Demand-
    Making Among Migrants in Iran." Paper presented at the
    74th annual meeting of the American Political Science
    Association. New York, N.Y. August 31-September 3,
    1978.

—————. "Social Mobilization and Domestic Violence in
    Iran: 1946-1968." Ph.D. dissertation, University of
    Michigan, 1973.

—————. "The Study of Political Unrest and Violence: The
    Middle East." Middle East Studies Association Bulletin,
    12 (May, 1978), 17-31.

—————, and Abrahamian, Ervand. "The Nonrevolutionary
    Peasantry of Modern Iran." State and Society in Iran.

Special issue of Iranian Studies, 11. Edited by Amin
Banani. Boston: Society for Iranian Studies, 1978.

Keddie, Nikki. "The Iranian Power Structure and Social Change
1800-1969: An Overview." International Journal of Middle
East Studies, 2 (January, 1971), 3-20.

————. "The Iranian Village Before and After Land Reform."
Journal of Contemporary History, 3 (July, 1968), 69-91.

————. "The Roots of the Ulama's Power in Modern Iran."
Scholars, Saints, and Sufis: Muslim Religious Institu-
tions in the Middle East since 1500. Edited by Nikki
Keddie. Berkeley: University of California Press, 1978.

————. "Stratification, Social Control, and Capitalism in
Iranian Villages: Before and After Land Reform." Rural
Politics and Social Change in the Middle East. Edited
by Richard Antoun and Iliya Harik. Bloomington: Indiana
University Press, 1972.

Kerckhoff, Alan, and McCormick, Thomas. "Marginal Status and
the Marginal Personality." Social Forces, 34 (October,
1955), 48-55.

Khamsi, Farhad. "Land Reform in Iran." Monthly Review, 21
(June, 1969), 20-28.

Khumanyi, Ruhullah. "The Message of Ayatollah Khomaini to the
Brave People of Iran on the Occasion of Moharram." Iran
Erupts. Edited by Ali-Reza Nobari. Stanford, Cal.:
Iran-America Documentation Group, 1978.

————. Vilayat-i Faqih. Tehran: n.d.

Khusravi, Khusrow. Pazhuhishi dar Jami'ih-yi Rusta'i-yi Iran.
Tehran: Payam, 2535/1976.

Kirkham, James, Levy, Sheldon, and Crotty, William.
Assassination and Political Violence. Washington, D.C.:
U.S. Government Printing Office, 1969.

Kornberg, Allan, and Thomas, Norman. "The Political
Socialization of National Legislative Elites in the
United States and Canada." Journal of Politics, 27
(November, 1965), 761-75.

Lambton, Ann K. S. Landlord and Peasant in Persia: A Study
of Land Tenure and Land Revenue Administration. London:
Oxford Univeristy Press, 1953.

————. The Persian Land Reform: 1962-1966. London:
Clarendon Press of Oxford University Press, 1969.

————. "A Reconsideration of the Position of the Marja'
Al-Taqlid and the Religious Institution." Studia
Islamica, 20 (1964), 115-35.

Lapham, Robert. "Population Policies in the Middle East and
North Africa." Middle East Studies Association Bulletin,
11 (May, 1977), 1-30.

Lapidus, Ira. "The Evolution of Muslim Urban Society."
Comparative Studies in Society and History, 15 (January,
1973), 21-50.

——————. "Muslim Cities and Islamic Societies." Middle
Eastern Cities. Edited by Ira Lapidus. Berkeley:
University of California Press, 1969.

——————. "Traditional Muslim Cities: Structure and Change."
From Madina to Metropolis: Heritage and Change in the
Near Eastern City. Edited by L. Carl Brown. Princeton,
N.J.: Darwin Press, 1973.

——————, ed. Middle Eastern Cities. Berkeley: University
of California Press, 1969.

Lee, Everett. "A Theory of Migration." Demography, 3 (1966),
47-57.

Lenczowski, George. "Iran: The Awful Truth Behind the Shah's
Fall and the Mullah's Rise." American Spectator, 12
(December, 1979), 12-15.

Lerner, Daniel. The Passing of Traditional Society:
Modernizing the Middle East. New York: The Free Press,
1964.

Le Tourneau, Roger. "Implications of Rapid Urbanization."
State and Society in Independent North Africa. Edited
by L. Carl Brown. Washington, D.C.: Middle East
Institute, 1966.

Levine, Ned. "Old Culture--New Culture: A Study of Migrants
in Ankara, Turkey." Social Forces, 51 (March, 1973),
355-68.

Lewis, Oscar. "Further Observations on the Folk-Urban
Continuum and Urbanization with Special Reference to
Mexico City." The Study of Urbanization. Edited by
Philip Hauser and Leo Schnore. New York: John Wiley,
1965.

——————. "Urbanization Without Breakdown." Scientific
Monthly, 75 (July, 1952), 31-41.

Linsky, Arnold. "Some Generalizations Concerning Primate
Cities." The City in Newly Developing Countries:
Readings on Urbanism and Urbanization. Edited by Gerald
Breese. Englewood Cliffs, N.J.: Prentice-Hall, 1969.

Lloyd, Peter. Slums of Hope? Shanty Towns of the Third World.
Middlesex, England: Penguin, 1979.

Lockhart, Laurence. Persian Cities. London: Luzac, 1960.

Lomnitz, Larrisa. Networks and Marginality: Life in a
Mexican Shantytown. New York: Academic Press, 1977.

Looney, Robert. A Developmental Strategy for Iran Through
the 1980s. New York: Praeger Publishers, 1977.

——————. The Economic Development of Iran: A Recent Survey
with Projections to 1981. New York: Praeger Publishers,
1973.

Lopreato, Joseph, and Hazelrigg, Lawrence. Class, Conflict, and Mobility: Theories and Studies of Class Structure. San Francisco: Chandler, 1972.

Lynch, Owen. "Political Mobilisation and Ethnicity among Adi-Dravidas in a Bombay Slum." Economic and Political Weekly, 9 (September 28, 1974), 1657-68.

——————. "Potters, Plotters, Prodders in a Bombay Slum: Marx and Meaning or Meaning Versus Marx." Urban Anthropology, 5 (Spring, 1979), 1-27.

Mahdavy, Hossein. "The Coming Crisis in Iran." Foreign Affairs, 44 (October, 1965), 134-46.

McCrone, Donald, and Cnudde, Charles. "Toward a Communications Theory of Democratic Political Development: A Causal Model." American Political Science Review, 61 (March, 1967), 72-79.

McGee, T. G. "Rural-Urban Mobility in South and Southeast Asia. Different Formulations . . . Different Answers?" Third World Urbanization. Edited by Janet Abu-Lughod and Richard Hay, Jr. Chicago: Maaroufa, 1977.

McLachlan, K. S. "Land Reform in Iran." The Cambridge History of Iran. Vol. 1: The Land of Iran. Cambridge, England: Cambridge University Press, 1968.

Mangin, William. "Introduction." Peasants in Cities: Readings in the Anthropology of Urbanization. Edited by William Mangin. Boston: Houghton Mifflin, 1970.

——————. "Latin American Squatter Settlements: A Problem and a Solution." Latin American Research Review, 2 (Summer, 1967), 65-98.

——————, ed. Peasants in Cities: Readings in the Anthropology of Urbanization. Boston: Houghton Mifflin, 1970.

——————, and Turner, John. "Benavides and the Barriada Movement." Shelter and Society. Edited by Paul Oliver. New York: Frederick A. Praeger, 1969.

Marx, Karl. The Class Struggles in France: 1848-1850. New York: International Publishers, 1972.

——————. The Poverty of Philosophy. New York: International Publishers, 1963.

——————, and Engels, Friedrich. The Communist Manifesto. New York: Appleton-Century-Crofts, 1955.

Mehran, Farhad. Income Distribution in Iran: The Statistics of Inequality. Geneva: International Labour Office, 1975.

Mehta, Surrinder. "Some Demographic and Economic Correlates of Primate Cities: A Case for Revaluation." The City in Newly Developing Countries: Readings on Urbanism and Urbanization. Edited by Gerald Breese. Englewood Cliffs, N.J.: Prentice-Hall, 1969.

Menashri, David. "Strange Bedfellows: The Khomeini Coalition." _Jerusalem Quarterly_, 12 (Summer, 1979), 34-48.

Merip Reports. Special issue, "Iran in Revolution," 9 (March-April, 1979).

Momeni, Djamchid. "The Population of Iran: A Dynamic Analysis." Ph.D. dissertation, University of Texas at Austin, 1970.

—————, ed. _The Population of Iran: A Selection of Readings_. Honolulu: East-West Center, 1977.

Monthly Review. Review of the Month, "Iran: The New Crisis of American Hegemony," 30 (February, 1979), 1-24.

Moore, Barrington, Jr. _Social Origins of Dictatorship and Democracy: Lord and Peasant in the Making of the Modern World_. Boston: Beacon Press, 1967.

Morse, David. "Unemployment in Developing Countries." _Political Science Quarterly_, 85 (March, 1970), 1-16.

Mumford, Louis. _The City in History: Its Origins, Its Transformations, and Its Prospects_. New York: Harcourt, Brace and World, 1961.

Nardin, Terry. "Conflicting Conceptions of Political Violence." _Political Science Annual: An International Review_. Edited by Cornelius Potter. Indianapolis: Bobbs-Merrill, 1973.

—————. "Violence and the State: A Critique of Empirical Political Theory." _Sage Professional Papers in Comparative Politics_, 2 (1971), 5-72.

Nelson, Joan. _Access to Power: Politics and the Urban Poor in Developing Nations_. Princeton: Princeton University Press, 1979.

—————. _Migrants, Urban Poverty, and Instability in Developing Nations_. Harvard University, Center for International Affairs, 1969.

—————. "The Urban Poor: Disruption or Political Integration in Third World Cities?" _World Politics_, 22 (April, 1970), 393-414.

Nettl, J. P. _Political Mobilization: A Sociological Analysis of Methods and Concepts_. London: Faber and Faber, 1967.

Nie, Norman, Powel, G. Bingham, Jr., and Prewitt, Kenneth. "Social Structure and Political Participation: Developmental Relationships." _American Political Science Review_, 63 (June, 1969), 361-78; 63 (September, 1969), 808-32.

Nobari, Ali-Reza, ed. _Iran Erupts_. Stanford, Cal." Iran-America Documentation Group, 1978.

Ollman, Bertell. "Marx's Use of 'Class.'" _American Journal of Sociology_, 73 (March, 1968), 573-79.

Organski, A. F. K. The Stages of Political Development. New York: Alfred A. Knopf, 1965.

Pahlavi, Muhammad Riza. Inqilab-i Sifid. Tehran: Bank Milli Press, 1345/1966.

Park, Robert. Race and Culture. Glencoe, Ill.: The Free Press, 1950.

Paydarfar, Ali. "Differential Life-Styles Between Migrants and Nonmigrants: A Case Study of the City of Shiraz, Iran." Demography, 2 (August, 1974), 509-20.

————. "Modernisation Process and Demographic Changes." Sociological Review, 15 (July, 1967), 141-53.

————. Social Change in a Southern Province of Iran. Chapel Hill: Institute for Research in Social Science, University of North Carolina, 1974.

Peeler, John. "Urbanization and Politics." Sage Professional Papers in Comparative Politics, 6 (1977), 5-56.

Perlman, Janice. The Myth of Marginality: Urban Poverty in Rio de Janeiro. Berkeley: University of California Press, 1976.

Pesaran, M. G. "Income Distribution and Its Major Determinants in Iran." Iran: Past, Present, and Future. Edited by Jane Jacqz. New York: Aspen Institute for Humanistic Studies, 1976.

Peshkin, Alan, and Cohen, Ronald. "The Values of Modernization." Journal of Developing Areas, 2 (October, 1967), 7-21.

Peterson, Karen. "Villagers in Cairo: Hypotheses Versus Data." American Journal of Sociology, 77 (November, 1971), 560-73.

Petras, James. Critical Perspectives on Imperialism and Social Class in the Third World. New York: Monthly Review, 1978.

Phillips, Doris. "Rural to Urban Migration in Iraq." Economic Development and Cultural Change, 7 (July, 1959), 405-21.

Portes, Alejandro. "Rationality in the Slum: An Essay on Interpretive Sociology." Comparative Studies in Society and History, 14 (June, 1972), 268-86.

————, and Walton, John. Urban Latin America: The Political Condition from Above and Below. Austin: University of Texas Press, 1976.

Pye, Lucian. "The Political Implications of Urbanization and the Development Process." The City in Newly Developing Countries: Readings on Urbanism and Urbanization. Edited by Gerald Breese. Englewood Cliffs, N.J.: Prentice-Hall, 1969.

Race and Class. Special issue, "The Iranian Revolution," 21 (Summer, 1979).

Ravenstein, E. G. "The Laws of Migration." Journal of the Royal Statistical Society, 48 (June, 1885), 167-227.

──────. "The Laws of Migration." Journal of the Royal Statistical Society, 52 (June, 1889), 241-301.

Redfield, Robert, and Singer, Milton. "The Cultural Role of Cities." Economic Development and Cultural Change, 3 (October, 1954), 53-73.

Robin, John, and Terzo, Frederick. Urbanization in Peru. New York: Ford Foundation, 1972.

Rhodes, Robert, ed. Imperialism and Underdevelopment: A Reader. New York: Monthly Review, 1970.

Richards, Helmut. "Land Reform and Agribusiness in Iran." Merip Reports, 43 (December, 1975), 3-18, 24.

Ricks, Thomas. "Islamic Republic and Iran Today." Ripeh, 3 (Spring, 1979), 1-16.

Riva, Diego Robles. "Development Alternatives for the Peruvian Barriada." Third World Urbanization. Edited by Janet Abu-Lughod and Richard Hay, Jr. Chicago: Maaroufa, 1977.

Rose, Arnold. "Incomplete Socialization." Sociology and Social Relations, 44 (1960), 244-50.

Ross, Marc Howard. The Political Integration of Urban Squatters. Evanston: Northwestern University Press, 1973.

Sabagh, George. "The Demography of the Middle East." Middle East Studies Association Bulletin, 4 (May, 1970), 1-19.

Safa, Helen. The Urban Poor of Puerto Rico: A Study in Development and Inequality. New York: Holt, Rinehart and Winston, 1974.

Safinizhad, Javad. Bunih. Tehran: Tus, 1353/1974.

Salamat, Mihdi, et al. Ilal-i Muhajirat va Barrisi-yi Awza'-i Farhangi, Iqtisadi, va Ijtima'i-yi Muhajirin-i Mantaqih-yi Yakhchiabad. Tehran: College of Social Work, 1350-1351/1971-1972.

Saran, N. "Squatter Settlement (Gecekondu) Problems in Istanbul." Turkey: Geographic and Social Perspectives. Edited by P. Benedict et al. Leiden: E. J. Brill, 1974.

Schnaiberg, Ann. "Rural-Urban Residence and Modernism: A Study of Ankara Province, Turkey." Demography, 7 (February, 1970), 71-85.

Sewell, G. "Squatter Settlements in Turkey: An Analysis of a Social, Political and Economic Problem." Ph.D. dissertation, M.I.T., 1966.

Sigal, Roberta. "Assumptions about the Learning of Political Values." Annals, 361 (1965), 1-9.

Sjoberg, Gideon. The Preindustrial City, Past and Present. Glencoe, Ill.: The Free Press, 1960.

173

Slotkin, J. S. "The Status of the Marginal Man." Sociology and Social Research, 28 (September-October, 1943), 47-54.

Sovani, N. V. "The Analysis of 'Over-Urbanization.'" Economic Development and Cultural Change, 12 (January, 1964), 113-22.

Stern, S. M. "The Constitution of the Islamic City." The Islamic City. Edited by Albert Hourani and S. M. Stern. Philadelphia: University of Pennsylvania Press, 1970.

Stokes, Charles. "A Theory of Slums." Land Economics, 38 (August, 1962), 187-97.

Stonequist, Everett. The Marginal Man: A Study in Personality and Culture Conflict. New York: Charles Scribner's Sons, 1937.

Suzuki, Peter. "Encounters with Istanbul: Urban Peasants and Rural Peasants." International Journal of Comparative Sociology, 5 (1964), 208-16.

Tehran, University of. Sukhanrani-ha va Guzarish-ha dar Nakhustin Siminar-i Barrisi-yi Masa'il-i Ijtima'i-yi Shahr-i Tehran. Tehran, 1343/1964.

——————. Institute for Social Research. Barrisi-yi Hashiyih Nishinan-i Tehran: Shinasa'i-Vahidha (Jami'ah-yi Amari). 1350/1972.

——————. Institute for Social Research. Raftar-i Karguzaran-i Iqtisadi. Tehran, 1964.

——————. Institute for Social Research. "Takvin-i Shahr-i Abadan," Ulum-i Ijtima'i, 1 (Tir, 1353/1974), 50-56.

Tehranian, Majid. "Iran: Communications, Alienation, Revolution." Intermedia, 7 (March, 1979), 6-12.

Tilly, Charles. From Mobilization to Revolution. Reading, Mass.: Addison Wesley, 1978.

Todaro, Michael. Internal Migration in Developing Countries: A Review of Theory, Evidence, Methodology and Research Priorities. Geneva: International Labour Office, 1976.

——————. "A Model of Labor Migration and Urban Unemployment in Less Developed Countries." American Economic Review, 59 (March, 1969), 138-48.

Touba, Jacquiline Rudolph. "The Relationships Between Urbanization and the Changing Status of Women in Iran, 1956-1966." Iranian Studies, 5 (Winter, 1972), 25-36.

Turner, John C. "Barriers and Channels for Housing Development in Modernizing Countries." Peasants in Cities: Readings in the Anthropology of Urbanization. Edited by William Mangin. Boston: Houghton Mifflin, 1970.

——————. "Uncontrolled Urban Settlement: Problems and Policies." The City in Newly Developing Countries: Readings on Urbanism and Urbanization. Edited by Gerald Breese. Englewood Cliffs, N.J.: Prentice-Hall, 1969.

United Nations. Conference on Human Settlements. <u>Urban Slums and Squatter Settlements in the Third World</u>. A/CONF. 70/RPC/9, 1975.

————. International Labour Office. <u>Employment and Income Policies for Iran</u>. Geneva: International Labour Office, 1973.

Vakil, Firouz. "Iran's Basic Macro-Economic Problems: A 20-Year Horizon." <u>Iran: Past, Present, and Future</u>. Edited by Jane Jacqz. New York: Aspen Institute for Humanistic Studies, 1976.

Van Nieuwenhuize, C. A. O. <u>Sociology of the Middle East: A Stocktaking and Interpretation</u>. Leiden: E. J. Brill, 1971.

Vekemans, Roger, and Giusti, Jorge. "Marginality and Ideology in Latin American Development." <u>Studies in Comparative International Development</u>, 5 (1969-1970), 221-34.

Vieille, Paul. <u>Marché des Terrains et Société Urbaine</u>. Paris: Editions Anthropos, 1970.

————. "Transformation des Rapports Sociaux et Révolution een Iran." <u>Peuples Méditeranéens</u>, 8 (Juillet-Septembre, 1979), 25-58.

————, and Banisadr, Abol-Hassan. <u>Pétrole et Violence</u>. Paris: Editions Anthropos, 1974.

Von Grunebaum, Gustav. "The Structure of Muslim Towns." "Islam: Essay on the Nature and Growth of a Cultural Tradition." Memoir 81. <u>American Anthropological Association</u>, 57 (April, 1955), 141-58.

Waterbury, John. "Cairo: Third World Metropolis." Parts I, II, III. <u>American Universities Field Staff Reports</u>, 18 (Nos. 5, 7, 8), 1973.

Weber, Max. <u>The City</u>. Translated by D. Martindale and G. Neuwirth. Glencoe, Ill.: The Free Press, 1958.

Weinbaum, Marvin. "Agricultural Policy and Development Politics in Iran." <u>Middle East Journal</u>, 31 (Autumn, 1977), 434-50.

Weiner, Myron. "Urbanization and Political Protest." <u>Civilisations</u>, 17 (1967), 44-50.

————. "Violence and Politics in Calcutta." <u>Journal of Asian Studies</u>, 20 (May, 1961), 275-81.

White, James. "Political Implications of Cityward Migration: Japan as an Exploratory Test Case." <u>Sage Professional Papers in Comparative Politics</u>, 4 (1973), 5-59.

Winham, Gilbert. "Political Development and Lerner's Theory: Further Test of a Causal Model." <u>American Political Science Review</u>, 64 (September, 1970), 810-18.

Yar-Shater, Ehsan, ed. <u>Iran Faces the Seventies</u>. New York: Praeger Publishers, 1971.

Yazdani, Husayn. "Alunaknishini dar Hashiyih-yi Shahrha."
    Khwandaniha, 36 (June 5, 1976), 14, 39; (June 8, 1976),
    15-16, 36.

Zabih, Sepehr. The Communist Movement in Iran. Berkeley:
    University of California Press, 1966.

————. Iran's Revolutionary Upheaval: An Interpretive
    Essay. San Francisco: Alchemy, 1979.

Zanjani, Habibullah, et al. Jam'iyyat Shinasi-yi Tatbiqi-yi
    Jahan. Tehran: University of Tehran, 1350/1971.

Zonis, Marvin. The Political Elite of Iran. Princeton:
    Princeton University Press, 1971.

INDEX

113. See also Dual economy
model; Land reform; Migration;
Political participation; Revo-
lution, Iranian; Squatter
settlement eradication;
Urbanization
Migration: cityward, 13, 28, 30,
40, 113; defined, 26-27;
determinants of, 28, 30, 44;
distance and, 44; economic model
of, 27; education and, 30, 43-44;
in Iran, 28, 30; laws of, 26.
See also Migrant poor
Mihrabad-i Junubi, 80
Mongols, 19
Mubashir, 32
Muhammad, Prophet, 93
Muharram, 63, 94
Mujahidin-i Khalq-i Iran, 115, 118
Mussadiq, Dr. Muhammad, 1, 33, 107
Mussolini, Benito, 113
Mustaz'ifin, 116

Narmak, 80-81
Nasaq, 33
National Democratic Front, 118
National Front, 1, 33, 91-92, 94,
118
Nelson, Joan, 63, 83-84
Niavaran palace, 80
Nie, Norman, 69, 74

Overurbanization. See Urbanization

Pahlavi dynasty, 88, 92
Pahlavi Foundation, 117
Pahlavi, Muhammad Reza Shah:
clergy and, 92-95; during
revolution, 88-95; housing
policy for migrant poor, 52;
land reform program, 33, 35-36,
112; petitioning of, 80;
political party, control of, 74,
101; voluntary association
policy, 62-63; trade union,
control of, 101, 104, 108;
view of migrant poor, 113-114
Pahlavi, Reza Shah, 20, 92, 105,
107
Paris, 94
Park, Robert, 4-5
Peasants. See Land reform
Peattie, Lisa, 7
Perlman, Janice, 7, 52, 82
Perón, Eva, 52

Persia. See Iran
Peru, 83
Petras, James, 8
Peterson, Karen, 60
Pofintern, 107
Political demand making. See
Demand making, political
Political mobilization, 82, 88, 94-
96, 112
Political participation: after
migration, 71-74, 82, 88, 94-97,
100; before and after land
reform, 70-71; defined, 69;
organizational affiliation and,
73, 100; political awareness and,
71-73
Political socialization, 74, 99,
103, 105, 154 n. 3
Portes, Alejandro, 7, 52, 82-83
Powell, Bingham, 69, 74
Prewitt, Kenneth, 69, 74
Primate city. See Urbanization
Pye, Lucian, 60

Qajar, Aga Muhammad Khan, 19
Qajar dynasty, 92
Qur'an, 19

Radicalism. See Migrant poor,
radicalism; Revolution, Iranian
Rank-size rule. See Urbanization
Rastakhiz-i Iran party, 74-75
Ravenstein, E. G., 26
Ray, 18-19
Religious organization. See Shi'i
Revolution, Iranian, 88-96, 110-
111, 115-119
Revolutionary Council, 117
Rio de Janeiro, 7, 44, 52
Regional Studies, Office of, 37
Rome, 36

Safar, 63
Safavid dynasty, 92
Safavid, Shah Sultan Husayn, 19
Safavid, Shah Tahmasp I, 19
Saltanat, 32
Sanjabi, Dr. Karim, 94
SAVAK, 93, 108
Shah. See Pahlavi, Muhammad Reza
Shah
Shahbaz-i Junubi, 87
Shari'ah, 11
Shi'i, 63, 91-95
Shiraz, 12-13
Simnan, 30

179